Beatrice Fischer, Matilde Nisbeth Jensen (eds.)

Translation and the Reconfiguration of Power Relations

Repräsentation – Transformation
representation – transformation
représentation – transformation

Translating across Cultures and Societies

herausgegeben von

Michaela Wolf
(Universität Graz)

This book series is designed to provide a forum for interdisciplinary approaches to the discussion of translation in its wider sense. Special emphasis is given to works which focus on the research of translation and interpreting in their role of (de-)constructing cultures and societies. Particularly welcome is the interaction with neighbouring disciplines (cultural studies, sociology, anthropology, gender studies, literary studies, comparative literature, historiography, etc.). All texts are peer-reviewed.

Die Reihe ist ein Forum für interdisziplinäre Ansätze in der Diskussion kulturmittlerischer Phänomene im weitesten Sinn. Besonders willkommen sind Arbeiten, die das Übersetzen und Dolmetschen in ihrer Rolle als Beitrag zur (De-)Konstruktion von Kulturen und Gesellschaften untersuchen. Die interaktive Zusammenarbeit mit Nachbardisziplinen (Kulturwissenschaften, Soziologie, Anthropologie, Gender Studies, Allgemeine Literaturwissenschaft, Vergleichende Literaturwissenschaft, Geschichtswissenschaft, etc.) ist ausdrücklich erwünscht. Alle Texte werden anonym begutachtet.

Band 7

LIT

Translation and the Reconfiguration of Power Relations

Revisiting Role and Context of Translation and Interpreting

edited by

Beatrice Fischer and Matilde Nisbeth Jensen

LIT

Gedruckt mit Unterstützung von:
Karl-Franzens-Universität Graz
Land Steiermark, Referat für Wissenschaft und Forschung
CETRA, Centre for Translation Studies

Titelbild- und Umschlaggestaltung: Sigrid Querch
Satz: Guntram Titus Tockner, Graz

Bibliographic information published by the Deutsche Nationalbibliothek
The Deutsche Nationalbibliothek lists this publication in the Deutsche Nationalbibliografie; detailed bibliographic data are available in the Internet at http://dnb.d-nb.de.

ISBN 978-3-643-90283-2

A catalogue record for this book is available from the British Library

Klosbachstr. 107
CH-8032 Zürich
Tel. +41 (0) 44-251 75 05
Fax +41 (0) 44-251 75 06
e-Mail: zuerich@lit-verlag.ch
http://www.lit-verlag.ch

LIT VERLAG Dr. W. Hopf
Berlin 2012
Fresnostr. 2
D-48159 Münster
Tel. +49 (0) 2 51-620 320
Fax +49 (0) 2 51-23 19 72
e-Mail: lit@lit-verlag.de
http://www.lit-verlag.de

Distribution:

In Germany: LIT Verlag Fresnostr. 2, D-48159 Münster
Tel. +49 (0) 2 51-620 32 22, Fax +49 (0) 2 51-922 60 99, e-mail: vertrieb@lit-verlag.de

In Austria: Medienlogistik Pichler-ÖBZ, e-mail: mlo@medien-logistik.at
In Switzerland: B + M Buch- und Medienvertrieb, e-mail: order@buch-medien.ch
In the UK: Global Book Marketing, e-mail: mo@centralbooks.com
In North America: International Specialized Book Services, e-mail: orders@isbs.com

CONTENTS

Acknowledgements

Editing an anthology for the first time requires the efforts of many different people. We would like to acknowledge these people here with gratitude, as this publication could not have come into existence if it was not for their help. We owe a great debt of gratitude to all the reviewers who spent their time giving very valuable feedback and sharing their valuable knowledge. We would also like to thank the CETRA board for their support and a special thank you to Reine Meylearts for her help whenever we were in doubt. We would also like to take the opportunity to thank the CETRA professor Sherry Simon both for her exellent lectures during the Summer School and for her contribution to this publication.

This publication became a proper book publication thanks to our publisher LIT and especially to Michaela Wolf, who has provided her tireless help. A very warm thank you goes to Nadja Grbić and her precious assistance, for swiftly lending us a hand in times of trouble. Many thanks also go to our colleagues in Austria, Australia and Denmark for their support and interest.

For their financial support, we would like to thank the University of Graz, the Land Steiermark (Abteilung Wissenschaft und Forschung) and the CETRA board. Without their funding, we would not have been able to publish a printed book publication.

September 2012

Beatrice Fischer & Matilde Nisbeth Jensen

BEATRICE FISCHER/MATILDE NISBETH JENSEN

University of Graz, Austria / Aarhus University, Denmark; Macquarie University, Australia

Introduction – The Power of Translation

This publication came into existence as a result of the CETRA Summer School in 2010. The CETRA Summer School was established in 1989 when José Lambert created a special research programme in Translation Studies at the University of Leuven, Belgium. Every year, this summer school gives PhD students and other new scholars in Translation Studies the opportunity to spend two weeks in Leuven interacting with each other and with prominent scholars within Translation Studies in the form of lectures, seminars and tutorials. CETRA is thus an excellent opportunity for new scholars to get to know senior Translation Studies scholars, learn relevant methods and through tutorials thoroughly discuss their very own research projects with established scholars who support and comment on the ongoing research projects of these PhD students. Each year, a CETRA publication is edited by at least one CETRA participant. Thus, after the summer school, all students are encouraged to submit a paper. This is where the story of this publication commences.

This volume brings together the research of 14 PhD students who participated in CETRA Summer School 2010. While the young scholars tackle Translation Studies topics from different perspectives, all papers shed light on translation as a powerful activity from a language and social perspective. Power can thus be seen as an overall theme in all papers. In this context, this collection presents questions and attempts to provide answers regarding the role of translators and translations in societies affected by globalisation and migration. The different sections of the book cover various related topics, such as the powerful impact languages have on translation, the institutional constraints in the context of translation, and the challenges within the framework of multimodal translation.

This collection covers questions of institutional censorship in the twentieth century in the form of literary censorship (Trupej), media censorship (Garnemark) and theatre censorship (Antochi). In the context of translation history, the role of interpreters in the First World War is investigated

(Heimburger). Other constraints that multimodal translation faces, especially language constraints, (Nolette, Di Pietro, Maumevičienė, Moroni) and constraints within the literary translation field in post-communist Romania (Tiron) are also dealt with in this volume. The issue of today's institutional constraints is broached in the context of public service interpreting (Foulquié), and in the way both the translation process and product are constrained within the EU framework in the context of medical translation (Nisbeth Jensen, Martinez Motos). As languages have a powerful impact on translation policies and thus products, i.e. the languages translators work in and from, two papers focus on the role of English as a Lingua Franca (Mealha, Cabrita). We will not introduce the papers in more detail here as the CETRA Chair Professor of 2010, Sherry Simon, introduces the papers and their content further in her introduction below.

But how is power relevant for Translation Studies? And how are questions of power dealt with in the context of the discipline? Answers to these questions seem to be necessary in order to better contextualise this anthology and to better position the collected papers of the young scholars in the field.

Power in the context of translation

With the cultural turn in Translation Studies by the end of the 1980s and beginning of the 1990s (see especially Bassnett/Lefevere 1990), the impact of translations on cultures became obvious: "Translation has been a major shaping force in the development of world culture" (Lefevere/Bassnett 1990:12). This perspective on translation simultaneously allowed for a stronger emphasis on ideology, politics, ethics and hegemony in the context of translation. As questions of power are closely connected to these topics, "[t]he key topic that has provided the impetus for the new directions that translation studies have taken since the cultural turn is *power*" (Gentzler/ Tymoczko 2002:xvi).

Within the cultural turn, focus in Translation Studies widened from an investigation of texts and contexts, such as the analysis of linguistic differences between source and target texts, to subtexts and translation-related decisions, i.e. ideology or the reasons why a text is translated or not, and who the translator of a text is. As a result of the cultural turn, scholars started looking at translation from a more critical perspective, which consequently lead to a new focus on theoretical self-reflection within the discipline of Translation Studies itself (Tymoczko 2007:44). The cultural turn thus widened Translation Studies research, and the emergence of an awareness of the strong influence of power in relation to translation was inevitable. In consequence, more research was for instance done within the discourse of postcolonialism (e.g. Spivak 1987) and feminism (e.g. Simon 1996; von Flotow 1997), two areas which are not only closely connected to questions of ideology, but also to power relations. Furthermore, research was also conducted linked to a broader view of power relations in the context of translation (e.g. Álvarez/Vidal 1996a; Arrojo 1997; Dimitriu 2006). Questions of power are thus not only relevant in these areas but also from a wider theoretical perspective as shown by the edited volume *Translation and Power* edited by Tymoczko and Gentzler in 2002.

But what does power in this context mean? How can this term be understood? In the context of Translation Studies, power cannot be understood from a traditional and simplistic view of how power operates, i.e. power is not exclusively exercised by institutions and other authorities traditionally seen as the proprietors of power, but power is also exercised by people seeking empowerment (Tymoczko 2007). However, power is not only related to oppression or empowerment; power is always present. Thus, power is a multilayered term that is

> intimately related to knowledge, information, and especially to the manner in which that information is conveyed and the way of articulating a wide range of discursive elements in the TT [target text] which behave according to extremely subtle strategies. (Álvarez/Vidal 1996b:6)

Therefore, power in translation is closely linked to constraints from different perspectives (e.g. hegemony, norms, language, target group). These power-driven translation practices can lead to oppression of discourse or people (e.g. censorship, institutional constraints, ideological constraints), but they can also be seen as a means to resist this oppression. In this context, power does not necessarily open out into a black-and-white thinking, an absolutist and dichotomous understanding of translation. It does not necessarily only mean the difference between the powerful and the powerless, but rather makes translation implicitly or explicitly partisan. In this context, translation can be characterised as

> an image of the original, particularly for those who have no access to the reality of the original. This image can undoubtedly be very different from the truth, insofar as the translator can distort and manipulate reality, because he

> is under the pressure of a series of constraints [...] typical of the cultures to which he belongs. (Ibid.:4)

The role of the translator is thus closely connected to the issue of power as the translator or interpreter often functions as a double agent caught between two camps, "representing both the institution in power and those seeking empowerment" (Gentzer/Tymoczko 2002:xix). However, instead of viewing this as problematic, within the paradigm of power, this position can be seen as a strength (ibid.) as translators always have the possibility to influence the text by emphasizing specific content or rearrange parts of the text:

> As a result, translators must make choices, selecting aspects or parts of a text to transpose and emphasize. Such choices in turn serve to create representations of their source texts, representations that are also partial. This partiality is not to be considered a defect, a lack or an absence in a translation; it is a necessary condition of the act. (Ibid.:xviii)

Furthermore, translators can also "artificially create the reception context of a given text. [They] can be the authority who manipulates the culture, politics, literature, and their acceptance (or lack thereof) in the target culture" (Álvarez/Vidal 1996b:2). Thereby, translators have the possibility to actively participate in the construction of knowledge across different languages and cultural borders. The role of translation is therefore not a mere reproduction of a source text into a target text, but a creative act that demands complex decision-making from the translator:

> Translation thus is not simply an act of faithful reproduction but, rather, a deliberate and conscious act of selection, assemblage, structuration, and fabrication – and even, in some cases, of falsification, refusal of information, counterfeiting, and the creation of secret codes. In these ways translators, as much as creative writers and politicians, participate in the powerful acts that create knowledge and shape culture. (Gentzler/Tymoczko 2002:xxi)

As noted by Gentzler and Tymoczko, power and translation is not only linked to translation products and the way translations influence or lead to cultural transformation and change, but power is also "inherent in the translation process itself" (ibid.:xxviii), e.g. seen in the relationship between the translator and the author, source text and translation. Also the selection process, through which powerful agents decide which works are worth being translated or not, is a powerful act in the context of translation. Many works are simply not (entirely) translatable because of a lack of money or time and therefore face economic and/or political constraints: "[T]he first expression of power in translation is, as has long been recognized, the decision whether or not to translate something and, if so, how much to pay for it" (Fawcett 1995:181).

As briefly outlined, translation faces very different power relations, which this anthology tries to revisit in the context of both the role of translators and interpreters and the contexts of translation and interpreting. The papers included in this volume therefore tackle a range of the abovementioned topics in the context of power relations in the translation process, such as who is chosen as a translator, how translators deal with institutional constraints, what influence translations have on cultures, and what this has to do with cultural dominance. Thus, the collected papers in this volume represent the huge diversity within the field of Translation Studies in relation to power.

References

Álvarez, Román/Vidal, Carmen África (eds.) (1996a) *Translation, Power, Subversion.* Clevedon-Philadelphia-Adelaide: Multilingual Matters.

Álvarez, Román/Vidal, Carmen África (1996b) "Translating. A Political Act". In Álvarez, Román/Vidal, Carmen África (eds.) *Translation, Power, Subversion.* Clevedon-Philadelphia-Adelaide: Multilingual Matters, 1-9.

Arrojo, Rosemary (1997) "Asymmetrical Relations of Power and the Ethics of Translation". *TEXTconTEXT* 11:1, 5-24.

Bassnett, Susan/Lefevere, André (eds.) (1990) *Translation, History and Culture.* London-New York: Pinter.

Dimitriu, Ileana (2006) "'Symbolic Power' and 'Worldmaking' in Politically Over-Determined Times: Translation and Social Practice under Dictatorship". In Wolf, Michaela (ed.) *Übersetzen – Translating – Traduire: Towards a 'Social Turn'?* Wien-Berlin: LIT, 55-64.

Fawcett, Peter (1995) "Translation and Power Play". *The Translator* 1:2, 177-192.

Gentzler, Edwin/Tymoczko, Maria (2002) "Introduction". In Tymoczko, Maria/ Gentzler, Edwin (eds.) *Translation and Power.* Amherst: University of Massachusetts Press, XI-XXVIII.

Lefevere, André/Bassnett, Susan (1990) "Introduction: Proust's Grandmother and the Thousand and One Nights: The 'Cultural Turn' in Translation Studies". In Bassnett, Susan/Lefevere, André (eds.) *Translation, History and Culture.* London-New York: Pinter, 1-13.

Simon, Sherry (1996) *Gender in Translation. Cultural Identity and the Politics of Transmission.* London-New York: Routledge.

Spivak, Gayatri Chakravorty (1987) *In Other Worlds. Essays in Cultural Politics.* London-New York: Routledge.

Tymoczko, Maria/Gentzler, Edwin (eds.) (2002) *Translation and Power.* Amherst: University of Massachusetts Press.
Tymoczko, Maria (2007) *Enlarging Translation, Empowering Translators.* Manchester: St Jerome.
von Flotow, Luise (1997) *Translation and Gender: Translating in the "Era of Feminism".* Manchester: St Jerome.

Sherry Simon

Concordia University, Montreal, Canada

Introduction by CETRA Chair Professor 2010

It is not surprising that the twin issues of political power and globalisation continue to preoccupy the participants at CETRA. Many of the papers presented in 2010 have their source in questions of power and agency: how do the constraints imposed by political power and the global weight of English influence activities of cultural exchange? These questions respond to the increasing awareness in Translation Studies for the need to understand the very broad contexts which regulate the practice of translation. The cataclysmic events of recent European history (from the fall of Communism to the rocky state of the European Union, the insecurities of the economy and the difficult questions of cultural identity and inclusion) make Europe a particularly unstable unit. Translation issues (in Europe) are profoundly embedded in the contentious conditions that create the needs for communication.

The images used by Franziska Heimburger in the opening article of the collection are particularly suggestive. What can the figures of the "go-between" and the "gate-keeper" tell us about the subjective experience and the objective situation of the translator? In the case of Heimburger's project which examines the military contribution of interpreters during World War I, these images allow a multilayered approach, revealing the variety of roles which military interpreters assumed in their relations with the military hierarchy as well as with local populations.

The idea of the gatekeeper takes on more sinister connotations when it is related to the practices of censorship in totalitarian regimes. Roxana-Mihaela Antochi takes on the subject of text selection policies in Communist Romania, focusing on the case of Spanish and Latin-American drama in the political context of Romania between 1945 and 1989. Rosario Garnemark looks at censorship in Francoist Spain. Rather than studying censorship at its most oppressive moments, Garnemark chooses to examine the "Apertura", a period beginning in 1963 of greater tolerance. During this period, translation was a result of negotiation among film distribution companies and the censorship authorities. The translations of three films by

Ingmar Bergman released during this period are studied: *Sommarnattens leende* (*Smiles of a Summer Night,* 1955), *Smultronstället* (*Fresas salvajes*, 1957) and *Såsom i en spegel* (*Como en un espejo*, 1961).

In contrast, Irina Elena Tiron approaches constraints from a very different angle when she discusses the transition of Romania from a Communist regime to a free market regime in 1989. Now it is the disappearance of censorship which defines the translation market. The regime before 1989 obeyed strict policies of translation censorship. With the collapse of the old regime, translation moved into a new role as a necessary daily practice in the cultural policy of Romania. There was a huge increase in the number of translations after 1989, and a new ethos of cultural exchange and plurality – reflecting the intensification of exchange at all levels – diplomatic, economic, political, intergovernmental, cultural.

In his article on the translation of racist discourse in Slovenia during the Socialist period, with reference to Mark Twain's *Adventures of Huckleberry Finn,* Janko Trupej focuses on the ideological pressures which allow or block access to other identities. He argues that the changing ideological affiliations of Yugoslavia and its changing attitude towards the United States may have influenced the translation of "racist discourse" in Mark Twain's *Adventures of Huckleberry Finn.*

In order to shed light on another dimension of cultural exchange, Dainora Maumevičienė's article on localisation uses examples from Lithuanian to show how the practice of localisation has broad roots in Lithuanian cultural practices. Ana Isabel Foulquié Rubio discusses yet another kind of constraint – one imposed by the particular situation of interpreting in police settings. She argues for recognition of the particular powers of the lawyer in this context – the possibility of lawyers to ensure the right to interpretation.

Another perspective on constraints in the context of multimodal translation is discussed in Elisa Moroni's paper on orality in the translation of Russian epics that focuses on the power of the context of reception to impose a new set of stylistic norms. Russian epic poetry, which was orally transmitted by generations of storytellers and systematically transcribed between the nineteenth and twentieth century, turns into a kind of *frozen* orality when it is translated. Although the translations aim to preserve oral features, this orality will be always different from that of the original performance, obeying the constraints of the academic or literary discourse into which it is integrated.

The study of dubbed sitcoms also deals with the clash of contradictory stylistic features. Giovanna Di Pietro's work on the paralinguistic and kinesic features of humour in dubbed sitcoms analyses the interplay between verbal and nonverbal communication in the creation of humour within the field of audiovisual translation from English into Italian. Multimodal analysis of one episode of the contemporary US sitcom *How I Met Your Mother* dubbed into Italian shows how there is often a disconnect between what is said and how it is said, between the words and the ways in which they are pronounced, the images and the bodily movements of the characters.

The paper by Nicole Nolette approaches constraints from yet another perspective, from the flipside in fact – introducing texts which are wilfully dissident, refusing the hegemony of a single language. In asking how these heterolingual plays can be translated, she shows how translation becomes a kind of linguistic performance. These games of translation intensify the play of languages, connecting with the mise en scène, and adding a new layer of verbal humour for the bilingual audience. The intentional dissonance of this kind of theatrical experience compares in interesting ways with the unintentional dissonances introduced in dubbing television sitcoms.

The contraints that are discussed in several other contributions have to do with the ways in which globalisation directs the flows of translation traffic. Two papers are devoted to the influence of English in contemporary Portuguese. Eduarda Melo Cabrita shows how the power of English is leading to lexical and stylistic inference in translation into Portuguese, particularly in the field of legal translation. The two terms which illustrate this interference are *consideration* (*consideração*) and *joint venture*, a false friend and loan-word, respectively. Isabel Ferro Mealha discusses a related issue, the use of English in non-translated medical Portuguese – emphasising the impact of English as a *lingua franca* in Portugal and particularly in medical Portuguese. In relation to similar issues of medical communication, Matilde Nisbeth Jensen focuses on the differing competencies of professional translators and pharmacist-translators in the preparation of Patient Information Leaflets in the EU. Raquel Martínez Motos studies patient package inserts in English and Spanish, and their apparent failure to fully achieve their communicative purpose.

The rich collection of articles published in this 2010 edition of CETRA confirms the broadening concerns of Translation Studies – not only in its geographical sweep but in the variety of situations, media and social concerns which it embraces. The collection also testifies to the quality of students attracted by the school and to the atmosphere of conviviality that is so central to the success of CETRA.

Translating as gatekeeping

Franziska Heimburger

Ecole des Hautes Etudes en Sciences Sociales, Paris, France

Of Go-Betweens and Gatekeepers: Considering Disciplinary Biases in Interpreting History through Exemplary Metaphors. Military Interpreters in the Allied Coalition during the First World War

Military interpreters were crucial to the functioning of the Allied Coalition on the Western Front during the First World War. The interpreters were French soldiers, who maintained the links between both the different military hierarchies, and also between the British troops and the local French civilians. In this case study, I examine the material concerning these interpreters (both archival material and published sources) in the light of two exemplary metaphors. On the one hand, the paper focuses on the metaphor of "go-between" which has recently found considerable application in transnational history, especially in colonial contexts. On the other hand, Translation and Interpreting Studies have long used the "gatekeeper"-metaphor which originally stems from organisational sociology. These two metaphors underline and illustrate different aspects of the case study and raise important questions regarding the articulation of different disciplinary angles on the history of translation and interpreting.

Keywords: gatekeeper, go-between, metaphors, military interpreters, history

History and Translation/Interpreting Studies as two different ways of exploiting a historical case?

For historians, language is what Evans calls "a constraint; but [...] also a vital and still unexploited field of study" (Evans 1998:34). In Translation and Interpreting Studies, there have been repeated calls for the establishment of a serious academic historiography of translation (most explicitly by Pym 1992:224). What happens when approaches from history and Translation/Interpreting Studies meet on the same body of historical material?

In the following, I shall examine how a corpus of sources on one case study in history – that of military interpreters in the Allied Coalition during the First World War – can be shaped by the use of different metaphors as interpretive hypotheses. During the First World War, a Franco-British coalition fought on French ground from 1914-1918 and was joined by US-American Forces in 1917. Communications between the coalition partners were essentially handled by a large number (exact figures are impossible to determine, but approximately 4000) of French rank soldiers who were detached as military interpreters to serve alongside the British and later US-American troops and assist them both in liaison with the French civilian population on the ground and in battlefield liaison in zones where the two armies were in contact, such as in the 1916 joint offensive on the Somme. This coalition has left a large variety of source material, ranging from the procedural and individual military documentation[1] to a great number of published and non-published memoirs, both by interpreters and by the British officers who worked with them.[2]

Intermediaries like military interpreters can be considered through any number of metaphors that insist on different aspects of their status "in-between" different cultural, social or indeed military entities. Michel de Certeau considers a wide range of such metaphors, articulated around the notion of "shifters" (Certeau/Giard 1983:11). Ruth Morris (1993) writes of "cyphers" and "intelligent participants", Cecilia Wadensjö (1998:61) among many other metaphors mentions "intermediaries", "mediators" and "non-persons", while a book by Ruth A. Roland (1999) carries the title: *Interpreters as Diplomats*. There has even been an entire chapter of an edited volume on the profusion of metaphors employed in the context of interpreting (Roy 2002).

Choice of metaphors is not only down to individual choice by the researcher, but is also heavily influenced by his or her disciplinary background and the biases introduced by the methodology and training he/she is familiar with. The choice of a given metaphor thus reveals important insights into the researcher's points of view. In the limited space of this paper which does not allow an exhaustive analysis of different types of metaphors, I shall examine the case of two metaphors, chosen because of their wide use. The

---

[1] Conserved, for the French case, at the Service Historique de la Défense (SHD), Château de Vincennes in the 7N and 17N series; for the British case, in the National Archives, Kew, W series; for the US-American case, in National Archives Record Administration RG 120 and 165.

[2] For the unpublished records, see for example: Imperial War Museum archival holdings: Audio recording 9476, reel 4, Interview with John William Boon (British officer who mentions working with his interpreter); Archives Départementales du Puy de Dôme, Correspondence of Jacques Bardoux (interpreter).

first, that of the "go-between", is commonly employed by historians working on transnational history and intercultural contexts and has recently been the focus of an edited volume with a long theoretical introduction (Schaffer et al. 2009). The second, that of the "gate-keeper", has its roots in organisational sociology and has since been widely applied in Translation and Interpreting Studies.

Studying interpreters by focussing on the entities they link: the "go-between" metaphor

According to the Online Collins dictionary (2006:741), a go-between is "a person who acts as agent or intermediary for two people or groups in a transaction or dealing". According to the Oxford English Dictionary (2006), a go-between is "an intermediary or negotiator".

The two dictionary definitions reveal both the great potential and the inherent limitations of the metaphor. We are dealing with a naturally evocative image which can be applied in a wide range of fields. We are also trying to grasp a concept which is too large and loosely defined to provide an analytical framework on its own. Nor does it have an established history of use in the humanities and social sciences.

For the purpose of this paper, I shall adopt the theoretical and methodological groundwork established in one particular historical study: a collective research project which resulted in a volume containing chapters on individual "go-betweens" from their chosen period, 1770-1820. This book, called a "collective xenobiography" (Schaffer et al. 2009:xxxviii), includes not only a series of chapters on individuals who acted as go-betweens but also a theoretical introduction which analyses the concept of the go-between.

According to the authors, go-betweens are individuals who create and/or maintain connections between culturally and, practically always, linguistically distant social entities. As the editors put it: "The go-between in this sense is thus not just a passer-by or a simple agent of cross-cultural diffusion, but someone who articulates relationships between disparate worlds or cultures by being able to translate between them" (ibid.:xiv).

Secondly, go-betweens are unique because of their knowledge of both sides and, as a further consequence, find themselves in a situation of ill-defined dual status between two larger entities. The editors of the aforementioned volume define one further characteristic of the go-between: a non-institutional position. They are constantly forging their own positions, inventing their own roles. We must consider especially the "relation between their strikingly improvised activities and the robust institutions they helped to produce" (ibid.:xi). This is closely linked to the specific period under study, since it is argued that there was an "era of the go-between" linked to the context of early colonial expansion which was later replaced by institutionally empowered brokers with official positions.

In the following, we shall examine how the characteristics of go-betweens according to the aforementioned study correspond with the source material on military interpreters during the First World War, in order to see to what extent the facets of this go-between metaphor are reflected.

The military interpreters were in their vast majority French rank soldiers who spoke English and were thus detached to serve alongside the British and later US-American troops. They had no formal training in interpreting, but very often had worked in a number of professional settings (ranging from shop assistant to missionary) either in an English-speaking country or elsewhere abroad. For the duration of their service as military interpreters, these men remained French soldiers, under the nominal authority of a French liaison officer, yet in their daily life, they assisted the British military structures and lived together with British officers, eating in their officers' mess, etc.

The following quotation from Winston Churchill's introduction to the memoirs of an interpreter provides a good starting point concerning the understanding of the interpreter's role:

> One may imagine the tact which was required in this anomalous figure, neither French nor English, neither officer nor soldier, nor indeed civilian, who collected the conversations of colonels and captains in the most deadly danger, formed his own view upon the local situation, and then was allowed that night to walk straight into the Army Commander's private quarters and tell him all that he had seen and heard. (Churchill, qtd. in Maze 1934:2)

This analysis by Churchill, a British officer who had worked in close contact with a number of military interpreters, shows evidence of the first two characteristics of go-betweens: creating connections by transmitting information and analyses, and using specific knowledge in an unclear situation.

This emphasis on dual identity is further reinforced by the following extract from the memoirs of a liaison officer:

> The liaison officer has to stand up to both sides and defend the thesis of the one to the other and vice versa. He deals with all complaints. To one side he is always a foreigner. To his own people he seems to be forever taking the side of the foreigner. His life is spent between the hammer and the anvil. (Spears 1930:340)

Finally, even their appearance betrayed the dual nature of their role. After serving in French uniform for the first couple of months (which was dangerous, as the very colourful French uniforms contrasted greatly with the khaki British kit), military interpreters wore regulation British khaki uniforms but retained their French *képi* and were provided with special buttons specific to the French corps of military interpreters, which they dutifully sewed onto their British uniforms in a rather telling rite of passage (see Cary 1956:134-135).

Schaffer et al. (2009) point out that the lack of institutional framework for the actions of the go-between is something which we find specifically at the beginning of the war. The interpreter Maze recounts, in a gripping narrative, how he was arrested under suspicion of being a spy (Maze 1934:30-31). As an individual with copious language skills and with a concrete military role as yet unknown to the hierarchy he dealt with, all his actions were a cause for suspicion. Similarly, Henri de Vibraye gives an account of just how unprepared he was for a role which was only just beginning to take on a clear outline:

> I asked about my tasks as an interpreter: I thought it meant transmitting messages from an English unit to a French unit and vice versa. Poireau explained that "liaison work" was the exception; the interpreters were "truchements"[3] between French civilians and the British army: during

[3] The choice of the term "truchement" in this extract is highly significant. While the etymology of the word is not definitely established, it has been used in French since medieval times both to designate actual interpreters and to designate intermediaries. The Trésor de la Langue Française (2012) gives examples including works by Montaigne to Chateaubriand. It characterises the profession long before the twentieth century-process of professionalisation of conference interpreting and the exclusive use of "interprète" in French gave it a coherent identity.

> combat activity you were left somewhere safe. (Vibraye 1937:23, my translation)[4]

It has now been shown how it is possible to substantiate the case for the use of the metaphor of the "go-between" in this historical case. Military interpreters created connections, not only between British and French military authorities but also between the British army and the French civilian population. In addition to their language skills, military interpreters had special knowledge of the coalition partner, and they attempted to transmit and use this knowledge. Finally, since the First World War seems to be the first case in history of a mass deployment of military interpreters in coalition warfare, we are very close to Schaffer et al.'s (2009) examples taken from the period of early colonial expansion. These individuals had certain skills but no formal training; they were go-betweens of the same type, creating their role and its scope "on the job".

The use of the "go-between" metaphor in historical writing reflects an important bias. In any given study, the two sides, institutions, camps or other fractions between which the "go-between" operates are usually well known and thoroughly studied in a historiographical context, while the work of the "go-between" is virtually unknown. In Schaffer et al. (2009), the case studies are part of of early colonial exploration and the power relations between local elites and new actors in colonial functions. The go-betweens are in practically all cases resurrected from the anonymity of history.

Using the metaphor of the go-between is therefore a tool with certain advantages. Its precise evaluation of the power relations between the two entities that are linked by the interpreter is of great interest for the case of First World War military interpreters. They were French soldiers under British authority and had to negotiate between these two differently situated powers during their service on the Western Front. On the other hand, this metaphor has limitations, which, as we have attempted to show, tend to be linked to larger disciplinary biases in history. On a very fundamental level, the metaphor of the go-between denies the intermediary agency, reducing the interpreter to a conveyor of information between two sides. We need to

---

4 "Je demandai qu'on me mît au courant du métier d'interprète : je croyais que cela consistait à transmettre des messages d'une unité anglaise à une unité française et réciproquement. Poireux m'expliqua que « faire la liaison » était un cas exceptionnel ; les interprètes étaient les truchements entre les populations civiles françaises et l'armée britannique : pendant les combats on vous mettait souvent dans un endroit tranquille".

turn to Translation and Interpreting Studies with their much greater understanding of the actual work of these intermediaries to further the analysis.

Getting to grips with the actions of the interpreter: the "gatekeeper"

Now, the focus lies on the second metaphor under consideration – that of the gate-keeper. In many ways, this concept puts us not only in a different disciplinary context, but also in a different situation on the methodological level. While the image of the gatekeeper seems similarly evocative at first sight, we cannot use it without referring to the considerable theoretical baggage it carries in the various branches of the humanities and the social sciences.

The first and subsequently most thoroughly exploited area of research where the metaphor has been used is the sociological analysis of publishing and editing. The gatekeeper image was used to characterise the role of the editor in deciding what gets published.

We can see an example in what Kurt Lewin wrote in one of the founding texts on gatekeepers in publishing:

> Gate sections are governed either by impartial rules or by "gatekeepers". In the latter case an individual or group is "in power" to make the decision between "in" or "out". Understanding the functioning of the gate becomes equivalent then to understanding the factors which determine the decisions of the gatekeepers, and changing the social process means influencing or replacing the gatekeeper. The first diagnostic task in such cases is that of finding the actual gatekeepers. This requires essentially a sociological analysis and must be carried out before one knows whose psychology has to be studied or who has to be educated if a social change is to be accomplished. Similar considerations hold for any social constellation which has the character of a channel, a gate, and gatekeeper. Discrimination against minorities will not be changed as long as forces are not changed which determine the decisions of the gatekeepers. Their decisions depend partly on their ideology – that is, their system of values and beliefs which determine what they consider to be "good" or "bad" – and partly on the way they perceive the particular situation. (Lewin 1951:186)

The use of the metaphor, however, goes further than providing a useful image. Crucially, it is an important tool in order to understand the articulation between the individual and the context he or she works in:

> The relation between social channels, social perception, and decision is methodologically and practically of considerable significance. The theory of channels and gatekeepers helps to define more precisely how certain "objective" sociological problems of locomotion of goods and persons intersect with "subjective" psychological and cultural problems. It points to sociologically characterized places, like gates and social channels, where attitudes count most for certain social processes and where individual or group decisions have a particularly great social effect. (Ibid.:187)

This pioneering work by Lewin was later developed for larger areas of the publishing world, including writers as well as editors (White 1966; Coser 1975; McGinty 1999; Rowley 2003). In Translation Studies, and indeed in Interpreting Studies, the metaphor of the gatekeeper has been taken up several times. We can cite Wadensjö's ground-breaking work on dialogue interpreting (1998), which relies heavily on the concept of the gatekeeper. She summarises the use of the metaphor and enlarges it for the dialogue situation she analyses:

> As do all professional intermediaries, interpreters work at providing a particular service. Simultaneously, they – of necessity – exercise a certain control. Obviously, there is a potential conflict between the service and the control aspects, which sometimes surfaces in dilemmas reported in the literature on institutional communication. It largely remains to be investigated how this conflict is handled in institutional interpreter-mediated talk, where the gatekeeping is, in effect, doubled. (Wadensjö 1998:68-69)

Since Wadensjö's work, the use of the gatekeeper metaphor has been most frequent in the subfield of research on legal interpreting, as several recent publications show (Hale 2008; Rosenberg/Seller/Leanza 2008).

Another field where we can now increasingly find research on interpreters using the gatekeeper metaphor: in the medical domain, concerning medical interpreters (Davidson 2001; Hsieh 2008). The recurrence of the metaphor in this field may be linked to its very frequent use in the medical field itself, for all sorts of biological processes.

From all these research approaches using gatekeepers, we can draw a number of conclusions about the characteristics generally used to designate the role of gatekeeper. First of all, the gatekeeper shares a good knowledge of both sides with many other metaphorical descriptions of in-betweenness. Gatekeepers are necessarily individuals with very detailed insight into the functioning and characteristics of the two sides they negotiate with. What sets them apart, however, is that they use this knowledge in order to decide which information and other elements are transmittted from one side to the other. The crucial aspect of gatekeeping is this control, a certain power which can be exerted by the gatekeeper. In the case of interlingual interpreters as gatekeepers, it is clearly their language competence which gives them this margin of movement, as their actions cannot usually be fully supervised by either of the two parties between whom they are acting as interpreters. Further, gatekeepers tend to have a fairly well-defined institutional position. Their control and power are mostly linked to the authorities that determine their work and give a definite structure within which to act.

One of the most recurrent cases of gatekeeping by military interpreters during the First World War concerns settling claims made by the civilian population. For any expenses or damages incurred by the British Army, the local inhabitants could make claims, which were usually settled via the military interpreter: "I also had to settle peasants' everlasting claims for damages done to their fields or barns, and although on many occasions they had my sympathy, I thought very often they were overdoing it and told them so" (Maze 1934:99).

We can see how the interpreter, as a French soldier, became a regulatory instance in the local economy of damage compensation between French civilians and the British military authorities. Interpreter Maze in this case would have decided which cases merited reimbursement and were thus passed on to the financial services of the British Army, and which cases were exaggerated claims and thus did not merit further attention.

This example is fairly limited in its scope, but there were other cases where gatekeeping could take on much larger proportions. The French military archives conserve a number of documents concerning a court case in which a military interpreter was tried for having accepted bribes from the local farmers in order to favour them in the sale of their horses to the British army.[5]

Tensions related to perceived or real gatekeeping by interpreters were recurrent and tended to be reflected in the evaluation of their work. The following evaluation of interpreter Peschier's work was given by his superior, a Liaison Officer: "Cannot be left for too long without supervision, as he ends up antagonising the local civilian population by excessively siding

---

[5] SHD Vincennes 17 N 457, dossier concerning interpreter Peschier.

with the English point of view. All this because he is very eager to please".[6] Gatekeeping could also occur on a more rhetorical level, and this is without doubt one of the most recurrent features. In many cases, the tone of the message had to be adapted in order to avoid unnecessary friction between the two military commands. An episode recounted in interpreter Maze's published souvenirs is one example among many:

> A tall French General, in a fever of agitation, was giving orders to officers arriving and departing – he said something about using their artillery and seventy-fives and then, looking at our transport in the middle of the reigning confusion, briskly stepped towards us, a map in one hand, a crust of bread in the other, and said: "Can't you see that you are congesting the whole of my retirement? You must get out of our way". His manner was anything but pleasant. I translated what he said in milder tones. Pointing to his map and addressing me, he added, "Tell your officer to get on this road as soon as he possibly can". With that he precipitately entered his car, which cut through the troops and disappeared. (Ibid.:33, emphasis added)

Here, the military interpreter makes a choice as to which part of the message he wants to transmit and thus chooses the functional content, while dropping the emotional charge which accompanied the original message. The interpreter thus decides to transmit only one part of the message he was charged to interpret.

These cases of gatekeeping are all fairly self-evident; at the same time we would like to argue that there is another level of gatekeeping which is more abstract. As the only Frenchmen among the British troops, it fell to the military interpreters to answer the many questions the British officers had about the foreign country they were fighting in, and it is at this level that they had a profound impact on the functioning of the coalition. Their perception of the reality of coalition warfare fed straight back into the same reality when they "interpreted" the reality of life in rural France for the British and, for many of the interpreters who published accounts of their work, both during and after the war, for the French public at large.

An example of how a military interpreter dealt with both the French and the British: Interpreter Boulestin had just come upon a curious scene: on the one hand, a concert party for British officers was in merry swing

[6] SHD Vincennes (French military archives), 17 N 477, evaluation of work by interpreter de Ricci dated 30th August 1917, our translation. Original quote: "Ne peut pas être laisé trop longtemps sans contrôle, car il finit par se mettre à dos la population civile en prenant parfois un peu trop le point de vue anglais – tout cela par zèle et désir de bien faire".

somewhere behind the lines, music and comedy acts alternating in the early evening. On the other side and at the same time, a group of French women had gathered to say the Rosary at a wayside shrine:

> Here I had, so to speak, materialized in one fugitive instant the fundamental and temperamental characteristics of the two allied races. It explained all; it illuminated, as the German lights did the trenches, the whole situation – the two kinds of patriotism, the amazingly different points of view, and ways of thinking, the serious articles in the French Press, England's jokes about herself in the comic newspapers, the heroic attitude of the French soldier, the sporting spirit of the British, the intense sentimentality of some Parisian writers who once had wit, talent and humour, the truly British "Business as usual". (Boulestin 1936:192-193)

Here the military interpreter, the same man who will later go back to the British officers' mess to answer many questions about France and the French, or, indeed, will publish a book to explain the contribution of the British to the Allied cause, gives a rare insight into the mental framework he has established in order to deal with the cultural differences he is confronted with every day. With this framework both for understanding the world around him, and for explaining it to others, the interpreter has a profound influence on the circulation of representations – one could say he is "gatekeeping ideas".

In 1915, two military interpreters, Richet and Herzog (later to become famous as a writer under the pseudonym André Maurois), published a translation of the souvenirs of the beginning of the war of the British officer alongside whom they served. Their introduction clearly delineates the kind of gatekeeping of ideas they intend to pursue by publishing for the French public.

> If some Frenchmen were to be led to better appreciate the immense effort of our friends from over there, and to better understand to what extent the English gentleman and the French gentilhomme are natural allies against the Herr Professor, our work will have been adequately rewarded. (Richet/ Herzog 1915:8, my translation)[7]

There seems to be no doubt that the gatekeeping metaphor is eminently suited to the case of military interpreters during the First World War. They

[7] "Si quelques Français y trouvent des raisons pour mieux apprécier l'effort géant de nos amis de là-bas, et pour mieux comprendre à quel point le Gentleman Anglais et le Gentilhomme Français sont des alliés naturels contre le 'Herr Professor', nous aurons reçu de notre travail la meilleure des récompenses".

had very detailed knowledge of the functioning and characteristics of both sides; they exerted a surprising amount of control over the information which was passed on; and they had a somewhat clearly defined position with respect to the military hierarchy on both sides of the coalition.

Testing the "gatekeeper" image on our case study has shown significant aspects of using metaphors in such a research setting: the predominant disciplinary metaphor in history, that of the "go-between", could not meaningfully cover the actual activities of the individuals or agencies while the "gatekeeper" provided a far more satisfactory coverage. However, we must also note that while the "gatekeeper"-metaphor is at its best in the analysis of minute details such as the memoirs can provide, the possibilities for linking these micro-elements of analysis to the larger context are severely limited, especially in a multi-variant setting such as that of Allied coalition warfare in the First World War. We might thus say that the use of the gatekeeper-metaphor on the historical case study of military interpreters quickly reaches its limits when it comes to generalising from individual situations where gatekeeping clearly happens.

Conclusion

While both metaphors seem to resonate with the source material concerning military interpreters during the First World War, they do so in a fundamentally different way which is linked essentially to disciplinary habits and biases. In short, historians and Translation/Interpreting Studies scholars, with their different skills, approach the material in very different ways, as our exemplary choice of two metaphors has shown.

Considering military interpreters during the First World War as go-betweens underlines their position as privileged witnesses of the Allied coalition and its functioning. It inserts their role into the context of the well-studied French and British armies and underlines the political nature of much of Allied coalition negotiations. Considering them as gatekeepers instead highlights the part they played as actors of the military coalition, influencing the day-to-day work and the public perception of the alliance.

Rather than being mutually exclusive, these metaphors provide complementary analyses to the case study. Only if we take into consideration both the actual work of an interpreter and the larger framework within which he or she works, can we get a complete picture of the interpreting setting. However, it can be stated that this short study has also showed the limitations of current historical approaches to transnational research objects which often remain focussed on the larger structures and are thus unable to comprehend what is happening on the actual level of exchange (an introduction to the current state of historiography can be found in Douki/ Minard 2007). Translation and interpreting history would do well to look at these particular approaches to elevate the study of individuals' contribution to a higher order by inserting it into established historiographical frameworks of power relations. We need to see both the go-betweens and the gatekeepers to get the whole picture.

References

Boulestin, Xavier M. (1936) *Myself, My Two Countries*. London: Cassell.

Cary, Edmond (1956) *La Traduction dans le monde moderne*. Université de Genève: Librairie de l'Université.

Certeau, Michel de/Giard, Luce (1983) "L'ordinaire de la communication". *Réseaux* 1:3, 3-26.

Collins Online Dictionary (2006), http://www.collinslanguage.com [3 July 2012].

Coser, Lewis A. (1975) "Publishers as Gatekeepers of Ideas". *The Annuals of the American Academy of Political and Social Science* 421, 14-22.

Davidson, Brad (2001) "Questions in Cross-Linguistic Medical Encounters: The Role of the Hospital Interpreter". *Anthropological Quarterly* 74:4, 170-178.

Douki, Caroline/Minard, Philippe (2007) "Histoire globale, histoires connectées: un changement d'échelle historiographique?". In Douki, Caroline/Minard, Philippe (eds.) *Revue d'histoire moderne et contemporaine* 54:4bis (special issue), 7-21.

Evans, Robert John Weston (1998) *The Language of History and the History of Language. An Inaugural Lecture delivered before the University of Oxford on 11 May 1998*. Oxford: Clarendon Press.

Hale, Sandra (2008) "Controversies Over the Role of the Court Interpreter". In Valero-Garcés, Carmen/Martin, Anne (eds.) *Crossing Borders in Community Interpreting: Definitions and dilemma*. Amsterdam-Philadelphia: John Benjamins, 99-121.

Hsieh, Elaine (2008) "'I am not a robot!' Interpreters' Views of Their Roles in Health Care Settings". *Qualitative Health Research* 18:10, 1367-1383.

Lewin, Kurt (1951) *Field Theory in Social Science Selected Theoretical Papers*. New York: Harper.

Maze, Paul (1934) *A Frenchman in Khaki*. Toronto-London: Heinemann.

McGinty, Stephen (1999) *Gatekeepers of Knowledge. Journal Editors in the Sciences and the Social Sciences*. Westport-London: Bergin & Garvey.

Morris, Ruth (1993) "The Interlingual Interpreter? Cypher or Intelligent Participant?". *International Journal for the Semiotics of Law* 6:3, 271-291.

Oxford English Dictionary (2006) Oxford: Oxford University Press.

Pym, Anthony (1992) "Shortcomings in the Historiography of Translation". *Babel* 38:4, 221-225.

Richet, Georges/Herzog, Emile (1915) "Avant-Propos". In Beith, John H. *Les Premiers cent mille.* Translated by Georges Richet and Emile Herzog. Paris: Nelson, 7-10.

Roland, Ruth A. (1999) *Interpreters as Diplomats: A Diplomatic History of the Role of Interpreters in World Politics.* Toronto: University of Toronto Press.

Rosenberg, Ellen/Seller, Robbyn/Leanza, Yvan (2008) "Through Interpreters' Eyes: Comparing Roles of Professional and Family Interpreters". *Patient Education and Counseling* 70:1, 87-93.

Rowley, J. (2003) "Knowledge management – the New Librarianship? From Custodians of History to Gatekeepers to the Future". *Library Management* 24:8, 433-440.

Roy, Cynthia B. (2002) "The Problem with Definitions, Descriptions, and the Role Metaphors of Interpreters". In Pöchhacker, Franz/Shlesinger, Miriam (eds.) *The Interpreting Studies Reader.* London-New York: Routledge, 345-353.

Schaffer, Simon/Roberts, Lissa/Raj, Kapil/Delbourgo, James (2009) "Introduction". In Schaffer, Simon/Roberts, Lissa/Raj, Kapil/Delbourgo, James (eds.) *The Brokered World: Go-betweens and Global Intelligence, 1770-1820.* Sagamore Beach: Science History Publications, ix-xxxviii.

Spears, Edward Louis (1930) *Liaison, 1914; a Narrative of the Great Retreat.* London: W. Heinemann.

Trésor de la Langue Française informatisé (2012), http://atilf.atilf.fr/tlf.htm [3 July 2012].

Vibraye, Henri de (1937) *Sans doute il est trop tard. Souvenirs du Front britannique.* Paris: Emile Hazan.

Wadensjö, Cecilia (1998) *Interpreting as Interaction.* London-New York: Longman.

White, David Manning (1966) "The 'Gatekeeper': A Case Study in the Selection of News". In Lewis, Anthony Dexter/White, David Manning (eds.) *People, Society, and Mass Communications.* New York: Free Press, 160-172

Roxana-Mihaela Antochi

University of Alicante, Spain

Behind the Scene: Text Selection Policies in Communist Romania. A Preliminary Study on Spanish and Latin-American Drama

The purpose of this paper is to discuss the selection policies at work in Communist Romania when it came to foreign drama chosen for performance, in particular the case of Spanish and Latin-American texts. To this end, it provides the overall political and cultural background of Romania between 1945 and 1989, with emphasis on the dynamics between theatres and the main institution in charge of censorship – the General Board for Press and Publications. A preliminary analysis of the place held by the Spanish corpus of plays in the general landscape of texts performed in the main Romanian theatres of this period is presented. The analysis is set within the conceptual framework of translation and censorship, by means of studying the scope of the ideological and cultural policies implemented in Romania and their effect on the translation policies at work in the country during Communist rule.

Keywords: censorship, selection policies, theatre, Spanish drama, Communist Romania

Introduction

The topic of the Communist period in Romania is, twenty-one years after the fall of the regime, still a highly controversial one. Attitudes ranging from vehement criticism to idealising nostalgia, crowned by the much debated results of a presidential commission's report on the period (Tismăneanu/ Dobrincu/Vasile 2006) make it even more relevant to raise questions about the actual situation in Romania between 1945 and 1989. If the political background is intricate, the cultural environment is no less complicated. Were all cultural manifestations regime-controlled? How did censorship really function? What sources of information were available to those involved in cultural activities in a country in which the dominant political party reportedly controlled it all? In other words, was Romania as closed a space as it is maintained by most scholars (among whom, Caravia 2000; Denize 2009)? Or were there also niches of dissent in the cultural world, cases in which censorship-related decisions had little to do with political matters, as recent studies on the literary institutions of the period seem to suggest (Macrea-Toma 2009)? The present paper intends to address such questions in relation to the theatre, which the Party saw both as an important tool for indoctrination, and as a very dangerous realm, due to the evanescent nature of its codes (which the Party had more difficulties in controlling than in the case of book publications, for instance). The types of plays included in the repertoire and performed on the Romanian stage provide interesting answers as to the approach to text selection taken by the deciding agents.

Against this background, I will first have a brief look at the political and cultural environment of the country in the period under analysis, as well as at the general composition of the theatre repertoire, and afterwards, I will address the issue of visibility in the case of the Spanish corpus, and the extent to which it respects the general requisites of repertoire composition. As mentioned above, in this study, I am focusing on translation policy as the most relevant indicator of the ideological constraints set upon translation and of the kind of cross-cultural relationships cultures negotiate as part of their self-image and the image of the "other". The analysis is set within the theoretical framework of translation and censorship, by means of studying the scope of the ideological and cultural policies implemented in Romania and their effect on the translation policies at work in the country between 1945 and 1989.

This preliminary study is part of a larger research project financed by the University of Alicante.[1] This project was triggered by the interest in looking at the (theatrical) contact zones between two ideologically different regimes but which were similar in their forms of repression, namely Communist Romania and Francoist Spain.

Theoretical framework

As already anticipated, this study attempts to offer a brief insight into the impact that ideology and censorship have on the process of translation during the Communist period in Romania (most specifically selection of

1 The study is funded through a Research, Development and Innovation scholarship for the training of doctoral researchers and an on-going three-month research grant at the Romanian National Archives.

texts for performance), by focusing on how the general level of "culture planning" influenced and restricted the choice of Iberian and Latin-American playwrights. Understood as a series of "deliberate acts of intervention in a current state of affairs within a social group" (Toury 2003:403), culture planning is of special relevance to the Romanian context because it "guides" and controls the policies of translation in such a way as to turn the selected texts into instruments of indoctrination. Otherwise stated, theatre as an entertainment industry is reconfigured and "readdressed by the state in pursuit of ideological goals" (Sturge 2010:74). Any field in the realm of culture (writing, publishing, performance, etc.) turns into "a device with a purpose" (Thomson-Wohlgemuth 2007:94), a tool used to implement an ideology. Hence, the texts are carefully selected in view of being used to enforce the new political order, and most choices are triggered by an "ideologically consonant" strategy (Sturge 2010:77). Consequently, the impact of ideology and censorship on the cultural life of the country, together with the changes it determines on the cultural policies applied at a national level has a direct influence on the types of texts that get to be translated and performed on the Romanian stage in the analysed period. In this respect, the "boundaries placed on cultural production", or, more specifically, "the limits imposed on culture by the regimes in their attempts to instrumentalize it" (Philpotts 2010:36) become a Procrustean bed for all walks of culture, which are forced to fulfil specific standards. Thus, text selection strategies become "mechanisms of political intervention" (Rundle/Sturge 2010:7), materialisations of the ideological principles that the dominant party wishes to disseminate within a given cultural field.

In totalitarian regimes, the concept of culture planning also entails, among others, the idea of "targets and guidance" together with the support given to and the "development of the right kind of literature" (Thomson-Wohlgemuth 2007:100). By looking at which texts by which Spanish-speaking playwrights are chosen for translation and performance in Communist Romania, one also succeeds in understanding the process of image projection for those specific authors, and, implicitly, for their respective cultural backgrounds. In other words, the elements considered "appropriate" turn into a sort of label for their countries of provenance, pointing out how the deciding agents at the receiving end wish to relate to certain geographical and political zones. Put differently, "text selection automatically filters the representation of a given culture and is, therefore, a key agent in the reception process" (Wolf 2002:50). This is not to say, however, that each and every one of the plays translated for the Romanian stage during Communism is to be reduced strictly to this role. Within the general framework of the translation policies the regime wishes to implement, and despite the organised and goal-oriented nature of the former, obviously not all translated plays are included in the repertoire for strictly ideological reasons. Particular and sometimes even puzzling cases do arise, which apparently have little to do with the general text selection criteria. These instances are mere exceptions, though, in an otherwise conformist environment.

Returning to translation policies, the act of selecting and choosing, which implies the existence of a grid against which texts are compared implicitly leads to the idea of blocking out and rejecting certain elements and favouring others. The selection mechanisms or the "exclusion procedures" (ibid.:60) may be enforced on military, political, moral, religious or corporate grounds:

> [T]he first category [of censorship] involves "acts of sedition […] but also control of public information on public airways; the second category includes blocking "criticism of regimes in power", while moral censorship "appeals to public decency". Religious censorship prevents "certain groups from worshipping in their own way", and corporate censorship "uses economic power to protect its interests". (Reinelt, qtd. in Pina Coelho 2010:217)

Regardless of their nature, they play a decisive role in how the chosen texts are perceived, since the target culture usually has no access to what is sifted out. In this respect, the understanding of censorship as "a form of manipulative rewriting of discourse by one agent or structure over another agent or structure, aiming at filtering the stream of information from one source to another" (Billiani 2007:3, emphasis added), is particularly relevant for the present study, as it points out the selection of what gets to be represented for and received by the general public. In the case of Romania, where censorship was institutionalised during almost the entire communist period, and in the specific instance of the theatre, as will become apparent in the following parts of this article, these selection mechanisms intervene to block the entry of supposedly pernicious elements, in the form of pre-censorship procedures, but also in order to control how the accepted plays were performed and delivered to the audience, by means of post-censorship forms of control (the so called "pre-premieres" in the case of the theatre).

A brief overview of the political context

The period in which Romania was under communist rule extends for five decades. Throughout this period, the fluctuations in the politics of the Romanian Communist Party (RCP), the changing attitudes in relation to both the Soviet Union and Romania itself have to do with a variety of aspects, ranging from developments in international politics, shifts within the Soviet Union, as well as adjustments in Romania's domestic and foreign affairs. Initially called the Romanian Workers' Party, before coming to power, this political organism conducted most of its activities in illegality (1924-1944). This, together with more general elements, characteristic of the Communist ideology, such as censorship, the manipulation of both national history and of the present, as well as the obsessive and constant control exercised on the people, are among the basic ingredients made use of by the Party.

Historically, the Communist regime in Romania can be divided into three periods (Tismăneanu 2005). The years between 1945 and 1958 are known as the Stalinist époque, and are defined by the progressive consolidation of a peripheral political party, which manages to reach power only thanks to Russian support, and tries to win over a highly sceptical and unwilling majority. Due to the presence of the Russian troops in the country, the RCP turns into a "dynamic group of pressure" (ibid.:110)[2], and by what is now labelled as an election fraud (Ionescu-Gură 2005:83, 109-110; Troncotă 2006:71), manages to collapse the influence and authority of its political opponents. After internal purges and fights for power, the sole ruler of the Party remains Gheorghe Gheorghiu-Dej, who between 1948 and 1956 emulates Stalin's politics and personality cult, thus exposing the Romanian culture to an intensive process of Sovietisation.

As far as the theatre life of the country is concerned, at the beginning of the period, the country was culturally independent from Moscow, as shown by the very small number of Russian plays presented to the Romanian audience. If in 1945, for example, there were only four Russian plays, their number grew to 26 in 1948 (when the Romanian performances barely reached twelve). The press is still the field for fierce protests against the interference of politics in the cultural domain but as soon as the Decree 102 of February 1945 takes effect, and the press purge succeeds in annihilating

---

[2] "un grup de presiune dinamic". All English versions of the quotations included in this paper are my own.

the publications of the opposition, such reactions will vanish. The same control will be extended over to libraries, bookshops and publishing houses through a decree published in May 1945.

Yet another law with great impact over the Romanian cultural world is the so-called "law of the theatres" (Law nr. 265 of July 1947), which brings about the beginning of state control in the field of public performances. As a result, the "guidance" of these institutions falls in the hands of the Ministry of Art, through the Theatre Board. Together with a 1948 decree which ensures total dominion over private theatres as well, these decisions turn the Party, through its propaganda and ideology committees, into the sole controller of theatrical activities. However, one of the most important institutions is yet to be born, namely the DGPT, the General Board for Press and Publications (Decree 28 of May 1949). With the state control of the publications comes the imposition of "socialist realism" as the appropriate approach in literature, which focuses on the figure of the New Man, the fight against bourgeois values and the construction of a socialist society (Denize 2009:140).

Stalin's death in 1953 generates a radical change in the approach of the Soviet Communist Party (CPUS) which distances itself from Stalin's politics. This year also triggers the so-called "small cultural thaw" in Romania, whose culture mimics a brief and superficial opening towards the West. The change is so convincing that eventually the Soviet troops are out of the country and 1958 marks the start of the second period in the evolution of the RCP (1958-1965), a period in which Gheorghiu-Dej consolidates even further his position in the country, where he maintains the Stalinist line while appearing to follow the new Soviet directives. In 1961, however, with the beginning of Khrushchev's second thaw, Gheorghiu-Dej decides to openly distance himself from Moscow.

Culturally, this year pinpoints a move away from the previous ideological policies, as well as the beginning of the "second wave of the absurd" in the theatre and the more visible presence of less dogmatic autochthonous playwrights. In terms of theatre censorship, this is the phase of orality, of "suggestions expressed mostly verbally", but also one full of "meetings, reunions, and indications" which left no doubt as to the desired ways of staging the repertoire (Popescu 2004:80). At the same time, this period is central for the consolidation of the Party's future leader, Nicolae Ceauşescu, who, until Gheorghiu-Dej's death in 1964, had managed to make himself irreplaceable to the entourage.

Hence, from 1965 until 1989, the leading figure of the Romanian Communist Party will be Ceauşescu, whose personality cult and extreme forms of control will be enforced by the much-feared secret police, the Securitate. In its turn, this third epoch in the history of the RCP is subdivided in two periods, during which Ceauşescu's politics are very different. Thus, between 1965 and 1971, Romania's image improves very much, thanks to good relations with the Western world as well as the positive projection of certain decisions made in the country such as a (yet another) so-called "cultural thaw". Notwithstanding, this is also the moment when the supervision of cultural manifestations, together with the dissemination and implantation of Ceauşescu's nationalist discourse begin.

All this apparent freedom ends in 1971, with Ceauşescu's visits to China and North Korea, and with the "theses of July" (Ceauşescu 1971). This moment marks the beginning of the most difficult years for the Romanian people (1971-1989), a time when the leader's personality cult reaches new heights and the control over and the repression of the population are unprecedented.

The repertoire

Decision boards

When it comes to theatre control in Communist Romania, two issues need to be considered: first, that it does not manifest itself in a uniform manner throughout the period (a fact explained by the numerous avatars of the RCP), and second, that censorship was present at two levels – text and performance –, the latter of which was extremely difficult to conduct given the plurivocality of the performed text. Initially, when censorship was yet a recent preoccupation of the new rulers, the means taken were usually restricted to textual censorship. In time, however, there was a marked change towards performance because of the paratextual strategies it involves:

> The scenic object, beyond its direct functional qualities, has a heavy symbolical charge; the image in its entirety, or a part of it, can gain multiple connotations, some of which contradict the literary text or project it in a

> hermeneutic dimension that is more or less visible, but that had passed totally unperceived until then. (Runcan 2006:301)[3]

It was precisely at that point when subversive messages could be sent which both actors and audience experienced as a "justificative catharsis" (ibid.), as the illusion of a rebellion and subsequent victory against the system. The paradox identified at the end of the seventies explains how the communist leaders related to the theatre and its dangers:

> In those times you could write poems and novels which had little to do with socialist realism, but in the theatre, where you had a room full of people, only "dramatic theatre" was acceptable. [...] The behaviour of this mass of people who, united, could react in an immediate and unpredictable fashion, was fear-provoking. (Maliţa 2006b:96)[4]

The same idea of the reactionary potential of the theatre world is underlined by playwright Radu Iftimovici, in a comparison between the stage, the novel and the screen:

> [As the novel, which one reads in the domestic space] the cinema was also considered less dangerous. Darkness separates people, and besides, at the cinema nobody claps their hands when they hear a good line, the people in the audience don't make audible comments, and the heroes move on a screen, which is a piece of cloth. In other words, the convention does not incite to violence. The situation is totally different in the case of the theatre, [where] you can see the actors move in front of you, you can hear them breathe, and their words are like daggers. The ovations bring about solidarity and the scene turns into a tribune that hosts dangerous political agitators. (Iftimovici 2008, no paging)[5]

---

3 "Obiectul scenic, dincolo de calitatile sale functionale directe, are o puternica incarcatura simbolica, imaginea de ansamblu sau o portiune din ea pot fi incarcate cu conotatii multiple, dintre care unele capabile sa contrazica textul literar sau sa il proiecteze intr-o dimensiune hermeneutica, mai mult sau mai putin vizibila, dar total nebanuita pana atunci".

4 "Aveai voie, la acea data, sa scrii poezii, romane, care nu mai aveau nimic de a face cu realismul socialist, dar in teatru, unde exista o sala plina, nu se admitea alta formula decat a teatrului "dramatic". [...] Atitudinea unei mase de oameni care, stranse la un loc, putea reactiona imprevizibil si imediat speria".

5 [Un roman se citea in mediul domestic]. Nici sala de cinema nu era socotita "mediu periculos". Intunericul izoleaza, la cinema nu se aplauda replicile, nu se vocifereaza, eroii se misca pe panza, conventia nu-ti da branci spre rascoala. Cu totul alta e atmosfera dintr-o sala de teatru [unde] le prinzi privirea, le auzi respiratia, cuvintele incitante patrund ca pumnalele. Aplauzele incita la solidarizare, scena devine o tribuna pe care se pot misca agitatori politici periculosi".

For these reasons, at times the censorship of the written word was more permissive than that of the performed material.

In terms of the control forced onto the theatres, starting from 1947, the Law of the theatres imposed a certain internal dynamics when it came to the repertoire. First, the list with the repertoire was discussed at the level of the theatre "Workers' Committee", whose members decided which plays to include. This committee came into being prior to the communist period, though under a different name, but if before 1947 its responsibilities had more to do with the literary quality of the texts and the profile of each theatre, with this law it took on more ideological and doctrinaire aspects (Preutu 2008:65). Moreover, its importance grew in time, especially starting with the mid fifties. Before that moment, the repertoire list was sent to the individual theatres by the Theatre Board, and the committee was less visible in the process. So, once the plays were chosen from that list, the resulting selection was sent to the Regional Committee for Culture together with an explanatory summary which in fact acted as an ideological justification for the inclusion of the play. This was followed by a meeting between the members of this Committee, theatre representatives and the regional Party secretary. Once the list was approved at this level, it was sent to the Regional Committee of the Party, where it became the responsibility of the secretary for propaganda and ideology. Only after this winding road, with both internal and external obstacles, did the repertory reach the Theatre Board in Bucharest. This, in its turn, analysed the suggestions made by the previous screening organisms and eventually contacted the theatre to confirm the final list with the plays (Runcan 2006:307).

Nonetheless, the control was far from being over. After the texts had been looked into by so many eyes, it was time for the actors to begin their work, and for the censors to start viewing the end result before it was presented to the public, and usually after that as well. The series of pre-premieres was addressed firstly to the Workers' Committee, who saw the staging before it was performed in front of the ideological Commission. The latter was usually formed by the theatre delegate of the Regional Committee, the secretary for propaganda, cultural magazine editors, the delegate of the General Board for Press and Publications and, for purely formal reasons, certain intellectuals whose inclusion was supposed to "professionally legitimize the commission, whose main and sometimes sole objective was ideological in nature" (Maliţa 2006a:7).[6] What should be stated, however, is that

> its intention was not to prohibit a play and cause a scandal, but rather to exhaust [...] especially the stage director so that he might operate the indicated changes and thus transform the text in a performance compatible with the party's ideological requirements, one that could be staged. (Ibid.)[7]

Contents: types of plays, origin, topics

The repertoire was composed mainly of contemporary Romanian plays, which held centre stage almost at all times. Even if at the beginning of the period, due to lack of national models in the socialist realist line, Russian texts were more numerous, soon Romanian ones became dominant. Still, throughout the period, the hierarchy was maintained for contemporary works: Romanian plays, Soviet texts, plays from other "communist sisterly states", and lastly, plays from Western and other countries. Both autochthonous and foreign texts had to help the formation and subsequent development of "the new man", strengthen the audience's education and political culture, attract a diverse public, etc. Also, it was mandatory to consider certain pragmatic aspects related to the number of actors the theatre had, its financial resources, the structure of the stage, etc. Along the same line, a balance between the number of comedies and tragedies was aimed at (with special emphasis on contemporary texts, an implicit way of promoting ideologically correct authors).

In terms of preferred topics, the theme of the new socialist world was very much encouraged, as were the critique of the bourgeois society and of capitalism. Besides these clearly indicated focal points, another source of continuous inspiration and information were Ceauşescu's discourses and the articles published in Party newspapers such as *Scanteia* and *Flacara Poporului.*

An interesting presence in the repertoire is that of the so-called collective plays. They were of two kinds: either a selection of fragments from plays by the same author, or miscellanea of fragments from the work of various playwrights, usually staged to celebrate anniversaries and key historical

---

6 "In completare, formal, erau invitati oameni de cultura, pentru legitimarea profesionala a comisiei, al carei principal, adesea unic, obiectiv, ramanea cel ideologic".

7 "intentia acesteia nu era de a interzice si a provoca scandal, ci de a determina, prin epuizare si exasperare, [...] pe regizor in special, sa opereze modificarile solicitate, pentru ca spectacolul sa devina compatibil cu exigentele ideologice ale partidului si, astfel, sa poata fi jucat".

moments. Poetry recitals were also performed in the Romanian theatres, but mostly starting with the seventies, and with Ceauşescu's nationalist line in politics.

The Spanish corpus

Before focusing on the Spanish group of plays which were translated and performed in Communist Romania, it is important to say a few words about the data which make up this research. The general corpus of this project is based on the archives of 37 national and state theatres from 26 Romanian cities, and it includes all the shows organised by these institutions between 1945 and 1989 – theatre performances *per se*, poetry recitals, novel and short-story adaptations for the stage, as well as the above-mentioned collective plays –, a total of approximately three thousand performances. Despite the fact that during this period many theatrical institutions were built and there were also numerous amateur troupes (made up of factory workers, miners etc.), those included in the corpus are the most important ones in the country, not only in those days, but also in the present. The national theatres (from Iaşi, Bucharest, Craiova and Cluj-Napoca – leading cultural cities) are the oldest and among the most prestigious ones in Romania. They date back to the nineteenth century and were the first to host performances in the country. The state theatres, in their turn, began being built in the mid-fifties, had ample capacity, were spread throughout the country and were meant to enhance access to cultural and propaganda events for the working class. In both cases, their troupes toured the country and the repertoires they prepared were highly representative for the selection policies of the regime. At the same time, these theatres are constant presences in the "official conversation" with the censorship bodies throughout the period, also providing broader scope for analysis and helping to establish connections among the different sublevels of the corpus.

In such a rigorously controlled, ideologically-centred cultural environment, what was the place held by Spanish-speaking authors? Who was selected and on what grounds? If in the case of the Latin-American playwrights, the choice was politically motivated, their Iberian counterparts obviously belonged to a totally opposed reference system, which makes their presence all the more interesting. What about access to their texts? If Romania was as closed a country as maintained by some researchers (for instance Denize 2009), how did contemporary texts reach the theatres, especially those produced in a country whose political orientation was radically different, so that they might be included in the repertoire? Put differently, what sources of information were available to theatre professionals in Communist Romania?

As archival material proves, apart from the Ministry of Culture and the Theatre Board, which could order translations and then introduce them in the repertoire circuit, as of 1958, a new organisation was founded – the Association of Art's People from Theatre and Music Institutions, in short the *ATM*. Its name is mentioned in various classified files of the GDPT as one of the main providers of translated texts available to the theatres under the label of "inner circulation material". The *ATM* also published a news bulletin (1965-1971), which contained well documented theoretical information about the latest trends in drama, news about the most recent premieres in the world (from neighbouring countries to the most distant states) and lists with plays available at the *ATM* library (be they already translated into Romanian, in their original language or in other translations). Besides, the treatment the *ATM* receives in the censorship files proves it was a tool for both Ministry and theatres when it came to repertoire design. These data show that, despite firm ideological control and limited access to direct information, Romanian theatres were not totally divorced from contemporary reality. Moreover, the presence of some Spanish authors who definitely did not fit the prescribed profile proves that state control was not completely ubiquitous and that the text selection policies were not *only* politically motivated.

The following graph (Figure 1) includes the number of plays originally written in English, French, Italian, German and Spanish which were selected for performance on the Romanian stage both in terms of the individual titles and the number of times they were premiered in theatres during the Communist period, and it clearly shows the dynamics established among the different groups of authors from non-communist states, as well as the limited visibility of Spanish texts on the Romanian stage.

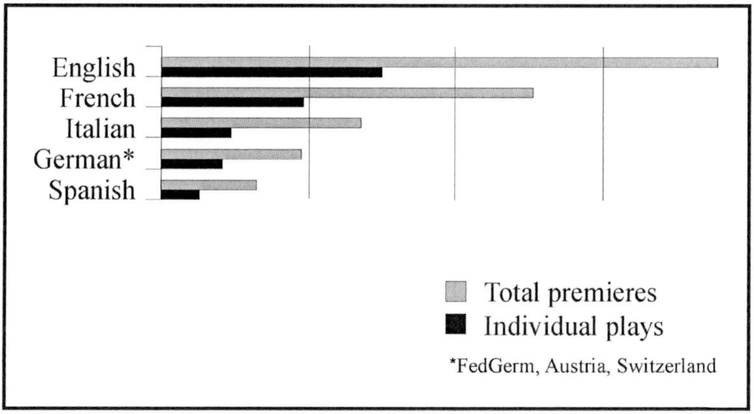

Figure 1: Plays by authors from non-communist countries

In terms of decades, the situation of the Spanish corpus is as follows: 1948-1949: three Spanish plays with three premieres; 1950-1959: 22 plays/31 premieres; 1960-1969: 41 plays/51 premieres (a poetry recital included); 1970-1979: 38 plays/42 premieres; 1980-1989: 13 plays/13 premieres and two poetry recitals. As seen, the period with most Spanish performances coincides with a cultural thaw, and it is also the moment when most foreign contemporary texts were present on the Romanian stage.

As for the authors included in the Spanish corpus and the number of plays selected from their work, they are: from Spain, 12 authors with 30 plays – Lope (10), Calderón (6), Tirso (1), Moreto y Cabaña (1), de Rojas (1), García Lorca (7 plays, 2 recitals), Casona (5), Buero Vallejo (5), Mihura (1), Arrabal (2), Sastre (1), Calvo Sotelo (1); from Latin-America, 9 authors with 10 plays – Argentina: Dragún (2), Mauricio (1), Cuzzani (1); Venezuela: Rengifo (1), Santana (1); Chile: Neruda (1 play, 1 recital); Cuba: Quintero (1); Mexico: Usigli (1); Colombia: Martínez (1).

The Latin-American authors are, without exception, connected with the communist cause. Militant members of their respective communist parties, critics of capitalism, and promoted in other communist countries, these names were more easily accessible, and their selection more traceable. In the case of the Spanish authors Lorca, Buero Vallejo, Sastre and Arrabal, their clear progressive profiles and/or leftist preferences also provide the needed explanation for their inclusion in the repertoire, apart from the literary value of their texts, given the fact that the presence of numerous lesser known names on the Romanian stage manifestly proves that literary quality alone was by no means a decisive factor. Casona, Mihura and Calvo Sotelo, on the other hand, are a more challenging option, due to their anti-communist militancy (Oliva 2002:151-156). Why were they selected and how did their texts reach the Romanian theatres? Casona, for example, is first performed in the mid and late fifties, in a period in which the communist regime had consolidated its control over the country, hence when there was no danger in staging an "outsider", and also when he was living in exile in Argentina. Mihura, in his turn, was staged towards the end of the second wave of the theatre of the absurd in Romania, and of the three premieres of his play *Carlota*, one was occasioned by the anniversary of an esteemed actress; put differently, reasons beyond ideology and literary quality sometimes had a say in the selection process. The first mention of Calvo Sotelo is in *Teatrul* magazine (1971), as president of the Spanish section of the *ITI* (the International Theatre Institute, which also had a Romanian branch) in a meeting with Mihnea Gheorghiu (an influential figure in the cultural life of the period) which took place four years prior to the staging of his work in Bucharest. The antibourgeois character of many of these plays, their light-hearted tone and/or their absurd touches, together with the historical moment when they were selected, all constitute equally valid explanations as to their performance in Communist Romania. One could not emphasise enough, however, the fact that, despite the interesting and even striking nature of these names, they never cease to be isolated, exotic islands in a sea of Communist militant writers and of ideologically innocuous authors.

Conclusion

These considerations are, as anticipated in the title of this article, of a preliminary nature. Further research needs to be carried out by accessing the *ATM* archives, which will certainly provide valuable information on the exact number of plays by Spanish and Latin-American authors that were available to Romanian stage directors, but were never performed. These data will help understand the broader picture and the inner workings of the text selection mechanism at work during the communist regime in Romania, as well as the connection established between the party's ideological stance and the materialisation of the translation policies at the level of drama.

So far, the study of the main cultural magazines of the period, together with the censorship files of the General Board for Press and Publications has shown that, contrary to the general belief, Romanian theatres had at their disposal extensive sources of information on the activity of the main theatres in the world, as well as access to recent publications in the field of drama, and original versions or translations of the latest plays published throughout the world. Apart from the firm ideological guidance provided by the Party, which restricted the repertoire choice, lack of funding for translations, along with internal conditionings forced the theatres to reduce the span of their interest in contemporary playwrights and stage more readily-accessible texts, such as those by Romanian authors (both classical and contemporary), Russian and Soviet authors or recent plays whose translation had been commissioned by the Ministry, the Theatre Board or by other theatrical institutions in the country. Overall, the vast majority of contemporary plays were mostly of Romanian and Soviet extraction, thanks to their ideological reliability; the remaining titles were divided among classical writers (be they autochthonous or foreign) and contemporary authors from non-communist countries. The preference was clearly manifested towards the former texts which, apart from their readily-available translation, were also "politically neutral" in relation to the party's ideology and were a guarantee for the quality of the performance, thus enforcing the theatre's educational role that the regime supported. To conclude, despite the government's attempt at completely subordinating the theatre to its propaganda and ideological institutions, it would be a coarse generalisation and a limiting view to say that its control was ubiquitous or that all choices were only ideologically-informed, as proven in the brief analysis of the Spanish corpus.

Set within the framework of translation and censorship, the Romanian context exposes the limits of seeing such a case from a purely ideological, state-dominated perspective, and raises new questions as to the real motivations behind the translation policies implemented in dictatorial regimes.

References

Billiani, Francesca (2007) "Assessing Boundaries – Censorship and Translation". In Billiani, Francesca (ed.) *Modes of Censorship and Translation.* Manchester: St Jerome, 1-25.

Caravia, Paul (2000) *Gândirea interzisă. Scrieri cenzurate, România, 1945-1989.* Bucureşti: Editura Enciclopedică.

Ceauşescu, Nicolae (1971) *Propuneri de măsuri pentru îmbunătăţirea activităţii político-ideologice, de educare marxist-leninistă a membrilor de partid, a tuturor oamenilor muncii.* Bucureşti: Editura Politică.

Denize, Eugen (2009) *Propoaganda comunistă în România: 1948-1953.* Târgovişte: Cetatea de Scaun.

Iftimovici, Radu (2008) "Amintirile unui pseudodramaturg" (III), http://www.zf.ro/ziarul-de-duminica/radu-iftimovici-amintirile-unui-pse [3 July 2012].

Ionescu-Gură, Nicoleta (2005) *Stalinizarea României: Republica Populară Română 1948-1950: Transformări instituţionale.* Bucureşti: ALL.

Macrea-Toma, Ioana (2009) *Privilighenţia. Instituţii literare în comunismul românesc. Editura Casa Cărţii de Ştiinţă.* Cluj-Napoca: Casa Cartii de Stiinta.

Maliţa, Liviu (ed.) (2006a) *Cenzura în teatru. Documente. 1948-1989.* Cluj-Napoca: Eefes.

Maliţa, Liviu (ed.) (2006b) *Viaţa teatrală în şi după comunism.* Cluj-Napoca: Eefes.

Oliva, César (2002) *Teatro español del siglo XX.* Madrid: Síntesis.

Philpotts, Matthew (2010) "The Boundaries of Dictatorship". In Rundle, Christopher/Sturge, Kate (eds.) *Translation under Fascism.* New York: Palgrave Macmillan, 235-251.

Pina Coelho, Rui (2010) "Safe Shakespeare: Performing Shakespeare during the Portuguese Fascist Dictatorship (1926-1974)". In Rundle, Christopher/Sturge, Kate (eds.) *Translation Under Fascism.* New York: Palgrave Macmillan, 215-232.

Popescu, Marian (2004) *Scenele teatrului românesc.* Bucureşti: Unitext.

Preutu, Cristina (2008) *Istoria Teatrului Naţional Vasile Alecsandri, Iaşi, 1965-1989.* BA Dissertation: Universitatea Alexandru Ioan Cuza Iaşi.

Runcan, Miruna (2006) "Mecanisme şi instituţii ale cenzurii în teatru". In Maliţa, Liviu (ed.) *Viata teatrala in si dupa comunism.* Cluj: Eefes, 299-312.

Rundle, Christopher/Sturge, Kate (2010) "Translation and the History of Fascism". In Rundle, Christopher/Sturge, Kate (eds.) *Translation Under Fascism.* New York: Palgrave Macmillan, 1-12.

Sturge, Kate (2010) "Flight from the Programme of National Socialism?" In Rundle, Christopher/Sturge, Kate (eds.) *Translation Under Fascism.* New York: Palgrave Macmillan, 51-83.

Teatrul. Revistă lunară editată de Comitetul de Stat pentru Cultură şi Artă şi Uniunea Scriitorilor din Republica Socialistă România 12:1971.

Thomson-Wohlgemuth, Gaby (2007) "On the Other Side of the Wall. Book Production, Censorship and Translation in East Germany". In Billiani, Francesca (ed.) *Modes of Censorship and Translation.* Manchester: St Jerome, 93-116.

Tismăneanu, Vladimir (2005) *Stalinism pentru eternitate. O istorie politică a comunismului românesc.* Iaşi: Polirom.

Tismăneanu, Vladimir/Dobrincu, Dorin/Vasile, Cristian (eds.) (2006) *Raportul Comisiei Prezidenţiale pentru Analiza Dictaturii Comuniste din România. (C.P.A.D.C.R).* Bucureşti: Humanistas.

Toury, Gideon (2003) "Culture Planning and Translation". In Petrilli, Susan (ed.) *Translation Translation.* Amsterdam-New York: Rodopi, 399-412.

Troncotă, Tiberiu (2006) *România comunistă. Propagandă şi cenzură.* Bucureşti: Tritonic.

Wolf, Michaela (2002) "Censorship as Cultural Blockage: Banned Literature in the Late Habsburg Monarchy". *TTR* 15:2, 45-61.

Rosario Garnemark

University of Oslo, Norway

Institutional Constraints on Translation: Ingmar Bergman, Francoist Censorship and the "Apertura"

> "But the history of translation suggests that, as a rule, translations have not been perceived as equal to their source texts at all and that, in addition, they are deployed in situations involving highly unequal power relations."
> Theo Hermans (1999:54)

By 1963, an era of greater tolerance in Francoist censorship, known as the "Apertura", had begun to exert a subtle effect on the prevailing ultra-Catholic discourse. The censorial activity developed during this period was characterised by the extensive negotiations undertaken between film distribution companies and censorship authorities; negotiations marked by evident asymmetrical power relations. In this article, I will analyse the institutional constraints imposed by censorship boards on film distribution companies, and the impact of their dialogue on the translation of three films by Ingmar Bergman released during this period: *Sommarnattens leende (Sonrisas de una noche de verano,* 1955*), Smultronstället (Fresas salvajes,* 1957*) and Såsom i en spegel (Como en un espejo,* 1961*).*

Keywords: censorship, audiovisual translation, Descriptive Translation Studies, Francoism, Ingmar Bergman

Introduction

In the past decade, research on translation has shown a growing interest in issues related to censorship.[1] André Lefevere, one of the initiators of the so-called "cultural turn" in Translation Studies, addressed the importance of studying translation as a phenomenon directly influenced by determining factors such as power, ideology, institutions and manipulation (Lefevere 1992:2). Moreover, his conceptualisation of patronage as "the powers

[1] See for instance the very extensive bibliography mentioned in the "Introduction" to Ní Chuilleanáin/Ó Cuilleanáin/Parris (2009:9-23) or the entry on "Censorship" (Merkle 2010) included in the *Handbook of Translation Studies Online.*

(persons, institutions) that can further or hinder the reading, writing, and rewriting of literature" (ibid.:15) exposes the role of institutional censorship as one possible form of patronage in the cultural transmission that takes place when texts are translated or "rewritten".[2] My contribution to this field of research, focusing on the case of Ingmar Bergman in Francoist Spain, aims to complement with new data the research into this particular period of Spanish history already available in volumes such as Labrum (1997), Vandaele (1999, 2006), Rabadán (2000), Tymoczko and Gentzler (2002), Billiani (2007), Muñoz Calvo, Buesa Gómez and Ruiz-Moneba (2008) and Seruya and Lin Moniz (2008).

The cultural turn in Translation Studies took its origin in Descriptive Translation Studies, which can be characterised by Toury's claim that translations are to be regarded "as facts of the culture which hosts them" (Toury 1995:24). In the case of film translations circulating within the Spanish cultural system[3] during the Francoist period, they were produced under the harsh scrutiny of official censorship, becoming thus highly influenced by their hosting ideology. When studying the censorship files for this particular period kept in the "Archivo General de la Administración" (Administration General Archive) in Alcalá de Henares (Spain), it becomes strikingly evident that a dialogue took place between the censorship authorities and the film distribution companies trying to import foreign movies into Spain. It was of course a rather one-sided dialogue marked by a very asymmetrical power relation, since final decisions were always settled by the censorship authorities. Still, it is worthwhile examining the dynamics in place during these negotiations in order to arrive at a greater understanding of how Francoist dialectics worked, which kind of arguments and counter-arguments were put forward and how these institutional constraints influenced the translation process.

In this article, I will focus on the trajectory of three films by the Swedish film director Ingmar Bergman (*Sommarnattens leende*, 1955; *Smultronstället*, 1957; *Såsom i en spegel*, 1961). I will discuss the kind of dialogue that was established between the censorship boards and the distribution

[2] Other types of rewriting may include, according to Lefevere, historiography, anthologies, criticism, editing or adaptations for film and television (1992:9).

[3] The concept of cultural system applied here is drawn from Even-Zohar's Polysystems Theory (1990) that understands culture as a dynamic and evolving phenomenon shaped as a system, in which translation plays a vital role. The cultural system interacts as it develops with other aspects of society (financial system, political system etc.).

companies attempting to get the films' approval. The three films have been chosen on the basis that they all were released in Spain during a period known as the "Apertura" in the chronology of Francoist censorship, although their importation procedures may have been initiated earlier. Vandaele defines this period in the following terms:

> *Apertura*, or "opening" (1963-69): Franco gradually lost his personal grip on the Francoist subgroups. A new group of capitalist "technocrats" now tried to renovate the Spanish economy, stimulating tourism and admitting more flexible censorship criteria. In cultural policy, they were helped by ex-, post-, or "liberal" fascists, who had also grown tired of Catholic moralism. (2010:87, original emphasis)

During the "Apertura" years, Spain opened up to tourism and foreign influences. Indeed, tourism became one of the major sources of revenue for the country (Gubern 1981:181). A shift towards more effective financial policies, led by a group of specialists or "technocrats", was also established in order to achieve improved levels of prosperity. This new sociopolitical climate put a strain on the old traditional "National-Catholic" values of authority, hierarchy, discipline, religious and military dominance, themselves little more than the negation of their opposite numbers, including freedom, equality, democracy, and even capitalism, liberalism or modernism (Terrón Montero 1981:89). In order for these strategies to succeed, it was important for the regime to project a public image of openness, as well as to hide its most repressive or anachronic aspects (Gubern 1981:181). The appointment of Manuel Fraga Iribarne as Minister for Information and Tourism in 1962 to replace the ultra-Catholic Gabriel Arias Salgado had an impact on film censorship policy as well. As Gutierrez Lanza explains: "It became necessary to avoid the international ridicule that the banning of various prestigious films was likely to provoke" (2002:152). The reappointment of José María García Escudero as General Director of Cinematography and Theatre in 1962[4] brought a relaxation in moral standards and a greater tolerance of social criticism. García Escudero promoted the publication in 1963 of the first official written code of censorship, but Gutiérrez Lanza, who has studied this period in depth, argues that "the code was too general, too ambiguous, and too open to interpretation" (2002:154). Gutiérrez Lanza

---

[4] García Escudero had already held this position between 1951 and 1952, but his views were then considered too "progressive", so he was forced to resign after six months (Gutiérrez Lanza 2002:146-147).

points out that the apparent progress and moderate tolerance of the "Apertura" concealed the fact that many of the legal, administrative and political mechanisms of the old apparatus were still in place (ibid.:154-155).

As far as this article is concerned, the "Apertura" presented itself as an appropriate framework within which to study the kind of dynamics that may have been in place between the different agents involved, since censors were prone to be more receptive and therefore more inclined to negotiate.

Sommarnattens leende (*Sonrisas de una noche de verano*, 1955)

This film depicts the sentimental and erotic adventures of several couples belonging to Swedish upper class at the beginning of the twentieth century. The main character is a lawyer Fredrik Egerman, married to a young woman more than half his age, Anne. Though Anne worships Fredrik, she feels a strong attraction towards his son, Henrik, a theology student with deep moral concerns. At the same time, Fredrik reconnects with actress Desirée Armfeldt, and former lover. Desirée is still in love with Fredrik and plans to get him back, drawing another couple into her scheme. This film was unusual in Bergman's filmography in that it was one of the few comedies he ever directed.

The first written record concerning the reception of this film in Spain, dating from November 29, 1962 is an official form filled in by the Director of Procines[5], the distribution company interested in importing the film into the Spanish market, and addressed to the General Director of Cinematography and Theatre. The submission of this form constituted a necessary initial step in the process that would grant the film access to the censorship machinery, which was highly bureaucratised and has been described as a carefully planned and institutionalised process (Gutiérrez Lanza 2002:143). It included general technical and artistic information about the film as well as additional data concerning the proposed translated title, the synopsis of the plot and the application fee paid.[6] Furthermore, the form required the

---

[5] All documents mentioned and cited can be found in the official censorship file for this particular movie, filed at AGA (Alcalá de Henares, Spain) with entry 36/03949, database IDD (03)121.002.

[6] It is interesting to mention that different fees or taxes were paid at different stages of the censorial process. The fee mentioned on this form referred to a sort of application fee, but other fees were payable, for instance every time a film was to be screened by a censorship board, or for the customs office to release a film into the country.

distribution company to confirm that "the copy of the movie placed at the customs office integrally coincides with the version being shown at the country of origin", and instructed the distribution company to produce a "signed and stamped written document declaring whether it is intended or not to voluntarily apply suppressions or adaptations to the film" (my translation).[7] This last statement leads us to think that self-censorship on the part of distribution companies, prior to official censorial activity, was somehow expected and may even have been tacitly encouraged, although the censors still wanted to be aware of its existence and monitor it. In this particular case, Procines claimed that they did not intend to introduce any modifications either in the dialogues or the images of the film to be assessed.

Another important piece of information included in these application forms was whether the film was to be dubbed or subtitled. To this effect, the distribution company was required to include with the application a "twofold complete and literal translation of the filmic text from its original version" for dubbing or "a twofold text with the subtitles intended for the projection of the movie in Spain" (my translation)[8], if the film was to be subtitled. Although dubbing had become the only possible film translation practice in Spain after being imposed by law in 1941 (Gutiérrez Lanza 2002:158; Vandaele 2010:99), there was a very limited use of subtitles for movies shown in the members-only "Cine-clubs", and later on in the so-called "Salas Especiales", special movie theatres of no more than 500 seats, created in 1967 in cities with a population of more than 50,000 (Gutiérrez Lanza 2002:154). In this particular case, the distribution company Procines expressed its intention to apply for the movie to be released in its dubbed version, thereby aiming to appeal to a greater audience. In the light of the requirements outlined above, Procines presented its translation of the filmic text, presumably rendered from a German version, since the original title is provided in German. The translator's initials ("M. L. F.") can also be read in the opening page of the translation. The fact that these initials will be found again in a translation of our third movie (*Como en un espejo*), with a heading

[7] "Que la copia de la película depositada en la Aduana coincide íntegramente con la versión que se proyecta en el país de origen" and "Escrito firmado y sellado en el que se declara si se prentende o no efectuar voluntariamente supresiones o adaptaciones en la película".

[8] "Traducción literal y completa por duplicado del texto de la película en su versión original" and "Texto por duplicado de los subtítulos con los que haya de ser proyectada la película en España".

that reads "Literal translation from German to Spanish"[9], can be taken as supporting evidence that this was a case of indirect translation (i.e. the source text for this translation was not the original Swedish text, but a German version). Despite the fact that the rules stated that translations be rendered from the original version (see above), this application was accepted, an indication that the authorities were not so inflexible in this respect after all. It is difficult to establish whether the distribution company decided to translate from an intermediate language such as German due to a lack of translators who were qualified to translate from Swedish, or if they had easy access to German versions due to special agreements with German importers. In any case, it is reasonable to assume that the movie was assessed on the basis of an indirect translation from German.

A new letter dated January 16, 1963 addressed by Procines to the censorship authorities, serves to complement the information contained in the previous application form and implies that, as of January 1963, the film had not yet undergone a proper assessment. The application form had probably been given its due consideration, but the censors' verdict concerning the film was still pending, and in this sense, the letter may be seen as a pragmatic strategy to draw extra attention to the film in question. In the letter, Procines asks that the members of the censorship board who are to assess this particular film read a note attached to the letter. The purpose of this almost-two-pages-long "note" is to alert the censors to some potentially problematic aspects of the film, in an attempt to soften the negative impact that these might have on the censors. A couple of cuts are even proposed, always leaving it to the censors' discretion whether to apply them or not. One of the arguments used by the distribution company to support the alleged innocuousness of the film is its humorous tone. At the same time, they admit that, Ingmar Bergman being the author of this movie, humour in this case does indeed conceal a deeper concern: the condemnation of self-centred behaviour, lies and conventionalisms in matters relating to sentimental relationships.

On January 29, 1963, a Classification and Censorship Board (Junta de Clasificación y Censura) finally met, presided over by Jose Mª García Escudero,[10] in order to assess the film. Although four of the 13 censors that

[9] "Traducción literal del alemán al español" (my translation).

[10] García Escudero was one of the figures directly involved in the shaping of the so-called "Apertura" (Gutiérrez Lanza 2002:152; Vandaele 2006:66-67), as pointed out above.

attended this assessment session were in favour of releasing the film for a wider audience, with an "adults-only" rating and with possible cuts, the other nine considered it too daring and inappropriate. The depiction of partner-swapping, adultery and incest (a step-mother running away with her step-son) was deemed too serious a matter despite the humorous tone deployed. The final verdict pointed to authorising its release only for the so-called Cine-Clubs. The rating was set for adults over 21. It was agreed that the film could be shown without modifications, probably since the potential audience would be extremely limited (Cine-clubs were members-only theatres, as mentioned earlier).[11] It is therefore fair to present this verdict as a failure on the part of Procines, since their efforts to mollify the censors through the note I mentioned earlier did not produce the required result. At the same time, one might quite reasonably posit that the arguments deployed by Procines did have some impact on at least some of the censors, since the four in favour of an ordinary commercial release of the film expressed very similar ideas to the ones put forward by Procines.[12]

The reaction of Procines to this verdict came only a few weeks later. On February 9, 1963, a new letter addressed by Procines informs the censorial authorities of the company's intention to appeal the decision. Special emphasis is put on the fact that the setting of the movie is Protestant Sweden, where marriage had different connotations and the practice of divorce was allowed. To no avail, Procines informed the censors that the movie had been awarded the Poetic Humour Prize at the 1956 Cannes Film Festival,[13] in an attempt to stress its humorous tone. It even declared its willingness to introduce some kind of explanatory or guiding message at the beginning of the movie in order to prepare the audience. On June 10, 1963, the decision of the board handling the appeal was unanimous, reiterating the film's prohibition for commercial release. No favourable voices were heard this time, the general tone being that the work was too immoral to be made

---

[11] Which brings to mind Merkle's statement that "the broader the intended audience is, the more rigorous the censorship" (2010).

[12] This particular censorship file contains the reports from virtually all the censors involved in this session (only two are missing), including written annotations by each censor, which provides us with first-hand information about what was on their minds.

[13] This is considered by many to be Bergman's international breakthrough, although it has been proved that by 1956 some Spanish critics were already aware of the importance of Bergman's filmography through Latin American connections (Fernández Cuenca 1961:7-9; Steene 2005:919).

accessible to a greater audience. This was the last instance of appeal, so the movie was presumably released in accordance with the original verdict, restricted to selected Cine-Clubs in a subtitled version.

Smultronstället (*Fresas salvajes*, 1957)

The movie portrays a journey that is both physical and metaphorical. It is the story of the redemption and self-acceptance of an old and selfish man who is starting to worry about his own death. Some of the characters he encounters on his trip make certain allusions to Catholicism and religion in general that may have been problematic for some ultra-Catholic censors from this period.

The opening documents of this particular censorship file are less detailed than for the previous one.[14] There is, for instance, no record of the application form, although we know from a receipt that the application fee was paid on June 7, 1960, by a distribution company called Radio Films. Since the first censorship documents pertaining to this film are two years older than for the other two films, we may speculate that the official forms may have undergone certain modifications between 1960 and 1962, and that in 1960, no official application form was as yet being used. In any case, a brief report issued internally accounts for the film having been projected during a censorship board session on June 15, 1960. Unfortunately, there are no written records about this particular assessment session, which may again mean that the level of documentation in 1960 was less extensive than it would become by 1962, and procedures less bureaucratised. A letter dated July 8, 1960, and addressed to the Director of Radio Films confirms that a censorship board met on June 15 in order to assess the film, reaching the decision to ban its release nationally. The purpose of this letter is to inform Radio Films of its recourse to appeal to a higher authority. Radio Films' appeal came on July 13, 1960, as documented by a letter that states its obligation to the Swedish distributor (Svensk Filmindustri) to take all possible administrative and legal steps in the interests of obtaining a release authorisation. A new document issued by the censorship authorities on December 15, 1960, informed Radio Films that a new session had been held

[14] All documents mentioned and cited can be found in the official censorship file for this particular movie, filed at AGA (Alcalá de Henares, Spain) with entry 36/03768, database IDD (03)121.002.

on October 31, 1960, in order to reassess this movie, following their appeal, resulting in the same verdict as the previous board: to ban the release of the film across the country.[15] It was as such that Radio Films' attempt to import the film into Spain in 1960 proved unsuccessful.

The next set of documents to be found in this censorship file dates from 1962. Two years after Radio Films' failed attempt to import the film, a new distribution company called Chamartin decided to try out a more aggressive tactic. In a letter addressed to the censorship authorities and dated October 26, 1962, Chamartin requested permission to produce its own dubbed version of the film and present it for assessment, taking responsibility for any consequences should the board rule that further modifications were needed or, in the last instance, decide to ban the film. The company even stated its awareness of its obligation to leave all copies of the dubbed soundtrack at the disposal of the censorship authorities should the movie be banned. It was a risk it was willing to take. The authorities' reply came a few days later, on November 5, 1962, authorising Chamartin to produce its own dubbed version prior to the movie being assessed by a board, but warning of the risks involved, given that the film had already been rejected twice in 1960. Chamartin was prompted to adhere strictly to the original version and not to alter any images or fragments of dialogue. A reply by Chamartin on November 30 confirmed that no images would be modified, but indicated nonetheless that two sections of dialogue would be altered after all, giving a detailed account of the sections concerned, in which ambiguous allusions are made to one of the characters being Catholic. Furthermore, there are reasons to believe that Chamartin was not going to produce its dubbed version from the original version of the film, as requested by the authorities, but from an English version, since the title mentioned in all the documents from 1962 is in English, as opposed to the documents from 1960, in which the original title is always written in Swedish. However, this thesis is difficult to prove, since there is no further evidence to support it.[16] If this was the

[15] Statistical research about the outcome of this type of appeal would be useful in order to establish how successful this measure really was. The fact that new fees had to be paid every time a new board gathered to assess a film gives us an indication that there was at least some economical interest in keeping the possibility of appeal alive.

[16] Anecdotically, the Spanish title proposed by Radio Films in 1960 ("El fin del viaje", which in my own rendering would be "The end of the journey") also differs from the 1962 title proposed by Chamartin ("Fresas Salvajes" or "Wild Strawberries", which was the final title used for its release).

case, and Chamartin's dubbed version was produced using an English intermediate translation, it is fair to say that the censorship authorities again overlooked their own stipulations to adhere to the original version, and gave Chamartin a free rein to decide on matters relating the directness of the translation.

On January 17, 1963, a censorship board met to assess the dubbed version produced by Chamartin and their verdict was favourable: no modifications were stipulated and the movie was to be released with a rating of adults over 16. Chamartin's tactic had paid off. This was obviously as much a result of the more tolerant and open attitudes being tested during the "Apertura" as it was a victory on the part of the distribution company. A couple of minor modifications in the dialogue cannot by themselves justify a shift which saw the film going from a complete ban in 1960 to being regarded as totally innocuous in 1963 (as expressed by all censors in the written records contained in the 1963 report, which is exhaustive). A more radical change of attitudes heralded by the "Apertura" lay behind this shift of opinion, something that Chamartin sensed and cleverly used in its favour.

Såsom i en spegel (*Como en un espejo*, 1961)

This film, set on a remote island during a period of 24 hours, depicts the progressive mental deterioration suffered by a woman named Karin, and the various reactions of her closest family members (her husband, her father and her brother). During her psychotic episodes, Karin claims that she can communicate through a wall with a group of people who are awaiting God. An incestuous relationship with her brother is also suggested, which made the film highly controversial in Francoist Spain.

This film's censorship file dates from 1962.[17] A full application form is included, dated May 22, 1962, and in exactly the same format as for the first movie analysed (*Sonrisas de una noche de verano*). Again, the distribution company, this time Exclusivas Floralva Distribución, pledges to provide an intact presentation of the film, although the company admits that some modifications may be needed, which it will be willing to apply should the censors so wish. A translation rendered from a German version, and clearly

[17] All documents mentioned and cited can be found in the official censorship file for this particular movie, filed at AGA (Alcalá de Henares, Spain) with entries 36/03910 and 36/03968, database IDD (03)121.002.

stated as such in a heading already mentioned ("Literal translation from German to Spanish"), is provided to the censorship authorities. As established earlier, the translator's initials ("M. L. F.") is also included, identical to the initials found in the translation of our first film. Once again, a case of indirect translation is totally overlooked by the censorship authorities, despite the fact that the official forms stipulated otherwise.

The next document, dated June 8, 1962, is a letter addressed by the censorship authorities to the Director of Exclusivas Floralva Distribución informing him of the outcome of the assessment session held on May 29, 1962, for which there are no written records to be found. The verdict in this case was not positive and the film's importation was not approved.[18] The letter goes on to inform Floralva about the option to refer the decision to a higher authority. The appeal arrived the following day, June 9, 1962. On the appeal form attached to the file, the Floralva representative informed the censorship authorities that a new translation had been produced, this time from the Swedish source text. Floralva argued that the flaws of the previous version were due to the fact that the dialogue had already been adapted in the German version used as source for the translation "on the grounds of perhaps stressing certain aspects of the plot in certain scenes"[19], leading to a translation in Spanish that was not completely accurate. The new translation done directly from the Swedish text would rectify these flaws and present a more "correct" version. Indirect translation is presented in this case as a deterrent to the correct assessment of the film. The speed of Floralva's response and its production of an allegedly new translation prompt us to question the "truthfulness" of the latter. No acronym was displayed this time on the opening page of the allegedly new translation rendered from the Swedish text; this could quite possibly be the work of the previous translator having simply altered certain controversial fragments in a flagrant case of self-censorship. It is a thesis that remains to be proved either way.

On July 14, 1962, a new letter issued by Floralva bore witness to the company's perseverance and to the lack of response on the part of the censorship authorities. Firstly, Floralva reminded the censors about the appeal

[18] The fact that the movie depicts a schizophrenic woman, who believes she sees God coming through a wallpaper in the form of a spider that tries to penetrate her was surely reason enough for the censors to ban the movie. Allusions to incest between the woman and her brother are also made.

[19] "Sobre la base quizás de resaltar en determinadas secuencias ciertos aspectos de la trama" (my translation).

presented on June 9. The letter then goes on to explain that, in the meantime, the movie had received praise at the 1962 Berlin Film Festival from the International Catholic Film Office (Oficina Católica Internacional de Cine, OCIC), as part of a tribute paid to Ingmar Bergman at the Festival. The letter also informs the censors about the positive feedback the film had received in the US and Germany, which paradoxically served to contradict Floralva's earlier claim that the German version might be somehow faulty.

None of these arguments, however, seemed capable as yet of eliciting any response on the part of the Spanish censors. On September 8, 1962, Floralva sent a new letter, with further reminders to the authorities of their pending appeal. This letter is very interesting for various reasons. First of all, Floralva refers to a letter by Bergman's Swedish agents at Svensk Filmindustri (SF), also sent to the censors together with its translation, in which SF provides Floralva with further arguments to be used in favour of the film. Apparently, the movie was not only commended by the OCIC at the 1962 Berlin Film Festival, but it was also chosen by the OCIC as a candidate for its Grand Prix. SF admits that it was still undecided whether the film would take part in the competition, but Floralva is urged to use this argument to convince the Spanish censors that the film adheres to the concept of the "Ideal Film" as set out by Pope Pius XII.[20] In addition to all of this, Floralva included a newspaper clip from La Vanguardia Española, dated August 23, 1962, in which a priest named Arturo Juncosa reviews the movie in positive terms, under a section called "God in modern-day film"[21]. Finally, Floralva included a reminder to the censorship authorities about the allegedly new translation presented with the appeal, in which the dialogues taken from the Swedish source text were said to "suit more accurately the strength and moral value that the movie in itself has"[22].

The outcome of Floralva's efforts is documented in a number of internal censorship documents, which are unfortunately not particularly comprehensive, but still allow us to draw a number of conclusions. On November 8, 1962, a board finally met to assess Floralva's appeal, and after reassessing the case on the basis of Floralva's numerous arguments, it decided to re-

---

[20] This concept took shape in two different speeches given by Pius XII in 1955 to international representatives of the film industry and makes reference to the ideal type of movie promoted by the Catholic Church (Martínez Bretón 1987:111).

[21] "Dios en el cine de última hora".

[22] "se adaptan con más exactitud a la fuerza y valor moral que en sí tiene la película".

verse the previous ban and authorise the dubbing of the film with a number of modifications.[23] On January 25, 1963, the censorship authorities gave the green light to the dubbed version presented by Floralva. A comment attached to this last document, reading "dubbing and adaptations approved according to the Board's decision and the technical difficulties that the agreement posed"[24] accounts for technical complications in the process of adapting the movie, from which a number of fragments had to be removed.[25]

Conclusion

The institutional constraints imposed by Francoist censorship boards on film distribution companies are clearly illustrated in the analysis of the three films discussed in this article. The negotiations undertaken by the parties involved had an impact on varying aspects of the translation process. The main factors explicitly discussed focused on the suitability of the contents depicted in the films,[26] where distribution companies always tried to anticipate or comply with the moral norms imposed by the Francoist regime. This had a direct impact on the selection of texts to be translated, which invokes Toury's definition of preliminary norms as affected by "factors that

[23] It should be mentioned that, even though the "Apertura" had not officially started yet in November 1962, García Escudero had already been appointed a few months earlier as "Director General de Cinematografía y Teatro" (General Director for Cinematography and Theatre), which may have had an influence on the decision to reverse the ban for this particular movie.

[24] "aprobado el doblaje y las adaptaciones de acuerdo con la decisión de la Junta y las dificultades técnicas que ofrecía el acuerdo".

[25] As part of his own research on Francoist censorship, González Ballesteros had very early access to the official censorship files. In his impressive work from 1981, he lists and categorises hundreds of censored films, giving details about the nature of the fragments censored. One of the films included is this particular one. According to his findings, three fragments were removed: one simulating some kind of ecstasy (almost orgasmic) when the main character has her first encounter with God; a second one in which her brother is peeping at pornographic magazines; and a third fragment that implies some kind of incestuous relationship between the two of them (1981:286). None of this information was included in the file that I had access to in 2009, which leads us to think that some information was "lost" or destroyed between 1981 and the present time.

[26] I have deliberately chosen not to elaborate on the problematic contents depicted or fragments censored in order not to deviate my attention from the main focus of this article: the negotiations undertaken by the different parties involved and their impact on the translation process. A more thorough analysis of aspects connected with content will be included in my doctoral dissertation currently in progress.

govern the choice of text-types, or even of individual texts, to be imported through translation into a particular culture/language at a particular point in time" (Toury 1995:58).

Implicitly, other issues were also negotiated, for instance the use of direct or indirect translations. Distribution companies seemed to benefit from a relatively high degree of freedom as far as the use of intermediate languages in translation was concerned. Even though official forms advised distribution companies to translate from the source language, I have demonstrated that they did not always comply with this requirement and sometimes chose to translate from intermediate languages, a practice that the censorship authorities did not seem particularly quick to call into question. Drawing once again on the concept of preliminary norms as defined by Toury, which also addresses "the threshold of tolerance for translating from languages other than the ultimate source language" (ibid.), it may be argued that censorship boards during the "Apertura" overlooked the requirement to adhere to the source text as long as the final translation did not turn out to be problematic. Given that distortion played such an important role in the censorial process, the source language used when translating probably seemed like a minor issue as long as the ideological agenda was fulfilled adequately.

On the other hand, issues connected with dubbing vs subtitling policies fell very much within the remit of the censors, since it was always the censorship board who decided on the distribution level and the potential audience for each film (the use of subtitles was limited to films released in Cine-Clubs or "Salas Especiales", as mentioned earlier). The fact that dubbed versions were favoured should not be a surprise if we accept Danan's statement that "[d]ubbing results from a dominant nationalistic system in which a nationalistic film rhetoric and language policy are promoted equally" (Danan 1991:613), which was certainly the case in Francoist Spain. That movies were dubbed in order to conform to domestic "National-Catholic" values only validates our opening claim (borrowed from Toury) about the target-oriented nature of translation.

References

Billiani, Francesca (ed.) (2007) *Modes of Censorship and Translation.* Manchester: St Jerome.

Danan, Martine (1991) "Dubbing as an Expression of Nationalism". *Meta* 36:4, 606-614.

Even-Zohar, Itamar (1990) *Polysystem Studies.* Durham: Duke University Press.

Fernández Cuenca, Carlos (1961) *Introducción al estudio de Ingmar Bergman.* Madrid: Filmoteca Nacional de España.

González Ballesteros, Teodoro (1981) *Aspectos jurídicos de la censura cinematográfica en España.* Madrid: Editorial de la Universidad Complutense.

Gubern, Román (1981) *La censura: Función política y ordenamiento jurídico bajo el franquismo (1936-1975).* Barcelona: Ediciones Península.

Gutiérrez Lanza, Camino (2002) "Spanish Film Translation and Cultural Patronage: The Filtering and Manipulation of Imported Material during Franco's Dictatorship". In Tymoczko, Maria/Gentzler, Edwin (eds.) *Translation and Power.* Amherst: University of Massachusetts Press, 141-159.

Hermans, Theo (1999) *Translation in Systems. Descriptive and System-oriented Approaches Explained.* Manchester: St Jerome.

Labrum, Marian B. (ed.) (1997) *The Changing Scene in World Languages: Issues and Challenges.* Amsterdam-Philadelphia: John Benjamins.

Lefevere, André (1992) *Translation, Rewriting and the Manipulation of Literary Fame.* London-New York: Routledge.

Martínez Bretón, Juan Antonio (1987) *Influencia de la Iglesia Católica en la cinematografía española (1951-1962).* Madrid: Harofarma.

Merkle, Denise (2010) "Censorship". In Gambier, Yves/van Doorslaer, Luc (eds.) *Handbook of Translation Studies Online.* Amsterdam-Philadelphia: John Benjamins, www.benjamins.com/online/hts/ [1 September 2010].

Muñoz Calvo, Micaela/Buesa Gómez, Carmen/Ruiz-Moneva, M. Ángeles (eds.) (2008) *New Trends in Translation and Cultural Identity.* Newcastle: Cambridge Scholars Publishing.

Ní Chuilleanáin, Eiléan/Ó Cuilleanáin, Cormac/Parris, David (eds.) (2009) *Translation and Censorship. Patterns of Communication and Interference.* Dublin: Four Courts Press.

Rabadán, Rosa (ed.) (2000) *Traducción y censura inglés-español: 1939-1985. Estudio preliminar.* León: Universidad de León.

Seruya, Teresa/Lin Moniz, María (eds.) (2008) *Translation and Censorship in Different Times and Landscapes.* Newcastle: Cambridge Scholars Publishing.

Steene, Birgitta (2005) *Ingmar Bergman: A Reference Guide.* Amsterdam: Amsterdam University Press.

Terrón Montero, Javier (1981) *La prensa en España durante el régimen de Franco. Un intento de análisis politico.* Madrid: Centro de Investigaciones Sociológicas.

Tymoczko, Maria/Gentzler, Edwin (eds.) (2002) *Translation and Power.* Amherst: University of Massachusetts Press.

Toury, Gideon (1995) *Descriptive Translation Studies and Beyond.* Amsterdam-Philadelphia: John Benjamins.

Vandaele, Jeroen (ed.) (1999) *Translation and the (Re)Location of Meaning.* Leuven: CETRA.

Vandaele, Jeroen (2006) *Estados de Gracia. Trasvases entre la semántica franquista y la poética de Billy Wilder (1946-1975).* Leuven: Katholieke Universiteit Leuven: PhD Dissertation.

Vandaele, Jeroen (2010) "It Was What It Wasn't. Translation and Francoism". In Rundle, Christopher/Sturge, Kate (eds.) *Translation Under Fascism.* London: Palgrave Macmillan, 84-116.

Actors in the processes of translation

IRINA ELENA TIRON

Katholieke Universiteit Leuven, Belgium

Alexandru Ioan Cuza University of Iaşi, Romania

Politiques culturelles en Roumanie postcommuniste: Place de la traduction

The fall of communism in Romania enabled changes at the level of structures, representations and mentalities, defining a new attitude of the society towards the cultural goods and values originating both from Romania and from abroad. This is equally echoed in the translation both as import and export of knowledge and cultural capital inscribed in the flow of cultural and symbolic values. Built on Bourdieu's theory on the (re)production of cultural knowledge, this article aims at exploring, without trying to reach the exhaustivity of such a comprehensive topic, the setting of a coherent cultural policy in post-communist Romania and its impact on the translation policies analysed within the publishing field. In the context of the development of the country's institutional, cultural and political structures after 1989, translation in the post-communist society becomes a common practice, an important tool for exporting autochthonous cultural capital and importing foreign capital.

Keywords: translation policies, translation flows, circulation of cultural and symbolic goods, internationalisation, post-communist Romania

Introduction

Dans le contexte de la mondialisation accélérée, de la circulation internationale des idées, le débat contemporain s'est élargi et intensifié autour des thématiques comme le dialogue interculturel, l'intégration des valeurs dans le circuit international des idées, la préservation de la spécificité culturelle, autrement dit, des problématiques qui tiennent de politiques culturelles:

> [L]a politique de la culture relève d'un effort constant de se définir et de se faire reconnaître sur la scène internationale, tout comme elle relève d'un besoin de créer un marché pour sa propre culture ou pour la culture des autres. (Mihalache 2005:9)

Par son pouvoir de véhiculer des savoirs, des mentalités, des représentations, des valeurs propres à une culture, la traduction implique des enjeux symboliques et influence le contexte culturel, économique et social de production et de réception. Elle est un lieu privilégié de contact entre langues et cultures hétérogènes, ainsi qu'un symbole de résistance face à la tendance symptomatique d'uniformisation manifestée par les langues et cultures dites dominantes.[1]

Dans ce qui suit, nous proposons une réflexion sur la traduction en tant que matrice culturelle, médiation et transfert de capital culturel et symbolique dans le contexte de la Roumanie postcommuniste. Sans prétendre à une présentation exhaustive d'un tel sujet vaste, notre analyse sera centrée sur trois aspects principaux qui structurent notre exposé. La présentation du contexte sociopolitique d'après la chute du régime communiste fera l'objet de notre première partie où l'accent sera mis sur la restructuration de la société et les défis lancés avec la transition vers la (re)modernisation du pays. La politique de la culture mise en place progressivement après la chute du régime dictatorial sera traitée dans la deuxième partie de l'exposé, pour finir par une présentation des conséquences qui en dérivent sur les politiques de traduction, analysables au niveau du champ éditorial postcommuniste (la troisième partie). Par politique de la culture, nous nous rapportons ici à la dimension écrite de la culture et plus précisément aux livres en tant que biens culturels et symboliques mis dans le circuit national et international des valeurs, le champ éditorial étant considéré comme champ privilégié de la circulation de ce type de biens culturels.

La théorie sociologique de Pierre Bourdieu (1977, 1992, 1999) sur la production et la reproduction des connaissances culturelles représente le cadre de référence de notre investigation du fonctionnement de la traduction comme pratique socioculturelle. Nous nous positionnons dans l'espace du transfert transnational de capital culturel et symbolique, régi par une hiérarchie des valeurs témoignant d'un type particulier de logique – politique, économique et/ou culturelle. À travers les effets de la mondialisation manifestés sur le marché du livre dans les pays d'Europe de l'Est après 1989, la traduction devient pour les entreprises éditoriales un moyen

[1] Les études de localisation – études traductologiques appliquées au contexte d'un pays particulier, avec son histoire et son climat politique distincts – pourraient être une réponse à la tendance de généralisation (Tymoczko 2000:27) qui menace des disciplines jeunes comme la traductologie, ainsi que le discours sur la mondialisation.

d'accumuler aussi bien du capital économique que du capital symbolique. Le champ éditorial et la traduction en tant qu'instrument privilégié d'acquisition de capital culturel, symbolique et/ou économique sont analysés dans la perspective des conditions sociales et des transformations subies par la Roumanie postcommuniste. Ainsi, sont envisagés le système d'agents et d'institutions concourant pour la production et la diffusion des idées et des biens culturels, les relations de pouvoir activées par diverses formes concurrentielles de capital définissant le champ culturel et éditorial de la Roumanie postcommuniste. Les maisons d'édition en tant qu'agents culturels sont engagées dans cet univers concurrentiel caractérisé par une distribution inégale de capital spécifique et dont l'enjeu principal est l'obtention de la distinction, garant de la consécration:

> [L]a logique du fonctionnement des champs de production des biens culturels comme champs de lutte favorisant les stratégies de distinction fait que les produits de leur fonctionnement, qu'il s'agisse de création de mode ou d'œuvre d'art, sont prédisposés à agir différentiellement, comme instruments de distinction. (Bourdieu 1992:231)

Par la mise en question de l'impact que la traduction subit sur la société en général et plus précisément sur le développement de la culture dans un cadre socioculturel précis, cet exposé se propose de contribuer, tant par le sujet investigué que par l'exercice méthodologique qui l'accompagne, au débat contemporain sur les transformations culturelles qu'ont subies les sociétés de l'Europe de l'Est après la chute du communisme. L'analyse de la traduction en tant que pratique sociale, faite de la perspective de la culture cible comme champ d'observation, a le mérite, entre autres, d'éclaircir le rapport entre culture, traduction et société dans des conditions historiques précises. Le chemin des recherches – interdisciplinaires – semble loin d'arriver à son bout, de multiples pistes d'investigations ayant été continuellement ouvertes les vingt dernières années.

L'après 1989: contexte sociopolitique

L'époque postcommuniste a marqué une transformation des conditions de production, de reproduction et de diffusion des œuvres et des biens culturels dans le circuit international des idées et des biens symboliques. La chute du communisme a représenté un bouleversement des structures et des systèmes antérieurs, avec des conséquences importantes sur la réception des idées transférées par le biais de la traduction. L'ouverture vers le monde occidental, vers le savoir libre, non-censuré, qui transgresse les frontières géographiques et culturelles, le développement des moyens de communication et de transmission de l'information, ces nouvelles conditions ont marqué une explosion du savoir après la chute du communisme. Ce qui s'est ensuit a été une euphorie générale qui semble avoir mis la société au défi de comprendre et consolider la démocratie, et, en même temps, de s'aligner sur les exigences de l'avenir.

La révolution de décembre 1989 a déclenché un dégel culturel, social, économique et politique, ouvrant la voie sur l'instauration de la démocratie, de la pensée et de la circulation du capital humain, culturel et politique libres. Conflit armé, coup d'État instrumentalisé par la complicité des pouvoirs externes, révolution volée, manquée, quel que soit le statut encore contesté de cet épisode emblématique de l'histoire récente de la Roumanie (Cesereanu 2009), ce qui s'est ensuit a représenté une rupture, un changement brusque, peu contrôlé des structures, des institutions, des représentations, engendrant un bouleversement de valeurs. Certains parlent d'une crise administrative plutôt qu'identitaire ou culturelle (Conseil de l'Europe 1999a). Le vide du communisme a laissé la place au (re)positionnement de la société envers les valeurs autochtones, le monde occidental et ses systèmes de référence. La voie de la transition s'est avérée être longue et sinueuse (on continue à discuter dans les mass-médias de la sortie de la transition), marquée par un rythme lent de progression et de mise en place de réformes censées (re)donner au pays le statut de démocratie moderne.

L'effondrement du communisme a dévoilé une société en transition troublée par des problèmes pointus comme l'identité nationale, le rapport à son propre passé récent (avec des débats importants sur les anciennes structures répressives comme la *Securitate*) et à l'altérité, les défis de l'État de droit, de la démocratisation du pays et de la société moderne, la perspective de l'adhésion aux structures européennes et euro-atlantiques (la Roumanie devient le candidat de l'Union européenne en 1995 et membre en 2007 et fait partie des structures de l'OTAN à partir de 2004) etc.

Les héritages du passé ont mis leurs empreintes sur le nouveau contexte socio-politico-culturel du pays, fonctionnant comme des tares et étant à l'origine du retard enregistré par le pays dans sa transition politique, économique et culturelle. Le dirigisme, l'absence de l'esprit d'entreprise, l'organisation déficitaire, les blocages systémiques, le manque de ressources – humaines, financières – spécialisées, capables de s'adapter facilement et rapidement aux nouvelles conditions sont autant de prolongements de l'ancien régime qui ont laissé des traces profondes sur le parcours de la société roumaine postcommuniste.

Le passage brusque vers la démocratie a (re)inscrit le pays dans le circuit des pays occidentaux. Les anciens pays communistes, y compris la Roumanie, ont été attirés par les prérogatives et les valeurs promues par la *société ouverte* (concept emprunté à Karl Popper 1945): démocratie, liberté, accès au savoir, progrès économique et culturel (Mihalache 2005:30). Cette nouvelle idéologie est vite devenue le *desideratum* et le credo de la société postcommuniste, dans le long chemin vers la démocratisation des valeurs et des mentalités. Une nouvelle époque a vu le jour, du dialogue et de la pluralité, de l'échange des valeurs spirituelles avec l'altérité. La société roumaine postcommuniste se trouvait confrontée à un nouveau contexte social, politique, économique et spirituel qui, a côté de l'enthousiasme du nouveau commencement et la multitude d'options qui s'ouvraient, apportait des défis importants. Dans l'absence d'un projet de modernisation du pays qui soit cohérent, conçu à long terme et, si possible, avant le lancement des offensives violentes (comme cela est passé dans d'autres pays), le processus de démocratisation a trouvé une Roumanie non-préparée, tant au niveau des ressources humaines qu'au niveau de l'appareil institutionnel. La transformation des anciennes structures dans des instances modernes s'est faite lentement et de manière incohérente. Cela fait la spécificité de la transition postcommuniste roumaine.

Vers la légitimation de la politique culturelle

Sans développer ici le sujet de l'histoire de la culture roumaine, qui ne fait pas l'objet direct de notre recherche, nous allons seulement préciser que la Roumanie se jouit d'une forte culture écrite et d'une longue tradition lettrée, caractérisée par continuité et rupture, en quête perpétuelle d'un compromis entre l'identité nationale et l'appartenance ou la référence à des structures sur-nationales, perçues comme modèles. Cela fait la spécificité de la *synthèse roumaine* (Conseil de l'Europe 1999a).

Dans l'atmosphère post-décembriste de bouleversement, de transition non-préparée vers de nouvelles structures, la culture devient un sujet d'actualité, fonctionnant comme matrice de (re)positionnement des valeurs nationales envers le patrimoine autochtone et/ou étranger. Le droit et l'accès à la culture sont mentionnés dans l'article 33 de la Constitution du pays (adoptée dans sa nouvelle forme en 1991 et amendée en 2003). Au niveau institutionnel, c'est le ministère de la Culture qui se charge de la protection et la mise en valeur de l'héritage culturel, la promotion de l'expression artistique et la diffusion, dans le pays et à l'étranger, des valeurs de la spiritualité nationale, ainsi que la favorisation de la circulation à l'intérieur du pays des valeurs de la culture universelle (Conseil de l'Europe 1999a:28).

Après une cinquantaine d'années de dirigisme étatique où la culture a servi de simple instrument de propagande dans les mains du régime totalitaire (à fonction politique et idéologique), la censure étant le moyen de contrôler et de dominer la création culturelle, dans toutes ses formes d'expression, la jeune démocratie crée les prémisses de la mise en place d'une politique culturelle autochtone qui représente les valeurs du pays tant à l'intérieur qu'à l'extérieur des frontières nationales.

La première décennie après la chute du régime répressif est caractérisée par des efforts constants d'adapter de manière rapide et efficace les structures administratives aux nouvelles conditions de développement du pays. L'instabilité du pays, en général, et du champ culturel, en particulier, est reflétée dans la structure-même du ministère de la Culture, institution qui compte, entre 1990 et 1998, neuf cabinets, tous à la recherche de la formule la plus appropriée pour (re)inscrire la culture roumaine dans le circuit des échanges des valeurs culturelles et spirituelles européennes. L'absence de communication avec l'extérieur, de circulation des biens cultures dans le circuit international, les répressions envers les artistes et leurs formes d'expression créative, toutes ces manifestations de la doctrine Jdanov et de la révolution culturelle maoïste ont laissé la place à une série de réformes initialement incohérentes, confuses, d'inspiration contradictoire, doublées par une dévalorisation de la culture au niveau du budget national (1990-1996), générant ainsi un bastion de résistance au changement (Conseil de l'Europe 1999b:6).

Après de nombreuses tentatives de décentralisation et de recentralisation du champ culturel (pendant les deux premiers mandats de Ion Iliescu, période dans laquelle les systèmes restent encore centralisés), nous pouvons affirmer que ce n'est qu'à partir de 1996 (avec l'avènement au pouvoir de la coalition démocratique) que se met en place une série de réformes en accord avec les nouvelles conditions sociopolitiques du pays. Ces réformes spécifiques d'une politique culturelle autochtone créent les prémisses de la décentralisation des ressources, des compétences, des responsabilités et de l'administration, assurant ainsi que l'intervention ministérielle se résume à fournir les lignes directrices et à créer les moyens de réalisation des projets culturels. Parmi les initiatives législatives les plus importantes adoptées dans cette période, il convient de rappeler:

- le décret-Loi n° 12 du 28 décembre 1989 sur la suppression du Conseil de la culture et de l'éducation socialiste et la création du ministère de la Culture, la première loi démocratique relative à la culture;
- la Loi n° 35/1994 instituant le timbre littéraire, cinématographique, théâtral, musical, folklorique et des beaux-arts (un "timbre littéraire" apposé à chaque exemplaire des livres publiés en Roumanie contribue au financement des prix littéraires mis en place par l'Union des Ecrivains, institution où sont inscrits la plupart des auteurs et des traducteurs);
- la Loi n° 8/1996 concernant le droit d'auteur et les droits connexes (l'une des plus modernes lois européennes en la matière, qui correspond à tous les standards internationaux);
- la décision du Gouvernement n° 134/1998 sur l'organisation et le fonctionnement du ministère de la Culture (cette loi est l'acte de naissance de cette institution en tant que structure moderne, cohérente, au service de la politique culturelle nationale);
- la Loi 186/2003 sur la promotion de la culture écrite (avec des précisions importantes sur les mesures fiscales censées soutenir et encourager l'exploitation du potentiel économique et culturel du secteur éditorial avec, par exemple, l'exonération de la TVA sur la vente des livres).

Un climat favorable s'est ainsi progressivement instauré pour privilégier des directions comme la protection et la promotion du patrimoine national, l'éducation de l'esprit artistique, la coopération nationale et internationale. Bien que l'héritage, les valeurs nationales redécouvertes après 1989 soient considérés une priorité dans la stratégie culturelle postcommuniste (Conseil de l'Europe 1999b), dans les conditions où ce secteur a été gravement affecté pendant le régime totalitaire, la dimension internationale de la culture roumaine a également été pleinement exploitée.

La politique culturelle roumaine s'inscrit progressivement dans le contexte intégrateur européen et mondial. Ainsi, la Roumanie est, depuis 1993, membre de quelques groupes d'experts du Conseil de l'Europe, a mis en place un projet PHARE (RO 9709) sur la dimension culturelle de la démocratie, fait partie des programmes européens Culture 2000 et Culture

2007-2013, a accueilli le Sommet International de la Francophonie (2006), a une commission représentative de l'UNESCO et est signataire de la Convention UNESCO sur la protection et la promotion de la diversité des expressions culturelles. Par cette Convention, la Roumanie exprime son support pour la création d'une plate-forme innovante de coopération culturelle internationale où est réaffirmé le droit souverain des États d'élaborer des politiques culturelles censées "protéger et promouvoir la diversité des expressions culturelles", d'une part, et "créer les conditions permettant aux cultures de s'épanouir et interagir librement de manière à s'enrichir mutuellement", d'autre part (article premier).[2] On y ajoute de divers partenariats culturels avec d'autres pays européens et du monde entier. Cette forte dimension de coopération internationale montre que, malgré les disfonctionnements internes et le rythme plutôt lent d'instauration des réformes démocratiques, la Roumanie a toujours eu une volonté d'ouverture vers le capital culturel et l'échange des valeurs dans le circuit mondial.[3]

En octobre 1997, le ministère de la Culture de Roumanie a soumis à l'UNESCO, via le Conseil de l'Europe, une proposition visant à mettre en place une analyse de la situation de la production et la distribution du livre dans son pays, qui soit le point de départ dans la formulation d'une nouvelle politique nationale du livre et de la lecture. Commencées à l'occasion de la Foire de Leipzig, alors que la Roumanie était le pays invité d'honneur, les discussions ont continué à la Foire de Frankfurt, en octobre 1998. Les débats ont porté sur l'importance de la création et de la mise en application par la Roumanie d'une politique intelligente du livre et de la lecture, afin de tirer profit du grand potentiel culturel et économique de ce secteur et de contrecarrer les effets concurrentiels de l'explosion de moyens audiovisuels. Des recommandations ont été conjointement faites par les représentants de l'UNESCO, mais aussi par des acteurs du secteur privé, pour la constitution d'un Conseil National du Livre et l'adoption d'une loi sur le livre qui

[2] Il convient de préciser, à ce point, le fait qu'en 1993, la Roumanie n'avait pas adopté le principe de l'exception culturelle, dans le cadre des négociations du GATT. Lorsqu'en 2001 l'UNESCO a lancé le débat international sur la diversité culturelle, nouveau concept pour l'exception culturelle, la Roumanie est parmi les premiers pays à signer la Convention (en 2006).

[3] Dans un Eurobaromètre de 2003 (Magyar Gallup Intézet 2003) sur le comportement culturel des pays candidats à l'Union européenne, la Roumanie est, à côté de la Slovénie, l'un des pays qui préfèrent que la politique culturelle soit majoritairement dans les mains de l'Union européenne (47% par rapport à 32% soutenant l'initiative nationale), tandis que les autres pays candidats considèrent que les décisions devraient être prises au niveau national, en tant que garantie de la préservation des valeurs culturelles autochtones.

propose des mesures fiscales favorables et des activités de formation à tout niveau de la production et de la distribution. Ces initiatives se sont concrétisées après 2000, avec, par exemple, la Loi 186/2003 sur la promotion de la culture écrite (connue aussi sous le nom de la loi du livre) qui contient des mesures fiscales incitatives à la production et à la distribution des livres. Une autre initiative à mentionner est la formation de l'Institut Culturel Roumain (la Loi 356/2003, amendée par la Loi 91/2004), avec un réseau de 17 centres culturels dans 16 pays et qui a sous sa responsabilité, depuis 2007, le Centre National du Livre dont l'activité principale est la promotion à l'étranger des traductions de littérature roumaine.

Dans le nouveau contexte socioculturel, l'un des objectifs de la politique culturelle de la Roumanie postcommuniste est la promotion et le soutien, au niveau (inter)institutionnel, par des structures nationales et internationales, des projets qui privilégient la dimension interculturelle.[4] Selon le *Compendium de politiques culturelles* publié sur le site du Conseil de l'Europe, le ministère de la Culture de Roumanie soutient la circulation des œuvres et créations culturelles, la promotion du dialogue international et la création culturelle dans le cadre du circuit mondial des valeurs. La traduction, dans ses deux hypostases d'*intraduction* et d'*extraduction* (Ganne/Minon 1992:55-95), en est une composante importante. Cela est l'une des conclusions d'une série de rapports rédigés par Centrul de Studii şi Cercetări în Domeniul Culturii (le Centre d'études et de recherches dans le domaine de la culture). La traduction est qualifiée de démarche à potentiel élevé de réussite pour la promotion de la culture roumaine dans l'espace européen, et cela notamment par la traduction, dans des pays à forte tradition de lecture et de production éditoriale, des œuvres de référence et par la promotion des écrivains "actifs"

[4] Parmi les institutions et les initiatives visant la promotion des traductions du monde occidental vers l'espace littéraire roumain, nous énumérons l'Institut de la Société Ouverte de Budapest (Fondation Soros), l'Université central-européenne de Budapest, le Centre for Publishing Development (pour la promotion des valeurs de la société ouverte), le *CEU Translation Project, EAST Translates EAST Project, Books for Civil Society Project, Popper Project, Gender/Women's Studies Translations, Roma Project Translation Grants, Fund for Central and East European Book Projects* (qui réclame "un marché commun de l'esprit européen"), l'Agence Universitaire de la Francophonie, l'Institut Français de Bucarest avec son "Programme d'aide à la publication *Nicolae Iorga*", le Programme d'aide à la traduction du Centre National du Livre ou d'autres programmes comme les "Bourses de séjour des traducteurs d'œuvres françaises", "À l'Est de l'Europe", le British Council avec son programme "British Books for Managers", l'Institut für die Wissenschaften vom Menschen de Vienne, avec son programme "Paul Celan Fellowships for Translators" (1997).

dans l'espace littéraire de ces pays (Centrul de Studii şi Cercetări în Domeniul Culturii 1).

Une analyse des industries culturelles créatives (Centrul de Studii şi Cercetări în Domeniul Culturii 3) amène en discussion les problèmes avec lesquels est confronté ce secteur, en vue de l'identification des solutions nécessaires. Sur le fond de multiples déficiences enregistrées dans le champ du livre, surtout au niveau de la production, la distribution, la promotion, le financement, la représentativité, les défis de la technologisation, les politiques publiques etc., la traduction – et notamment l'extraduction – est envisagée comme secteur d'investissement, par des programmes de financement, des bourses de mobilités etc.

Après avoir passé en revue de manière superficielle une série d'initiatives mises en place progressivement après décembre 1989, nous pouvons conclure que la Roumanie postcommuniste a vécu une ouverture de perspective et de références, ce qui a mené à la réinscription de la culture nationale sur le circuit international de l'échange des valeurs et des idées (par rapport à la période du régime communiste) et cela notamment par la mise en pratique d'une politique culturelle adaptée, d'un côté, aux nouvelles conditions de développement du pays et, de l'autre, aux défis de la globalisation. La traduction est l'un des signes de cette tendance d'internationalisation de la politique culturelle roumaine pour joindre le dialogue interculturel initié avec la chute du régime dictatorial et la globalisation de la communication et de la consommation. Dans ce qui suit nous allons analyser la manière dont cette ouverture se manifeste au niveau des politiques éditoriales de traduction.

Politiques de traduction: éthos d'ouverture

Après la chute du communisme, sur le marché éditorial roumain se met en place progressivement une logique qui relève du marché international du livre (Popa 2008:257-286) qui transforme fondamentalement le fonctionnement du marché des idées et des biens culturels et symboliques. Lorsque l'État fournisseur cesse la production et la distribution engagées des livres, l'économie de marché reprend le contrôle sur le commerce du livre. Le désengagement du pouvoir fait place aux mécanismes concurrentiels du marché libre. Dans ce nouvel espace, la détention de capital économique est un facteur essentiel qui assure la distinction sur le marché, le profit, la rentabilité, le livre étant un objet à double enjeu (économique et symbolique), à la fois marchandise et signification.

Le projet de la Roumanie postcommuniste vise la réduction du décalage culturel (mais également social et économique) existant entre la Roumanie et les sociétés développées, ainsi que la synchronisation aux tendances contemporaines. Au niveau des politiques éditoriales de traduction, ce phénomène a entraîné une importation massive de livres de sciences humaines et sociales[5], domaine en général interdit ou contrôlé par le régime socialiste, le seul autorisé à rédiger le programme culturel de l'*homme nouveau* et de *la société socialiste multilatéralement développée.* Ainsi, s'est ressentie une forte demande de livres de psychologie, sociologie, sciences politiques, anthropologie, études culturelles, droit, relations internationales, histoire, économie, mais aussi dictionnaires, encyclopédies, livres d'informatique, d'apprentissage des langues étrangères, de littérature pratique, guides et livres traitant de différents aspects d'intérêt quotidien. Cette demande témoigne de l'existence d'une demande latente et du changement de la société en termes de préoccupations, références, nécessité de combler les vides du passé et de se mettre à jour avec des thématiques abordées par/dans la société de consommation. La Roumanie postcommuniste est sous le signe du "paradoxe de la continuité et de la discontinuité" (Alexandrescu 1998, cité en Mihalache 2005:134), à la recherche d'une identité située au carrefour d'autres modèles culturels, sociaux, idéologiques, économiques, une identité accablée entre un passé de privations, rigoureusement dirigé vers de fausses valeurs, et un présent confus dont les changements n'ont pas été assumés dans la conscience du peuple, avec des conséquences importantes sur l'avenir et le devenir de la société postcommuniste.

[5] L'importation massive et parfois irrationnelle, au sens où elle n'est pas toujours filtrée par l'esprit critique, fait penser à la thèse de l'imitation des formes sans fond, promue par Titus Maiorescu et les intellectuels regroupés, en 1886, autour de la société littéraire et culturelle *Junimea*.

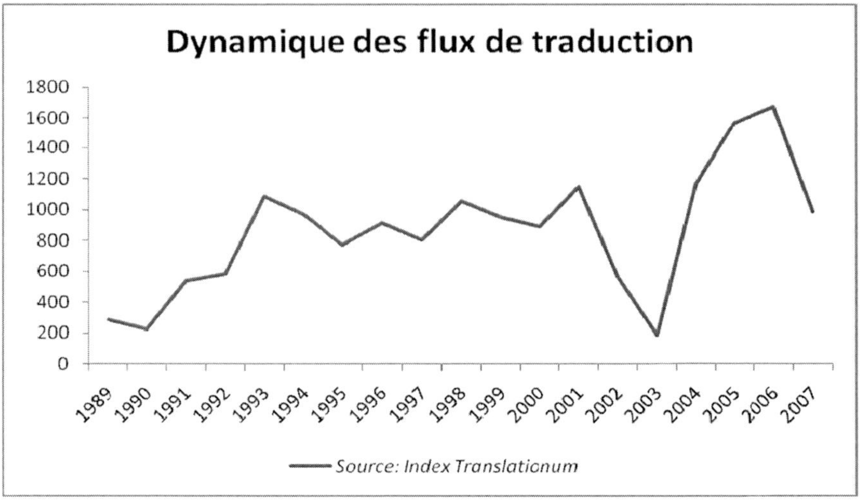

Figure 1: Dynamique des flux de traduction dans la période 1989-2007

La fête du livre et de la lecture du début des années 90 (voir la représentation graphique de la dynamique des flux de traduction dans la Figure 1), similaire à la situation enregistrée sur le marché éditorial russe (Thiesse/ Chmatko 1999), va de pair avec la libéralisation du champ éditorial et a comme effet une croissance quantitative significative des flux de traduction[6] et des agents de ce secteur. Le catalogue des maisons d'édition de Roumanie (Catalogul editurilor din România 2007) recense presque 5 000 maisons d'éditions (d'État, subventionnées et privées) inscrites au Registre du commerce dans la période janvier 1990 – août 2007. Cette hausse s'explique, d'un côté, par la demande croissante des lecteurs et, de l'autre, par des conditions économiques et juridiques particulières, caractéristiques à la libéralisation progressive du marché. Des phénomènes comme l'instabilité du marché et des services, l'inflation, la dépréciation de l'économie nationale, l'absence d'une législation cohérente (par exemple dans le domaine de la protection de la propriété intellectuelle) ont créé les prémisses de l'investissement et du profit à court terme, transformant les livres en de pures marchandises, garantissant l'enrichissement immédiat des agents

[6] 283 traductions en 1989 et 1472 en 2005, ce qui revient à une croissance quantitative de 501%, selon les données répertoriées dans la base de données d'*Index Translationum*. Pour l'évolution des flux de traduction dans la période 1989-2007, voir Figure 1.

commerciaux. Le livre est vu comme marchandise profitable, ce qui résulte en une explosion de maisons d'édition de type petit commerce. Parmi les éditeurs il y en a qui se lancent à la recherche des *deals* éditoriaux, des *booms*, qui privilégient le succès immédiat traduit par des grosses ventes. La professionnalisation (trop) lente du secteur privé et notamment des ressources humaines, la faible efficacité de l'organisation associative du champ, la lourde fiscalité, l'inadéquation de la législation fiscale et économique pour inclure l'exception culturelle, i.e. le commerce des biens culturels et symboliques (le secteur éditorial est plutôt associé aux services qu'à la production/création, avec des effets importants au niveau de la fiscalité), tous ces éléments ont influencé le développement du marché du livre dans la société postcommuniste (UNESCO/le Conseil de l'Europe 1998).

Maison d'édition	**Production éditoriale (%)**
Humantias	20%
Polirom	18%
Univers	13%
Teora	10%
RAO	9%
Nemira	5%
Paralela 45	3%
Corint	2%
Institutul European	2%
Curtea Veche	2%
Cartea Romaneasca	2%
All	2%

Figure 2: Production des maisons d'édition dans la période 1990-2007 (sélection)

Dans ces conditions d'instabilité générale du pays, l'activité éditoriale elle-même est soumise à une forte fluctuation. L'industrie du livre est perçue comme une niche, mais le critère quantitatif est progressivement remplacé par le critère qualitatif, grâce à l'apparition d'un lectorat de plus en plus sélectif et de l'institution d'un climat de forte concurrence entre les éditeurs, obligés à mettre en place des stratégies originales et des standards hauts de performance. Ainsi, seul un petit nombre des maisons d'édition créées après 1989 ou même avant ont réussi à rester actives sur le marché, en imposant aux lecteurs un catalogue diversifié et également intéressant, capable d'influencer le goût public. Selon une analyse de l'UNESCO sur le marché du livre en Roumanie (UNESCO/le Conseil de l'Europe 1998), seulement une vingtaine de maisons d'édition possédaient une infrastructure consolidée (services de rédaction, de production, de marketing et parfois de distribution) et des lignes de catalogue bien déterminées. Sept éditeurs publiaient plus de 50 titres par an, tandis que deux ou trois éditeurs dépassaient 100 titres annuels. Le paysage éditorial semble ne pas avoir enregistré des changements majeurs de nos jours (voir Figure 2 pour la distribution, selon leur production, des principales maisons d'édition, dans la période 1990-2007).

La libéralisation a mené à la privatisation et même à la disparition de beaucoup d'entreprises d'État, y compris de quelques grandes maisons d'édition ayant servi à la diffusion de l'idéologie totalitaire (Dacia, Cartea românească, Kriterion, Minerva, Univers). Dans ce nouvel espace fortement concurrentiel, le principe de rentabilité et les mécanismes de réglage du marché se sont mises les empreintes sur le fonctionnement du champ, ajustant le volume à la demande, par exemple, avec des chutes considérables des tirages.[7]

Après l'an 2000, le système économique commence à donner des signes de revirement, grâce à l'accélération des mécanismes de transition à l'économie de marché, au développement du secteur privé et du secteur des services, en général, à la croissance positive du PIB, et cela après une régression entre 1996 et 1999, générée par les coûts élevés payés pour la transition à l'économie libre, concurrentielle. Dans ce nouveau climat, les maisons d'édition, structurées autour de la polarisation entre grande et petite production et distribution (Bourdieu 1999), mettent en place des politiques éditoriales de traduction reflétant leur positionnement envers le capital culturel universel, la politique nationale et/ou internationale de la culture, les logiques du marché de la circulation des idées (privilégiant la composante

---

[7] Dans le rapport du Centre d'études et de recherches dans le domaine de la culture sur l'indice de la vie culturelle en Roumanie, dans la période 1998-2007 (Centrul de Studii şi Cercetări în Domeniul Culturii 2), on remarque une évolution constante de la production éditoriale (sous-indice de la culture écrite) jusqu'en 2006 et une tendance descendante des tirages des livres, interrompue par des sommets en 2001-2002 et 2003-2005. Cela montre une production éditoriale diversifiée, un marché du livre dynamique, mais avec un volume diminué, ce qui pourrait donner des indices sur le pouvoir d'achat ou sur le rapport inégal entre offre et demande.

culturelle, la composante commerciale, ou un équilibre entre les deux). L'opposition entre commercial et non-commercial fonctionne comme un système de classement, comme des catégories de perception et d'appréciation, le principe générateur qui justifie des décisions, des jugements, *la formule génératrice des choix* (ibid.:18) dont rend compte le catalogue éditorial et qui se fait l'écho d'une prise de position dans le cadre du champ même. Un grand éditeur comme Polirom, par exemple, assume une politique éditoriale multifonctionnelle, visant "une gestion de la synchronie articulée sur la diachronie" (Jeanrenaud 2005:208), afin de court-circuiter le temps d'accumulation de capital symbolique, combler les vides accumulés pendant l'époque communiste et aligner la production éditoriale sur les tendances du marché international du livre. La maison d'édition Humanitas, grâce au capital culturel et symbolique de son père fondateur, philosophe et homme de culture réputé, concentre ses choix de titres à traduire autour de la logique des placements sûrs, misant sur un public élitiste mais toujours en extension, auquel est proposé un catalogue diversifié. D'autres éditeurs, plus petits et le plus souvent localisés en dehors de l'espace de la capitale, noyau culturel qui concentre la plupart des éditeurs (49, 7%, selon les données du Catalogue des maisons d'édition de Roumanie, publié par la Bibliothèque Nationale), choisissent des stratégies de niche afin de combler les vides du marché. C'est le cas, par exemple, de la maison d'édition à vocation européenne Institutul European de la ville de Iaşi, qui privilégie des titres du monde académique et des domaines qui mettent en valeur le capital de l'Union européenne. Les petits éditeurs agissent généralement en découvreurs, à la recherche d'œuvres d'avant-garde et explorant des aires culturelles et linguistiques peu connues, à la différence des grands éditeurs commerciaux, doués de fort capital économique et symbolique, qui se permettent des investissements chers (y compris les coûts de l'importation, par la traduction, des *best sellers* internationaux) et fonctionnent comme un label de capital symbolique sûr pour les écrivains et les traducteurs collaborateurs.

La plupart des éditeurs optent pour un catalogue généraliste afin d'attirer un public large, couvrant une gamme variée d'intérêts. Ainsi, la maison d'édition Paralela 45, créée dans la province, se proclame "un éditeur encyclopédique", ayant étendu son profile du livre didactique vers la littérature roumaine moderne et contemporaine. Curtea Veche Publishing s'est spécialisée initialement dans le développement personnel et, à présent, est considérée un chef de fil du marché des livres d'éducation financière et sociale (selon les données présentées sur le site internet de l'éditeur), ayant, entre autres, exclusivité sur la publication en Roumanie des livres de Jamie Oliver.

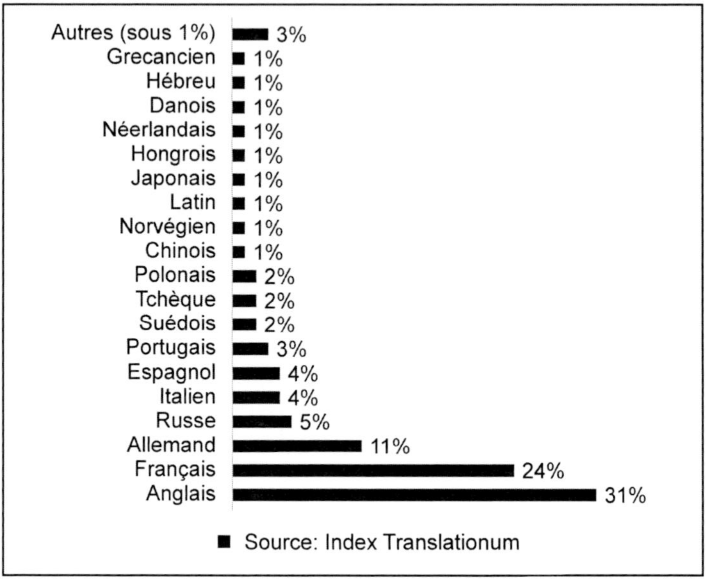

Figure 3: Distribution des langues sources 1989-2007

Dans le contexte du développement des structures institutionnelles, culturelles, politiques, et sur le fond de l'ouverture générale du pays après 1989, la traduction devient une pratique quotidienne de la société roumaine post-communiste, une composante importante de la politique culturelle de la Roumanie, outil d'exportation du capital culturel autochtone et d'importation de capital hétérogène (pour une répartition des principales langues traduites, voir la Figure 3 ci-dessus),[8] inscrit dans l'espace international de la circulation des idées et des biens symboliques. Bien que la traduction comme pratique linguistique, sociale et culturelle se soit intensifiée progressivement après la chute du communisme, le déséquilibre entre intraduction et extraduction reste d'actualité, ce qui témoigne, entre autres, du statut de

[8] Dans une analyse des industries du droit d'auteur en Roumanie (Centrul de Studi şi Cercetări în Domeniul Culturii et al. 2008), par exemple les industries créatives, y compris l'édition de livres, est mentionnée l'expansion constante des imports de ce type de biens, tandis que les exports ont suivi une tendance générale descendante. Autrement dit, la Roumanie importe des biens culturels plus qu'elle ne les exporte, ce qui s'applique également au secteur des traductions.

culture minoritaire, périphérique de la culture roumaine, et de la forte hiérarchisation du système mondial des traductions de livres (Heilbron 1999). Relativement autonome, ce système serait constitué par les dynamiques structurelles entre groupes linguistiques occupant des positions distinctes dans l'hiérarchie systémique: centrales (l'anglais comme langue véhiculaire hyperdominante, mais aussi le français, l'allemand et le russe), semi-périphériques et périphériques. Dans cette perspective, il faut garder à l'esprit le fait que ces échanges à l'échelle internationale s'insèrent dans des rapports inégaux, asymétriques entre cultures, rapports qui sont influencés par les relations géopolitiques et les intérêts économiques souvent au cœur de cette circulation transnationale des idées et des biens culturels.

Tout en rejetant l'approche culturaliste – selon laquelle le processus de globalisation éditoriale favorise le métissage des cultures et la diversité éditoriale – ainsi que l'approche économiste qui prend le livre comme une simple marchandise issue d'un marché comme les autres, Gisèle Sapiro (2009) conteste l'existence même d'un espace de circulation libre des livres, affirmant que le commerce du livre est au contraire le lieu de rapports de forces entre aires linguistiques, territoires nationaux, mais aussi imaginaires et symboliques. La problématisation de la globalisation devrait prendre en considération une perspective spatiale plutôt qu'idéologique et donc privilégier les relations territoriales, nationales ou linguistiques, en fonction de "différentes logiques commerciales, politiques et culturelles qui régissent la circulation transnationale des livres" (ibid.:300).

L'évolution du champ éditorial roumain et la place accordée à la traduction suit le même scénario enregistré dans d'autres anciens pays communistes. Dans son analyse de l'évolution du champ éditorial polonais après 1989, Elżbieta Skibińska (2009) conclut sur l'existence de trois étapes principales, marquées par des fonctions distinctes assumées par les traductions: un développement "sauvage", une régularisation suivie d'une stabilisation, avec la consolidation de grands groupes. Quant aux nouveaux éditeurs russes, Thiesse et Chmatko (1999) remarquent les transformations importantes subies par le champ éditorial après la chute du régime répressif: l'institution des rapports capitalistes, l'explosion du domaine privé, la restriction du marché, les lacunes législatives, la prépondérance des stratégies d'accumulation de capital économique, des principes de rentabilité et de profit immédiat qui vont de pair avec la promotion de la littérature de masse, la reconversion au niveau du profil des agents, l'ajustage de l'offre aux consommateurs, la course aux subventions etc. Le champ éditorial bulgare à l'époque postcommuniste est, selon Svetla Moussakova (2005) dominé par le souci d'adaptation aux exigences du marché (surtout privé), les aides à la traduction jouant un rôle essentiel. Devant les modèles culturels massivement importés par les traductions, le champ littéraire national s'est montré faible, ce qui a donné naissance à un mouvement de réveil de la conscience identitaire et à un mouvement culturel d'affirmation identitaire, les nouveaux éditeurs s'assumant une mission culturelle de défense et de promotion de la production nationale.

Conclusion

Les tendances de croissance quantitative des traductions après 1989 révèlent un éthos d'ouverture de la langue et de la culture roumaines dans le contexte de pluralité idéologique, sociale et culturelle. Avec l'instauration d'un nouveau contexte sociopolitique, les discussions et les débats sur la politique culturelle du pays reviennent en actualité. Progressivement se met en place une politique cohérente de la culture avec des acteurs et agences spécialisés, suivant deux directions importantes: nationale et internationale. Cette bivalence est au cœur même du profil culturel de la société roumaine postcommuniste.

En tant que composante importante de la culture écrite, la traduction dans la société roumaine postcommuniste acquiert un rôle de plus en plus important dans la construction et l'entretien du dialogue (inter)culturel. Cette évolution remarquable a plusieurs origines: l'intensification des échanges et des relations entre les États (diplomatiques, économiques, politiques), la création des politiques culturelles communes, au niveau interinstitutionnel (par exemple au niveau de l'Union européenne), le développement du champ du livre, en général, et du champ des traductions, en particulier, avec notamment la professionnalisation croissante du métier de traducteur. Nous pouvons donc conclure, avec Mihalache, sur l'importance de la traduction à l'époque postcommuniste, "ensemble de phénomènes à même d'instaurer, dans une société anciennement totalitaire, un éthos de l'ouverture, du dialogue et de la pluralité d'opinions" (Mihalache 2005:201).

Les traductions en tant que biens culturels et symboliques sont les produits d'une certaine *alchimie sociale* (Bourdieu 1977:9), entreprise complexe à laquelle collaborent les agents qui, animés par la croyance dans les règles du jeu, contribuent au dynamisme et à l'énergie du champ culturel dont les potentialités sont (re)activées avec le nouveau contexte socio-politico-culturel de l'effondrement du régime communiste répressif.

References

Bourdieu, Pierre (1977) "La production de la croyance". *Actes de la recherche en sciences sociales* 13, 3-43.

Bourdieu, Pierre (1992) *Les règles de l'art. Genèse et structure de champ littéraire.* Paris: Seuil.

Bourdieu, Pierre (1999) "Une révolution conservatrice dans l'édition". *Actes de la recherche en sciences sociales* 126-127, 3-28.

Catalogul editurilor din România (2007) Editura Bibliotecii Naţionale a României. Centrul Naţional ISBN Bucureşti.

Centrul de Studii şi Cercetări în Domeniul Culturii (1) *Promovarea culturii româneşti în spaţiul european,* http://culturadata.ro/Cercetari%20finalizate.html [1 November 2010].

Centrul de Studii şi Cercetări în Domeniul Culturii (2) *Indicele vieţii culturale în România 1998-2007*, http://culturadata.ro/Cercetari%20finalizate.html [1 November 2010].

Centrul de Studii şi Cercetări în Domeniul Culturii (3) *Schiţa unei politici de stimulare a creativităţii: Propuneri de la creatori, ONG-uri şi firme din sectorul cultural,* http://culturadata.ro/Cercetari%20finalizate.html [1 November 2010].

Centrul de Studii şi Cercetări în Domeniul Culturii/Dărăşteanu, Cătălin/Mucică, Delia/ Pârvu, Rodica/ Vasile, Valentina/Zaman, Gheorghe (2008) *Contribuţia economică a industriilor bazate pe copyright în România,* http://culturadata.ro/Cercetari%20finalizate.html [1 November 2010].

Cesereanu, Ruxandra (2009) *Decembrie '89. Deconstrucţia unei revoluţii.* Ediţia a II a. Iaşi: Polirom.

Conseil de l'Europe (1999a) *Programme européen d'examen des politiques culturelles nationales. La politique culturelle en Roumanie.* Rapport national, http://www.coe.int/t/dg4/cultureheritage/culture/reviews/CC-CULT99-33ARomania_FR.pdf [3 July 2012].

Conseil de l'Europe (1999b) *European Programme of National Cultural Policy Reviews. Cultural Policy in Romania. Report of a European Group of Experts*, http://www.coe.int/t/dg4/cultureheritage/culture/reviews/CC-CULT99-33B Romania_EN.pdf [3 July 2012].

Conseil de l'Europe (2011) *Compendium: Cultural policies and Trends in Europe. Romania,* www.culturalpolicies.net/web/romania.php [3 July 2012].

Ganne, Valérie/Minon, Marc (1992) "Géographies de la traduction". In Barret-Ducrocq, Françoise (ed.) *Traduire l'Europe.* Paris: Payot, 55-95.

Heilbron, Johan (1999) "Towards a Sociology of Translation: Book Translations as a Cultural World-System". *European Journal of Social Theory* 2:4, 429-444.

Index Translationum, http://databases.unesco.org/xtrans/stat/xTransStat.html [3 July 2012].

Jeanrenaud, Magda (2005) "La traduction entre l'accumulation et la distribution de capital symbolique. L'exemple des Éditions Polirom". In Dinu-Gheorgiu, Mihai/Dragomir, Lucia (eds.) *Littératures et pouvoir symbolique*. Piteşti: Editura Paralela 45, 203-223.

Magyar Gallup Intézet (2003) *Candidate Countries Eurobarometer. Public Opinion in the Candidate Countries. New Europeans and Culture,* http://ec.europa.eu/culture/pdf/doc973_en.pdf [3 July 2012].

Mihalache, Iulia (2005) *Le modèle occidental et ses traductions dans une société postcommuniste: le cas de la Roumanie*. Ottawa: PhD Dissertation.

Moussakova, Svetla (2005) "Figures de traducteurs-éditeurs. Vers une nouvelle représentation des élites littéraires en Bulgarie". In Dinu-Gheorgiu, Mihai/Dragomir, Lucia (eds.) *Littératures et pouvoir symbolique*. Piteşti: Editura Paralela 45, 223-235.

Popa, Ioana (2008) "D'une circulation politisée à une logique du marché. L'importation des littératures d'Europe de l'Est". In Sapiro, Gisèle (ed.) *Translatio – Le marché de la traduction en France à l'heure de la mondialisation*. Paris: CNRS Éditions, 257-286.

Popper, Karl Raymund (1945) *The Open Society and Its Enemies*. London: Routledge.

Sapiro, Gisèle (2009) "Mondialisation et diversité culturelle: les enjeux de la circulation transnationale des livres". In Sapiro, Gisèle (ed.) *Les contradictions de la globalisation éditoriale*. Paris: Nouveau Monde éditions, 275-302.

Skibińska, Elżbieta (2009) "La place des traductions sur le marché éditorial polonais après 1989". In Sapiro, Gisèle (ed.) *Les contradictions de la globalisation éditoriale*. Paris: Nouveau Monde éditions, 335-369.

Thiesse, Anne-Marie/Chmatko, Nathalia (1999) "Les nouveaux éditeurs russes". *Actes de la recherche en sciences sociales* 126-127, 75-90.

Tymoczko, Maria (2000) "Translation and Political Engagement: Activism, Social Change and the Role of Translation in Geopolitical Shifts". *The Translator* 6:1, 23-47.

UNESCO/Conseil de l'Europe (1998) *Les Gouvernements aiment les livres (les livres électroniques aussi). La situation du livre en Roumanie*. Rapport de mission UNESCO, http://www.manuscritdepot.com/edition/documents-pdf/conseil-europe.1.pdf [3 July 2012].

JANKO TRUPEJ

University of Ljubljana, Slovenia

Translating Racist Discourse in Slovenia during the Socialist Period: Mark Twain's *Adventures of Huckleberry Finn*

In the second half of the twentieth century, attitudes towards the acceptability of racist discourse against African Americans changed significantly. Thus, especially in the USA, many literary works containing such discourse were accused of racism. However, in countries with no direct experience of these racial issues, the perception of such works may be different. Focusing on the Slovenian translations of Mark Twain's *Adventures of Huckleberry Finn* (1884) (one of the books most frequently challenged on the grounds of racism), I shall try to determine whether domestic or foreign political and social changes during Slovenia's socialist era had any significant effect on how racist discourse was translated. In the case of translation shifts, the possible effects on the readers' perception of the addressed issues are discussed.

Keywords: translation shifts, norms in translation, racist discourse, *Adventures of Huckleberry Finn*, US-American literature

Introduction

Since the emergence of Translation Studies as an independent discipline, norms have been a prominent topic of research. Few translation scholars would still argue that translation is merely a linguistic process, and nowadays, it is widely acknowledged that norms govern the translation process to a great extent. As the cross-cultural process of translation bridges the gap between different time periods and cultures – and consequently between different norms – it often involves decision making concerning the question which elements of the source text to transfer, and which to suppress. Venuti (1998:67) claims that particularly elements affirming the norms dominant in a society at a certain point in time are retained, whereas potentially threatening elements are left out. Similarly, Lefevere (1992) speaks of "rewriting", which is employed to make translations (as well as original texts) acceptable to the contemporary ideology. Norms in literature are shaped by events in society, and in the case of rapid changes, they may also change quickly. In Yugoslavia (and Slovenia, as a part of it), this happened after World War II, when the socialist regime seized power. The government employed censorship of original and translated literature[1] to prevent ideas perceived as a potential threat to the newly established political system from reaching the general public (see Dović 2008a). In this paper, I will try to determine whether racism was also considered a threat deemed unacceptable by the new regime and thus censored in translation.

Historical background and research methodology

A number of historical facts support the hypothesis that during socialism certain racist elements present in original works underwent modification in their translation into Slovenian. First of all, because the Slovenian nation had faced oppression throughout its history, a certain degree of sympathy with other oppressed nations or races may be presupposed, which during the period of socialism (see Jeffs 2007:487-488) may also have been influenced by parallels between the oppression of African Americans and that of the working classes.[2] The African American Civil Rights Movement, which after 1955 was publicised worldwide, may also have been influential, since it not only brought about a change in the acceptance of racism in the USA, but raised awareness about this problem across the world. Furthermore, Yugoslavia was a founding member of the Non-Aligned Movement, and one of the principles of this intergovernmental organisation was opposition to racial discrimination (see Bakić-Hayden/Hayden 2007:456; Jeffs 2007:485).[3] This stance was reflected in Slovenian periodical publications, where the treatment of African Americans in the United States was frequently criticised by political commentators (see Orel 1963:2; Ravnikar

---

1 Elements indicating German superiority were sometimes censored in translation (Kocijančič Pokorn 2008a). Also, religious elements in children's literature (original and translated), were frequently censored (Mazi-Leskovar 2003; Kocijančič Pokorn 2008a, b; Svetina 2009), as part of efforts to weaken the influence of the Catholic Church, which traditionally had been very influential.

2 When discussing the situation of African Americans in the South of the United States, Bratko (1963:1067) speaks of "capitalist racist hatred" ("kapitalistična rasna mržnja"), thus linking the struggles of African Americans to those of the working classes. (All texts from sources written in Slovenian are translated by the author).

3 Smailagić (1970:3) claims that "racism and imperialism complemented one another" ("imperializem in rasizem se dopolnjujeta").

1964:2; N.N. 1968:2). Even prior to the formation of the Non-Aligned Movement, there is evidence that the new socialist government in Yugoslavia was opposed to racism against African Americans (see Puc 1947:296) and racism in general (Škerlj 1949:53-65).[4]

In this case study, I shall focus on the racist discourse against African Americans in two Slovenian translations of Mark Twain's novel *Adventures of Huckleberry Finn*, which in the twentieth century became controversial on account of its use of the racial slur "nigger", and the alleged stereotypical portrayal of black characters. Before the textual analysis, I consider Twain's status in Slovenia in pre-socialist times, in order to then compare it to his later status. The texts were analysed in accordance with the approach proposed by van Doorslaer (1995:256): the original text and its translations were read independently, and potentially interesting elements were chosen for further comparison. As suggested by van Leuven-Zwart (1989, 1990), the potential effects of the microstructural shifts on the macro level of the text (characterisation, plot etc.) were considered afterwards.[5] Following the textual analysis of *Adventures of Huckleberry Finn*, the reception of this novel in Slovenian periodical publications was also examined.

Mark Twain in Slovenia before the socialist period

The records maintained by the Slovenian Academy of Sciences and Arts (SAZU) show that Twain's name was first recorded in Slovenian periodical publications in 1880, although the first translation of one of his works (an adaptation of The Prince and the Pauper) was published as late as 1910, the year of the author's death. There followed a translation of The Adventures of Tom Sawyer entitled Mali klatež Tom Sawyer (1921), which remained the only other Twain translation until 1947, when a retranslation of the same novel was published. Early reviews of Twain's work were generally positive, e.g. describing him as a "man of the people"[6] (N.N. 1910:5), and praising his "strong characterisations and healthy sense of humour"[7] (N.N. 1920:3).[8]

---

[4] For claims of xenophobia and certain racist tendencies in Slovenia, see Atanasovski (1984:4), Bakić-Hayden/Hayden (2007:450) and Jeffs (2007:485-489).

[5] In this paper, I will not make use of her elaborate categorisation of translation shifts.

[6] "ljudska duša".

[7] "močna karakterizacija in zdravi humor".

[8] Although his humour was also criticised at times (see N.N. 1924:2).

However, the lack of translations indicates that, in Slovenia, Twain was not considered an important author. This is also evident from the fact that Adventures of Huckleberry Finn was first translated in 1948 (64 years after its original publication), despite the popularity and prestige it already enjoyed in the USA, as well as in several other countries (see Brown 1984). In Slovenia, it is still not perceived as part of the world literature canon; therefore, the amount of attention and critical discourse it generates in the USA (see Grosman 2004:144, 157-162) may seem surprising to many Slovenian literary scholars.[9] Lefevere claims that the degree of liberty taken when translating depends on the status of a certain text in the target culture: if it enjoys high prestige, the translation tries to be as literal as possible; if not, parts of the text are more likely to be changed (1992:90-91). Considering that Twain did not enjoy high status, we can presuppose that the latter was the case with Adventures of Huckleberry Finn.[10]

Translating racist discourse in Adventures of Huckleberry Finn

At the time of the novel's original publication in the United States, it was criticised for various reasons, including immorality, lack of humour, coarseness, roughness and inelegance (N.N. 1885; qtd. in Leonard/Tenney 1992a:2). Nevertheless, the frequent use of the racial slur "nigger" was not considered a significant problem at that time; "the pertinent objection to "nigger" was its vulgarity, not its racist implication" (Leonard/Tenney 1992a:6-7). However, the frequent use of this offensive term,[11] and the representation of black characters as "superstitious, childlike and generally insubstantial"[12] (ibid.:2) are among the main objections made by Twain's

[9] An analysis of the strategies for translating racist discourse may also show whether shifts affected the novel's reception in Slovenia.

[10] Venuti claims that a translation of a bestseller says more about the domestic culture for which it was created than about the foreign culture it is supposed to represent (1998:125).

[11] Opponents of "nigger" have gone as far as counting the number of its occurrences in the text: the number amounts to approx. 213 (Williams 1992:231).

[12] Jim (the runaway slave with whom Huck travels) is the only African American character playing a significant role; other African American characters appearing or mentioned (see Twain 1884/2008:4, 7, 26-27, 43-44, 68-69, 83, 85, 90, 92, 96, 98, 102-103, 111, 119, 133, 156, 158, 162, 166-170, 172, 179, 187-188, 198-199, 209, 212-215, 218, 223-224, 227, 241-242, 250-251, 254, 261) have no significant influence on the story and the protagonist Huckleberry Finn.

US-American audience against the novel in the latter part of the twentieth century.

In other cultures, varying degrees of importance may be ascribed to the issues of racism. Grosman notes that readers in target cultures that have had no direct experience with slavery and the oppression of African Americans cannot relate to the issues addressed in Adventures of Huckleberry Finn in a manner similar to that of US-American readers (2004:145). This is illustrated by a case study conducted in 1990 by Grosman, in which Slovenian students of English at the University of Ljubljana were asked which chapters of the novel they found to be the most memorable. The majority chose chapters from either the beginning or the end of the book, while they were not as impressed by the middle section, which is generally the most revered in the source culture (Grosman 1995:35).

Because of intercultural differences, a similar case can be argued for the severity of the epithet "nigger". In English, it has come to be widely regarded as one of the most offensive words, and has been stigmatised since the middle of the nineteenth century (Leonard/Tenney 1992a:6; Hill 2008:51). However, its severity varies in other languages. In Slovenian, a common pejorative term for a black person is "zamorec", which can be explained as "somebody coming from the other side of the [Mediterranean] sea" (Bezlaj/Snoj/Furlan 2007:846; Pogačnik 1981:172). Prior to the second part of the twentieth century, "zamorec" was used frequently; a search in the *Slovenian Digital Library* (*Digitalna knjižnica Slovenije* 2011) for the period from 1850 to 1950 returns 1624 instances of "zamorec",[13] as opposed to 672 occurrences of "črnec" (another Slovenian term for a black person). In the nineteenth century, "zamorec" was not regarded as offensive (Pleteršnik 1894:854), and although it later ceased to be the standard term used for black people, even as late as 1962, it was not marked as pejorative (Bajec et al. 1962:981). However, in the latter part of the twentieth century, the connotation gradually began to change, and its usage began to decline.[14] The *Dictionary of Standard Slovenian Language* (*Slovar slovenskega knjižnega jezika*) notes that the contemporary use of this term is usually offensive (Bajec et al. 1994:1604). Nevertheless, "zamorec" does not carry the connotations of

[13] It was also used by Slovenian national poet France Prešeren (Pogačnik 1981).

[14] From 1950 onwards "zamorec" appears 76 times in the *Digital library*, whereas "črnec" appears 168 times.

hundreds of years of slavery and oppression, as "nigger" does in English, which is why the severity of this racial slur is diminished in Slovenian.

The translation of 1948

The translation entitled *Pustolovščine Huckleberryja Finna* was published three years after a socialist government had been established in Slovenia. It was translated by Pavel Holeček (1882-1964), who was educated as a classical philologist, and spent most of his career as a grammar school teacher in Celje. He translated literary works from English, German and Czech. Among the authors he translated are Ernest Thompson Seton, Jack London, Mark Twain, Rudyard Kipling, H. G. Wells and Zane Grey (Špes/ Kovačič 1990:10-14).

My analysis shows that Holeček used a variety of approaches when translating the term "nigger". The microstructural comparison of the original and the first Slovenian translation of *Adventures of Huckleberry Finn* illustrates that in several instances the level of racist discourse present in the original is reduced in the translation. The most frequent means by which this is achieved is the omission of the racial slur "nigger" from the text, of which there are several instances (Twain 1884/2008:26-27 (7×), 53, 118, 128, 148, 156, 158, 168 (2×), 172 , 192 (2×), 215, 221 (2×), 241, 250, 255; 1948:45 (7×), 84, 174, 188, 216, 229, 231, 245 (2×), 250 , 278 (2×), 312, 323 (2×), 352, 369, 376). For example, when the protagonist Huckleberry Finn[15] describes the aftermath of a dinner party, in the original he states: "And when it was all done me and the hare-lip had supper in the kitchen off of the leavings, whilst the others was helping the niggers clean up the things" (Twain 1884/2008:156). In the translation, he[16] fails to mention the black servants[17] (Twain 1948:229).

In several instances, instead of "nigger", the translator opted to use either the first name of the character addressed (Twain 1884/2008:195 (4×), 214, 224; 1948:282 (3×), 283 (1×), 311, 327) or a personal pronoun (Twain 1884/2008:7, 73, 172, 214, 215, 224; 1948:15, 112, 250, 311, 312, 327).

[15] Throughout the story he is called "Huck".

[16] Since Huck narrates the story, it is with him that these shifts most often occur. However, at times this is also the case with negative characters: the racist passage in which Pap Finn (Huck's father) complains about a free "nigger" from Ohio not behaving as he should (Twain 1884/2008:26-27) is deleted in its entirety (Twain 1948:45).

[17] "Ko so gostje odšli, sva z 'zajčjo ustnico' v kuhinji večerjala".

Emphasising the role African Americans played in society, "nigger" is sometimes interchanged with "slave"[18] (Twain 1884/2008:41, 116, 119, 143, 166, 207; 1948:65, 172, 177, 209, 243, 301), or a range of Slovenian variants for "black servant"[19] (Twain 1884/2008:4, 98, 223, 254; 1948:11, 148, 326, 375). Also, instead of using the diminutives of "zamorec", "nigger girl" is changed into "little sister"[20] (Twain 1884/2008:198; 1948:286), "little nigger boys" into "black boys"[21] (Twain 1884/2008:198; 1948:286), and "little niggers" into "little black comrades"[22] (Twain 1884/2008:198; 1948:286).

Several translation solutions appear only once. Instead of "nigger", the Slovenian version reads:

- "fellow blacks"[23] (Twain 1884/2008:7; 1948:15)
- "foreign guests"[24] (Twain 1884/2008:7; 1948:15)
- "black souls"[25] (Twain 1884/2008:167; 1948:245)
- "black hind"[26] (Twain 1884/2008:212; 1948:308)
- "black man"[27] (Twain 1884/2008:212; 1948:309)
- "fugitive"[28] (Twain 1884/2008:225; 1948:328)

Other instances of shifts include Huck referring to an African American who had done him a service as a "good nigger"[29] (Twain 1948:166) instead of only "nigger" (Twain 1884/2008:111). Also, towards the end of the story, the doctor, whom Jim had helped to nurse the injured Tom Sawyer, instead of saying that Jim "ain't a bad nigger" (Twain 1884/2008:255), says in the translation: "ain't a bad man"[30] (Twain 1948:375). Despite the numerous shifts which lower the level of racist discourse, I have also found various

---

18 "suženj".

19 "črni služabniki" (Twain 1948:11), "črni služabnik" (ibid.:148), "črni sluga" (ibid.:326), "črna služinčad" (ibid.:375).

20 "sestrica".

21 "črna dečka".

22 "mali črni tovariši".

23 "črni rojaki".

24 "tuji gostje".

25 "črne duše".

26 "črni hlapec".

27 "črnec".

28 "begun".

29 "dober zamorec".

30 "ni hudoben človek".

translation shifts that intensify it instead. In several instances, this occurs when the negative characters (Pap Finn, the King and the Duke) refer to African American characters. Instead of translating "nigger" as the aforementioned less offensive Slovenian version ("zamorec"), severity is instead increased, as follows:

- "damned black killer"[31] (Twain 1884/2008:53; 1948:83)
- "black riff-raff"[32] (Twain 1884/2008:162; 1948:236)
- "stinking black rabble"[33] (Twain 1884/2008:167; 1948:244)
- "black good-for-nothings"[34] (Twain 1884/2008:179; 1948:262)

Such shifts are not limited to the translation of "nigger". When talking about the slaves, who he thinks have stolen a large amount of money, the Duke refers to them as "the black dogs"[35] (Twain 1948:245), instead of "they" (Twain 1884/2008:168). The Duke and the King also ascribe additional negative characteristics to the slaves by saying that "nigger women are disorderly"[36] (Twain 1948:236), which is not stated in the original (Twain 1884/2008:162). Furthermore, in some instances, they use "zamorec" ("nigger") (Twain 1948:172, 209, 244, 245) instead of the personal pronouns used in the original (Twain 1884/2008:116, 143, 167, 168).

However, it is not only the negative characters' discourse that is at times more racist. In the translation, Huck replaces the personal pronoun "he" with the less offensive Slovenian version of "nigger" ("zamorec") in several instances when referring to Jim (Twain 1884/2008:7, 53, 181, 212; 1948:14, 83, 122, 309) or other black characters (Twain 1884/2008:102; 1948:154).[37] Furthermore, instead of referring to Jim and to other African American characters by their names, he often uses "nigger" (Twain 1884/2008:7, 18, 39, 82, 113, 198, 224, 228, 231, 241, 255; 1948:14, 32, 62, 125, 168, 286, 327, 332, 337, 352, 375).

31 "prekleti črni ubijalec".

32 "črna sodrga".

33 "smrdljiva črna drhal".

34 "črni malopridneži".

35 "črni psi".

36 "zamorke so zanikrne".

37 Peripheral characters also sometimes make this substitution in the translation (Twain 1884/2008:169, 191, 251, 256, 257; 1948:246, 277, 369, 377, 378).

There are also more explicit instances:

- When Huck and Jim lose sight of each other on the Mississippi, Huck reports: "I did wish the fool would think to beat a tin pan, and beat it all the time, but he never did" (Twain 1884/2008:75). In Slovenian, instead of "he never did" Huck states: "but this was too much for his black brains"[38] (Twain 1948:116).[39]
- Realising that Jim would soon be free, instead of only referring to him as to a "free man"[40] (Twain 1884/2008:81), in the translation, Huck adds "free nigger"[41] (Twain 1948:125). Shortly afterwards, as Huck asks himself who was to blame for this, in the original he replies with: "Why, *me*" (Twain 1884/2008:81), whereas in the translation the following statement is added: "I committed the crime of helping a nigger who had escaped"[42] (Twain 1948:125). In the Slovenian version, Huck thus explicitly accuses himself of a crime.

Tom Sawyer also sometimes displays more racism, twice reducing Jim to the level of an animal:

- Instead of saying that the glorious chances given to Jim to escape from captivity were "wasted on him" (Twain 1884/2008:237), Tom calls Jim a "stupid animal"[43] (Twain 1948:346).

Instead of referring to Jim as "the runaway nigger" (Twain 1884/2008:225), he uses "rotten black dog"[44] (Twain 1948:328).

As a consequence of these explicit intensifications of racist discourse, the negative, as well as the positive characters appear more racist in the translation. This especially affects the reader's perception of the relationship between the two protagonists; the reader can much less appreciate the affection between Huck and Jim, and the latter's role in the former's moral growth.

---

[38] "ali to je bilo za njegovo črno pamet že preveč".

[39] Although, instead of calling Jim a "fool", in the translation Huck says: "I expected Jim would be smart enough […]" (Original: Pričakoval sem, da bo Jim toliko pameten [...]) (Twain 1948:116).

[40] "svoboden človek".

[41] "svoboden zamorec".

[42] "[J]az sem zagrešil zločin, da sem pomagal zamorcu, ki je pobegnil".

[43] "neumna žival".

[44] "pokvarjeni črni pes".

However, perhaps the most significant translation shifts occur where Jim is concerned. Several times, when referring to himself or other black characters, he uses "nigger" (Twain 1948:63, 65 (2×), 68 (3×), 69, 155-56 (3×), 326, 361) instead of the personal pronouns used in the original (Twain 1884/2008:39, 41, 43-44, 103, 223, 246). In three of these instances, patronising adjectives are added. In the Slovenian translation, Jim thus calls himself:

- "poor, old nigger"[45] (Twain 1884/2008:39; 1948:63)
- "poor, silly nigger"[46] (Twain 1884/2008:223; 1948:326)
- "poor nigger"[47] (Twain 1884/2008:246; 1948:361)

In the translation, Jim therefore evidently sees himself as a passive, helpless, unintelligent person and is consequently perceived as such by the other characters;[48] Huck also calls him "poor old man"[49] (Twain 1948:77) and "poor nigger"[50] (Twain 1948:375), instead of "Jim" (Twain 1884/2008:50, 255). Consequently, Jim's frequent displays of good reasoning skills and intelligence seem less believable, as is also the case with Huck's expressions of admiration for Jim. Since Jim's strength, dignity and upright moral stance were the characteristics that affirmed him as a character and thus lifted his

[45] "ubogo [sic], staro [sic] zamorec".

[46] "ubog, bebast zamorec".

[47] "ubogo [sic] zamorec".

[48] Jim's unimportance is also evident from the lack of depictions; he appears in only 4 of 26 illustrations (Twain 1948:73, 119, 341 387) and is not depicted on the cover. In comparison, in the translation published in 1962 he is featured in 10 of 29 illustrations (Twain 1962:15, 61, 77, 105, 125, 176, 269, 335, 347, 357), but does not appear on the cover. In the 1974 edition of this translation he is pictured in 14 (Twain 1962/1974a:3, 32, 48, 74, 112, 127, 163; 1962/1974b:3, 12, 32, 120, 164, 178, 184) of 27 illustrations and does appear on the cover of both the first and the second book. In accordance with the stereotype, all three artists depict him with full lips. In both translations, racist stereotypes about the superstitions of African Americans (see Twain 1884/2008:7, 17, 40, 42-43, 86, 213, 224 ; 1948:15, 31, 64, 66-67, 133, 310, 327; 1962/1974a:12, 27, 60, 64-65, 126; 1962/1974b:116, 133) and negative remarks about African American (see Twain 1884/2008:71, 73, 74, 82, 158, 199, 212, 213, 215; 1948:109, 112, 114, 126, 231, 289, 308, 311, 312; 1962/1974a:104, 107, 109, 120; 1962/1974b:34, 96, 114, 117, 118) characters remain largely intact. A notable exception is Holeček's omission of the passage in which Pap Finn complains about the misbehaviour of a free "nigger" from Ohio, which Gradišnik left intact (Twain 1884/2008:26-27; 1948:45; 1962/1974a:40-41).

[49] "ubogi starec".

[50] "ubogi zamorec".

whole race, the meaning potential of the novel may be gravely changed because of these shifts.[51]

The translation of 1962

In 1962, *Adventures of Huckleberry Finn* was translated anew by Janez Gradišnik (1917-2009), who is widely regarded as one of the greatest Slovenian translators. Shortly after graduating from the University of Ljubljana in 1940, he was mobilised, but was soon captured, and sent to a prisoner-of-war camp in Germany. After being released in 1942, he lived in exile in the Independent State of Croatia until the end of World War II. In the immediate post-war years, he was employed by one of the newly established Yugoslavian ministries in Belgrade, and after returning to Slovenia, by the publishing company DZS. However, because of his affiliation with the political dissident Edvard Kocbek, he was monitored by the Yugoslavian secret police, and after being forced out of his job in 1952, he decided to pursue a career as a freelance translator. He translated works by important authors of world literature, among them Ernest Hemingway, Thomas Mann, Mark Twain, Heinrich Böll, Franz Kafka and James Joyce. Gradišnik received numerous awards for his work, including the most prestigious Slovenian award for culture: the Prešeren Award (Pibernik 2009:110-113).

Published one year after the formation of the Non-Aligned Movement, Gradišnik's retranslation entitled *Prigode Huckleberryja Finna* differs significantly from the previous translation. Here, racist discourse is not intensified, but it is softened in several instances. In this translation also, the less severe pejorative term for a black person ("zamorec") serves as the translation for "nigger", and the use of this offensive word is often omitted by using either the neutral term for a black person ("črnec") (Twain 1884/2008:26 (2×), 41, 82, 83, 85 (2×), 116, 128, 143, 158, 166, 261; 1962/1974a[52]:40-41 (2×) 61, 120, 122, 123-124 (2×), 169, 184; 1962/1974b:13, 34, 45, 187), personal pronouns (Twain 1884/2008:7, 168; 1962/1974a:12, 1962/1974b:49) or omission from the text (Twain 1884/2008:214, 255; 1962/1974b:117, 179).

---

[51] Grosman (2004:147) claims that the characterisation of Jim is altered most severely because of the way his language was translated. In the translation, Jim uses the infinitive forms of verbs, because of which he appears to be illiterate and may be perceived merely as a comic figure by young readers.

[52] The 1974 edition of the novel was published in two parts: the reference "1974a" refers to part 1 and "1974b" refers to part 2.

Another translation shift is the standardisation of Jim's African American Vernacular English. The translator briefly comments on this in the afterword, explaining that Jim speaks "quite normally", because the practice of making the language of "niggers" sound incoherent was wrong (1962/1974b:194). He thus indirectly criticises the strategy used in the preceding translation. Grosman nevertheless claims that precisely this standardisation of Jim's and other characters' dialects significantly influenced the status change of *Adventures of Huckleberry Finn* in Slovenia. As the many dialects in the novel were lost in the translation, "important linguistic signs about characters' social position, relationships and distance were assimilated beyond recognition" (Grosman 1995:33-34). She further argues that, through the way Jim articulates himself in the original, his humanity is revealed to Huck, but because of the standardisation, he is "robbed" of part of this humanity, which diminishes his role in Huck's moral growth, and consequently, the focus of the reader shifts from Jim (and the racism related issues) to Huck and the adventure aspect of the story (Grosman 2004:147-148).

However, the translation shifts in racist discourse had not yet been taken into consideration by Grosman. The aforementioned shifts, including the use of the less severe Slovenian variant of "nigger", significantly reduce the severity of the racism displayed in the novel. Sutton notes that in the case of "softening of white bigotry in Twain's book, readers can conclude that life wasn't so bad for blacks in the South" (1984:44; qtd. in Leonard/Tenney 1992b:14). Therefore, the issue of racial prejudice becomes less important in the translation; this seems to be partly why the focus shifts to the adventure story.

The comparison between the two translations has shown that substantially different strategies for translating racist discourse were employed, and that this fact may have influenced the reception of the novel in Slovenia.

Conclusion

The results suggest that there was an awareness of the problem of racism towards African Americans in Slovenia before the start of the Civil Rights Movement and the formation of the Non-Aligned Movement. However, taking previous research on censorship in Slovenia into consideration (e.g. Kocijančič Pokorn 2008b), we can presume that translators were not directly pressured by their editors to approach racial issues with sensitivity.

The publishing houses were state-controlled,[53] and censorship was seldom enforced directly, as Dović (2008b:163) notes:

> [T]he new rulers were later content with (less obvious) control over the nationalized cultural institutions, in which a communist majority had been installed. The system, based on non-transparent interventions that thus created an atmosphere of dread and self-censorship, functioned almost perfectly: the retroactive (suppressive) measures only had to be applied in exceptional cases.

The question still remains of why in the first translation of *Adventures of Huckleberry Finn* the racist discourse is at times intensified. In an attempt to further investigate the cause, I shall examine the reviews of this translation, and also consider the political situation of the period.

In the first years of the socialist regime, the socially critical dimensions of Twain's writings are evidently perceived as more important than his humour. In the newspaper *Primorski dnevnik,* an anonymous author criticises US-American publishers for not giving Twain the status he deserved, especially in view of his anti-imperialist writings (N.N. 1948a:3). Similar sentiments are expressed in the few published reviews of the 1948 translation of *Adventures of Huckleberry Finn.* In an openly ideologically charged review, Željeznov attacks the imperialist tactics of US-American publishing houses, which according to him were flooding book markets in Europe with worthless US-American literature, whilst withholding Twain's works of much higher quality. This reviewer further claims that the reason US-Americans "hated" Twain's work is his criticism of the USA; he did not portray it as the "saviour of the world, a good motherland, a hospitable country willing to offer its protection to anyone"[54] (Željeznov 1948:444). Instead, in *The Adventures of Tom Sawyer* and *Adventures of Huckleberry Finn,* Twain addressed "the problems of slavery, [...] strict and shallow conventionalism and conservatism, which stifles every progressive idea and devel-

---

[53] Both translations of *Adventures of Huckleberry Finn* were published by Mladinska knjiga, the main Slovenian publishing house for children's and young adult literature, which was founded in 1945 by the newly established government. In socialist Slovenia children's literature played a significant role in children's "emotional, aesthetic education" (Bohanec 1958:368), and Mladinska knjiga was an important factor in this process. It published magazines, textbooks and – most importantly – books, including those which were on school reading lists; Janez Gradišnik's 1962 translation of *Adventures of Huckleberry Finn* was obligatory reading for students in the seventh grade of primary school (O. S. 1966:212).

[54] "rešiteljico sveta, dobro mater, deželo, ki vsakogar gostoljubno sprejme v svoje varstvo".

opment"[55] (ibid.:445). Similarly, when commenting on the translation, an anonymous reviewer in *Obzornik* writes that Twain exposed the "hypocrisy, dissimulation and selfishness of American society"[56] (N.N. 1948c:222).[57]

There is a range of possible reasons for these anti-US-American sentiments. Holeček's translation was published at a time when the Cold War between the USA and the USSR was just beginning. The newly formed socialist Yugoslavia was a close ally of the USSR, and its literature was also considerably influenced by Soviet literature (Gradišnik 1996:59). The newly ignited interest in Twain's work in Yugoslavia is of no surprise, since Twain was among the most popular US-American authors in the Soviet Union, owing to his social criticism (see Wysiolek 1964:10).

Perhaps even more important than the Soviet influence were the relations between Yugoslavia and the West; in the first post-War years, there were serious tensions between Yugoslavia and the Allies, and the strained relations may have been the reason for the translation shifts in the first translation of *Adventures of Huckleberry Finn*. As a capitalist system, the USA was perceived as an ideological adversary to any socialist government, a position which is reflected in comments made about the USA in Slovenian periodical publications: the injustices committed by US-American capitalists against their workers were openly criticised by commentators (N.N. 1954:4), as was US involvement in foreign affairs (N.N. 1961:1, Ravnikar 1964:2). The United States was frequently described in negative terms, for instance as a country "having made the huge step into the abyss of modern, immeasurable capitalism"[58] (Fatur 1951:648), in which could be found the "ruthless entrepreneurship of American liberalism in its overripe capitalist stage"[59] (Kralj 1954:940). However, after the Tito-Stalin split in 1948, relations between Yugoslavia and the United States gradually improved (Lukic/Lynch

---

55 "o problematiki suženjstva, [...] o strogem in puhlem konvencionalizmu in kenservativizmu, ki je dušil sleherno misel in razvoj naprej".

56 "svetohlinstvo, licemerstvo in koristoljubje ameriške družbe".

57 As far as the quality of the translation is concerned, the lack of metatexts is seen as the main deficiency. An anonymous reviewer in *Slovenski poročevalec*, while describing the translation as "good", criticises the lack of introduction, which could have educated younger readers about the author and the time period. Because of this he or she is of the opinion that adults would enjoy the book more (N.N. 1948b:4). Željeznov also notes that an introduction would have put certain issues into context (1948:445).

58 "ogromni korak v žrelo modernega, neizmernega kapitalizma".

59 "brezobzirnemu podjetništvu ameriškega liberalizma v njegovi prezreli kapitalistični fazi".

1996:303), and thus by the time the second translation was published in 1962, anti-US sentiment was present to a lesser extent.

Above, I have shown that the contemporary political situation did have an effect on how the racist discourse in *Adventures of Huckleberry Finn* was translated during the socialist period in Slovenia. In the first translation, racism was at times intensified, which likely happened because of the anti-US-American sentiment of the time period. The second translation was published after Yugoslavia had distanced itself from the Soviet Union, and its relations with the United States were significantly better than at the time of the first translation. Thus, the racist discourse was not intensified, but often softened instead. The example of the Slovenian translations of *Adventures of Huckleberry Finn* also shows that such translation shifts may significantly alter the reader's perception of a literary work in which racist discourse plays an important part. The case study suggests that relations between Slovenia and the United States substantially influenced the translation strategies for US literature during different periods; further investigation on the representation of the West in Slovenian translations should thus be considered for future research.

References

Atanasovski, Gligor (1984) "Tuji študentje v Sloveniji". *Tribuna* 34:3, 4.

Bajec, Anton et al. (eds.) (1962) *Slovenski pravopis*. Ljubljana: DZS.

Bajec, Anton et al. (eds.) (1994) *Slovar slovenskega knjižnega jezika*. Ljubljana: DZS.

Bakić-Hayden, Milica/Hayden, Robert M. (2007) "Orientalistične različice na temo 'Balkana': simbolna geografija v nedavni jugoslovanski politiki kulture." In Jeffs, Nikolai (ed.) *Zbornik postkolonialnih študij*. Ljubljana: Krtina, 441-459.

Bezlaj, France/Snoj, Marko/Furlan, Metka (eds.) (2007) *Etimološki slovar slovenskega jezika*. Ljubljana: Mladinska knjiga.

Bohanec, Franček (1958) "Knjižne police za otroke". *Jezik in slovstvo* 3:8, 362-368.

Bratko, Ivan (1963) "Črncem pravijo 'nigri'". *Sodobnost* 1:12, 1057-1075.

Brown, Robert B. (1984) "One Hundred Years of HUCK FINN". *American Heritage Magazine*, http://main.americanheritage.com/content/one-hundred-years-huck-finn [3 July 2012].

Digitalna knjižnica Slovenije (2011) Narodna in univerzitetna knjižnica, http://dlib.si [3 July 2012].

Dović, Marijan (ed.) (2008a) *Literatura in cenzura: Kdo se boji resnice literature?*. Ljubljana: Slovensko društvo za primerjalno književnost.

Dović, Marijan (2008b) "Literature and Censorship, Truth and Fear". In Dović, Marijan (ed.) *Literatura in cenzura: Kdo se boji resnice literature?*. Ljubljana: Slovensko društvo za primerjalno književnost, 159-165.

Fatur, Bogomil (1951) "Ameriška literatura in Sinclair Lewis". *Novi svet* 6:7-8, 638-662.

Grosman, Meta (1995) "Multicultural Perspectives on Huckleberry Finn - Including a Look at the Lack of Primary Socialization in Huck's Development". In Grosman, Meta (ed.) *American Literature for Non-American Readers*. Frankfurt am Main-Berlin-Bern-Bruxelles-New York-Oxford-Wien: Peter Lang, 33-47.

Grosman, Meta (2004) *Književnost v medkulturnem položaju*. Ljubljana: Znanstveni inštitut Filozofske fakultete.

Hill, Jane H. (2008) *The Everyday Language of White Racism*. Malden-Oxford: Wiley-Blackwell.

Jeffs, Nikolai (2007) "Kje, kdaj, zakaj postkolonialne študije." In Jeffs, Nikolai (ed.) *Zbornik postkolonialnih študij*. Ljubljana: Krtina, 461-503.

Kocijančič Pokorn, Nike (2008a) *(Avto)cenzura v prevodih otroške in mladinske književnosti: ste prepričani, da ste res brali Winnetouja?*. Maribor: Filozofska fakulteta, Presented at Oddelek za prevodoslovje, 5 March 2008.

Kocijančič Pokorn, Nike (2008b) "(Post)communist Censorship in Translation – Religion as a Taboo". In Kralova, Jana/Jettmarová, Zuzana (eds.) *Tradition Versus Modernity: From the Classic Period of the Prague School to Translation Studies at the Beginning of the 21st Century*. Praha: Univerzita Karlova v Praze, 175-185.

Kralj, Vladimir (1954) "Irwin Shaw – dobri ljudje". *Naša sodobnost* 2:10, 937-941.

Lefevere, André (1992) *Translation, Rewriting and the Manipulation of Literary Fame*. London-New York: Routledge.

Leonard, James S./Tenney, Thomas A. (1992a) "Huck Finn and the Authorities". In Leonard, James S./Tenney, Thomas A./Davis, Thadious M. (eds.) *Satire or Evasion? Black Perspectives on Huckleberry Finn*. Durham-London: Duke University Press, 13-15.

Leonard, James S./Tenney, Thomas A. (1992b) "Introduction". In Leonard, James S./Tenney, Thomas A./Davis, Thadious M. (eds.) *Satire or Evasion? Black Perspectives on Huckleberry Finn*. Durham-London: Duke University Press, 1-11.

Lukic, Reneo/Lynch, Allen (1996) *Europe from the Balkans to the Urals: The Disintegration of Yugoslavia and the Soviet Union*. Oxford: Oxford University Press.

Mazi-Leskovar, Darja (2003) "Domestication and Foreignization in Translating American Prose for Slovenian Children". In Clas, André/Oittinen, Riitta (eds.) *Meta* 48:1-2 (special issue), 250-265.

N.N. (1910) "Kraljevič in berač". *Soča*, 16 July 1910, 5.

N.N. (1920) "Mark Twain: Mali klatež Tom Sawyer". *Slovenski narod*, 24 December 1920, 3.

N.N. (1924) "Cezar in Kleopatra". *Slovenski narod*, 4 April 1924, 2.

N.N. (1948a) "Mark Twain na indeksu". *Primorski dnevnik*, 28 September 1948, 3.

N.N. (1948b) "Mark Twain, Pustolovščine Huckleberryja Finna". *Slovenski poročevalec*, 15 May 1948, 4.

N.N. (1948c) "Pustolovščine Huckleberry Finna". *Obzornik* 3:5, 222.

N.N. (1954) "Trusti, monopoli in ameriško delavstvo". *Dolenjski list*, 5 November 1954, 4.

N.N. (1961) "Naš komentar". *Ptujski tednik*, 27 January 1961, 1.

N.N. (1968) "Tedenski zunanjepolitični pregled". *Celjski tednik*, 14 November 1968, 2.

O. S. (1966) "Moja knjižnica". *Naša žena* 26:6, 212.

Orel, Tine (1963) "Pogled po svetu". *Celjski tednik*, 17 May 1963, 2.

Pibernik, France (2009) *Janez Gradišnik 1917-2009*. Celje: Celjska Mohorjeva družba.

Pleteršnik, Maks (1894) *Slovensko-nemški slovar*. Ljubljana: Knezoškofijstvo.

Pogačnik, Jože (1981) "Črni zamorec v Prešernovi baladi o Lepi Vidi". *Jezik in slovstvo* 26:5, 171-175.

Puc, Mira (1947) "Večerja v Beli hiši". *Novi svet* 2:3-4, 290-302.

Ravnikar, Marjan (1964) "Pogled po svetu". *Celjski tednik*, 6 November 1964, 2.

Smailagić, Nerkez (1970) "Vidiki ideologije 'nove levice'". *Problemi, časopis za mišljenje in pesništvo* 8:85, 2-6.

Svetina, Peter (2009) "Mladinska književnost med krščanstvom in socializmom: dve zgodbi ene Bratovščine Sinjega galeba". *Jezik in slovstvo* 54:5, 15-30.

Škerlj, Božo (1949) O *človeških rasah in o rasizmu*. Ljubljana: Slovenski knjižni zavod.

Špes, Irena/Kovačič, Breda (1990) *Profesorji – prevajalci s celjske gimnazije*. Celje: Gimnazija.

Twain, Mark (1948) *Pustolovščine Huckleberryja Finna*. Translated by Pavel Holeček. Ljubljana: Mladinska knjiga.

Twain, Mark (1962) *Prigode Huckleberryja Finna*. Translated by Janez Gradišnik. Ljubljana: Mladinska knjiga.

Twain, Mark (1974a) *Prigode Huckleberryja Finna 1*. Translated by Janez Gradišnik. Ljubljana: Mladinska knjiga.

Twain, Mark (1974b) *Prigode Huckleberryja Finna 2*. Translated by Janez Gradišnik. Ljubljana: Mladinska knjiga.

Twain, Mark (1884/2008) *Adventures of Huckleberry Finn*. Oxford-New York: Oxford University Press.

van Doorslaer, Luc (1995) "Quantitative and Qualitative Aspects of Corpus Selection in Translation Studies". *Target* 7:2, 245-260.

van Leuven-Zwart, Kitty M. (1989) "Translation and Original: Similarities and Dissimilarities, I". *Target* 1:2, 151-181.

van Leuven-Zwart, Kitty M. (1990) "Translation and Original: Similarities and Dissimilarities, II". *Target* 2:1, 69-95.

Venuti, Lawrence (1998) *The Scandals of Translation: Towards an Ethics of Difference*. London-New York: Routledge.

Williams, Kenny J. (1992) "Mark Twain's Racial Ambiguity". In Leonard, James S./Tenney, Thomas A./Davis, Thadious M. (eds.) *Satire or Evasion? Black Perspectives on Huckleberry Finn*. Durham-London: Duke University Press, 228-237.

Wysiolek, Edward (1964) "Rusi imajo svojo podobo o Ameriki". *Ljubljanski dnevnik*, 15 July 1964, 10.

Željeznov, Dušan (1948) "O dveh Mark Twainovih knjigah v slovenščini". *Mladinska revija* 3:10, 444-445.

DAINORA MAUMEVIČIENĖ

Vilnius University, Lithuania

Linguistic Insights into Localisation

Globalisation and the development of global markets and information communication technologies have laid the foundation for the enhancement of cross-cultural communication among countries. Many international companies are successfully exploiting the advantage of real-time communication provided by the Internet in order to properly reach their target consumers and offer them products/services that "speak" their language. This is possible when localising the products/services to the target country and its consumers. Localisation has been called a prerequisite for successful marketing, cross-cultural communication and a new paradigm within Translation Studies; however, there remains a lack of discussion about localisation among translation scholars. Since localisation can be treated as a linguistic phenomenon, this paper explores and presents linguistic insights into localisation by providing definitions and an understanding of the phenomenon within local and global contexts. Furthermore, the paper attempts to disclose the linguistic aspects of localisation by focusing on the roots of localisation in terms of translation theories and the features of localisation.

Keywords: localisation, internationalisation, culturalisation, adaptation, Lithuanisation

Introduction

Globalisation and the development of the global market foster the adaptation of new products to target markets by means of localisation. The term *localisation* could be briefly defined as the linguistic and cultural adaptation of a product (*product* is widely understood as any type of product, i.e. a book, a film, a website, software, etc.) to a particular country, region and language. Thus, book translation, or the subtitling or dubbing of a movie could be perceived as a type of localisation, the meaning of which is usually narrowed down just to software localisation.

Localisation as a new direction within Translation Studies has been considered and discussed within the academic publications of translation (O'Hagan/Ashworth 2002; Cronin 2003; Gil/Pym 2006; Gouadec 2007; Pym 2008) and computer science researchers (Dagienė 2004; Dagienė/

Grigas 2006), translators (Sprung 2000a) localisers (Esselink 2000, 2006; Sprung 2000b; Dagienė 2004) and software developers (Brooks 2000). Much of the discussion has focused on whether localisation should be perceived as a wider process that incorporates translation alongside other stages of product development, or rather as a new form of translation marked by the digital medium. Pym (2010:136) has recently defined localisation as a new translation paradigm; however, he states that "there has been remarkably little debate about localisation among translation theorists" due to the nature of localisation, which has been perceived as technological and industrial. This, indeed, reveals the urgency of discussing localisation within the scope of Translation Studies. Therefore, the aim of this article is to reveal linguistic insights into localisation by examining its understanding based on the relationship between translation and localisation in the context of translation theories.

This article employs a descriptive method and synthesis of scientific publications while discussing linguistic insights into localisation. Localisation was born out of the "marriage of language and technology" (Esselink 2006:20) and could be metaphorically called the offspring of language; thus, the linguistic aspects of localisation should be traced due to the "linguistic genes" they have inherited. Since the primary concern of this article is to disclose the linguistic aspects of localisation, it will explore the way localisation is defined and perceived in terms of the relationship between translation and localisation. The paper will also examine translation theories (i.e. the theory of Schleiermacher, Vinay and Darbelnet, Venuti and *Skopos* etc.) to highlight and emphasise the linguistic aspects of localisation.

Definitions of localisation

The term localisation (or the American English version localization) appeared within the context of studies about localisation around the 1990s, and later entered the domain of Translation Studies (e.g. Pym 2004). The way localisation is defined depends on those who describe it and their diverse perspectives on the phenomenon. Since localisation originated from the unification of language and technologies, both translation theorists and software developers/localisers emphasise different aspects and define localisation differently. Therefore, there is no solid consensus on the definition of the term due to divergent understandings of the phenomenon. Localisers are proponents of a practical approach and are not interested in theorising, as it seems they are more concerned with profit rather than definition making. On the other hand, definitions that are suggested by theories are sometimes far removed from practice, highly theoretical and not validated by practical evidence, thus, they might appear too artificial and distant from practice. Still, definitions provided by theory are necessary for the sake of having a common understanding of what phenomena and concepts are about. It has been observed that the polemics of defining localisation centres on the perception of the relationship and differences between translation and localisation, which are blurred (Munday 2008:191). Translation theorists (O'Hagan/Ashworth 2002; Gil/Pym 2006; Gouadec 2007; Pym 2008) who aim to disclose the phenomenon of localisation within the scope of Translation Studies seek to present versatile aspects of localisation; therefore, their works would subscribe to both views (translation as part of localisation and translation encompassing localisation).

Coming back to the polemics of localisation perception, one group of authors (Brooks 2000; Esselink 2000, 2006; Sprung 2000a; Austermühl 2001; Dagienė 2004; Pym 2004, 2008; Dagienė/Grigas 2006; Zeller 2006) claim that translation is only a part of localisation. These authors argue "that translation is only one of the many modifications a program has to go through" (Gil/Pym 2006:14), and treat localisation as a process of software adaptation/preparation/modification (Sprung 2000b; Austermühl 2001; Cronin 2003; Pym 2004; Zeller 2006). Researchers presenting arguments for translation as a part of localisation identify localisation-specific aspects such as internationalisation (the process of preparing a product to be localised during the process of product development); the model "one-to-many" (Pym 2010:126), which means that after internationalisation, the product can be translated and adapted to several target languages/cultures (e.g. Lithuanian, or any other); the use of technologies (translation memories, terminology management systems and computer aided/assisted translation); and the scope and complexity of the entire process (Esselink 2000; Pym 2008, 2010).

The other group of authors (O'Hagan/Ashworth 2002; O'Hagan 2006; Gouadec 2007) define translation as the core of localisation, which might be regarded as a new form of translation marked by the digital medium. For example, Gouadec (2007:38), describing the technical and linguistic aspects of localisation, supports the view that localisation is a variety of translation. O'Hagan and Ashworth (2002:12) claim that localisation is a part of globalisation, where translation is the core of both localisation and globalisation;

however, discussing the issue more thoroughly, the authors agree that localisation involves both activities: software engineering and translation. The scholars prove their point of view by stating that when "translation moved from a paper-based [activity] to a digital medium such as computer software, the process came to be called localization, as it required special engineering adjustments in addition to translation of texts" (ibid.:71). Moreover, the authors define it as a "comprehensive adaptation of the Message into the Receiver's environment in terms of both language and cultural context" (ibid.). If the majority of the above definitions on localisation dwell on a product-based approach, O'Hagan and Ashworth apply a communicative approach by emphasising the adaptation of the message sent to the receiver. Such an approach views localisation as an act of communication in which a sent message has to be modified to meet the particular cultural and linguistic norms of its recipient. This view of localisation as an act of communication is borrowed from Translation Studies that describes translation as an act of communication (Nida 1964; Kade 1968).

Defining the term localisation, both translation theorists and software developers/localisers usually turn to the definition provided by LISA (Localization Industry Standards Association). The association states that "localization involves taking a product and making it linguistically and culturally appropriate to the target locale (country/region and language) where it will be used and sold" (LISA 1998:3). Such a definition is too broad since "taking a product" might mean any product localised and fails to mention translation at all. It seems that "making it linguistically appropriate" hides a hint and reference to the translation undertaken to make the product suitable to the target language. The definition seems to understate the significance of translation as an activity, limiting it to a small "subset of localization" (Sprung 2000a:xvii) due to the fact that this definition is provided by LISA – the premier organisation for the globalisation, internationalisation and localisation (GIL) industries. The acronym GIL does not embrace the letter T, which stands for translation, to form the acronym GILT, because the letter L, i.e. localisation, has become a superordinate term for translation (Munday 2008:191). And even when GILT encompasses translation (T), it is the last word, making it also the least important – for the words that come first are the most significant in human perception (Lakoff/Johnson 2003:132).

The perception of localisation as a superordinate term for translation is overturned by O'Hagan (2006:39), who shifts translation from the periphery (being the least important term in GILT) to the core (the centre) of translation, localisation and globalisation. The core is always the most significant; therefore, translation becomes the essential part of localisation. The author of the article also adheres to the viewpoint that any type of product adaptation is carried out by means of translation. Book translation, or the subtitling or dubbing of a movie could be perceived as a type of localisation. However, the meaning of localisation is usually narrowed just to software or website localisation. Moreover, within the project of localisation, software users tend to judge the acceptability of a product through its language, as they notice the language first of all. If a message on the screen is not understood, users will immediately get frustrated and will not care about the design of the product or the difficult programming code that allows them to perform various commands.

Linguistic aspects of localisation in terms of translation theories

There has been much discussion about the perplexity of localisation perception. The question of whether localisation is something new or just a fancy name for a new and advanced form of translation has also been raised (Pym 2008:2). The answer to this question could be presented by probing into translation theories and revealing the points where localisation merges with translation and unfolds its linguistic aspects.

First of all, it could be stated that localisation is nothing new and deserves to be discussed within the scope of Translation Studies. Indeed, the first germs could be observed within the theory of Schleiermacher (1813/ 2004), who argues that texts should be translated by bringing the author to the language of the reader or the reader to the author. When talking about localisation, the process of bringing the writer to the reader or, more appropriately, the product to the reader, is rather important – as otherwise, the product will remain unused. Moreover, there is no single author, but rather a group of authors, as most products are developed by a team. And the author or writer whom Schleiermacher has in mind could be replaced by the product, the reader by the receiver or user thereof. As localisation is the adaptation of a product for a specific culture and language, the method of translation suggested by the scientist would be based on the strategy of moving the writer to the reader, as it is necessary to move the product to the specific culture, language and receiver (the consumer/ user of the product). For example, Microsoft products were moved to the Lithuanians in 2001 so as to be used in Lithuania.

Vinay and Darbelnet's *Comparative Stylistics of French and English,* written in French in 1958, among other things tells a story of the authors and their observations about different road-signs and their translations on the road that were recognised while travelling from New York to Montreal (Vinay/ Darbelnet 1995:1-6). The authors of the book discuss the issue of equivalence and the way it could be achieved when translating from French into English, but the story in the preface fits well to illustrate the situation of signs being localised in different cultures and languages. The sign with the phrase *Wet paint* could serve as an illustration here. No Lithuanian would understand the phrase were it to be literally translated into Lithuanian as *Šlapi dažai,* but if the Lithuanian past participle *Dažyta* (*painted*) was used, which indicates a completed action instead of a quality, it would be quite understandable.

Furthermore, the linguistic aspects of localisation are visible in Venuti's theory on the translator's invisibility (Venuti 1995). Discussing the role of the translator within the process of translation and the way s/he becomes in/visible, Venuti, following Schleiermacher's ideas of text translation, introduces two strategies of translation: *domestication* (the neutralisation of the foreign text's culture and values and their rendering in the culture and values of the target language) and *foreignisation* (the translation of a text without localisation, which allows readers to feel that they read a translated text). As an example, consider a cartoon based on an Eastern tale about a boy who visits the Sun to elicit an answer to the question of how to become a man. The cartoon is dubbed into Lithuanian, but the image of the Sun as a man is quite shocking for Lithuanian children. This is because the Lithuanian noun *saulė* (*the Sun*) is feminine and is associated with women and mothers, whereas for example in the Eastern cultures (e.g. Kirghiz), the Sun is associated with a man. If the picture of the sun were redrawn, the cartoon would be domesticated for the Lithuanian audience. *Domestication* is thus close to localisation, as the process is the same as text/product adaptation to a specific culture, language and country. For instance, the Google webpage is a good example of domestication/localisation. When opening the page, one clearly sees *Google Lietuvos, Google Deutschland, Google España*, etc. – the name of the country appears beneath the logo. Although Google appears to speak every language, the Lithuanian page is not as clearly domesticated/localised as some of the others; it remains open whether the

Lithuanian webpage should indicate the name of the country by saying *Google Lietuva* (this would conform to the other examples above), or state that "Google belongs to Lithuania" (*Google Lietuvos*) as the webpage claims.

The idea of *domestication/foreignisation* could be further developed by adding the concept of *culturalisation*, developed by O'Hagan and Ashworth (2002), who describe translation-mediated communication and discuss the issues of localisation. According to them, localisation is simply "culturalization of the Message" sent to the receiver (ibid.:71). These theorists regard translation as an act of communication (translation-mediated communication) where the message, through translation, is sent to a receiver. And if localisation is a new form of translation, a communicative approach to localisation can be applied as well, in which the message that is sent to the receiver/user of the software must be adapted or culturalised to a particular language and culture with the aim of being understood.

The paradigm shift from a focus on source texts towards a focus on the target text offers new insights into localisation and reveals other linguistic aspects of localisation. *Skopos* theory (1980s), with a functional approach to translation, highlights the purpose of the target text to be achieved and communicated within a particular target culture (Munday 2008:79-82). *Skopos* theory suggests that translation strategies are decided by the needs of the target text/language/culture. Such a functional approach works well with localisation as it is demonstrated in articles about website and software localisation (Charalampidou 2007; Fernández Costales 2009) wherein the product produced and its target users become more important than the prototype. Any message that is communicated through an IT product (website or software) has to achieve a particular purpose so that receivers of the message would know what they are supposed to do with it. Therefore, the message or software has to be culturally and linguistically adapted (Pym 2008:2).

Furthermore, Descriptive Translation Studies emphasise the fact that "translating depend[s] very much on the cultural situation involved" (Pym 2008:2), and localisation is highly dependent on the cultural situation involved in localising a product. For example, the localisation of products is often not so warmly received within Lithuanian culture. There are several reasons for this. First of all, it often means the invasion of English into Lithuanian, manifested through the spread of English loan words such as *file* (*failas*) or *domain* (*domenas*). Moreover, many Lithuanians perceive their national identity linguistically, meaning that the Lithuanian language is conceived of as part of what it means to be Lithuanian. Products that are localised are usually US-based, i.e. they come from the US-American culture and penetrate the Lithuanian by making the two languages (and two differently designed cultures) clash. This invasion of the English language by means of US products is perceived as a threat to national identity. Therefore, when seeking to avoid the rejection of a product, the linguistic adaptation that is usually carried out via translation becomes of crucial importance.

Linguistic aspects of localisation in terms of localisation features

The previous section aimed at indicating linguistic aspects of localisation that can be traced within translation theories. This part of the article will discuss other aspects of localisation revealed through its features, such as the size, scope and complexity of the process, internationalisation and the translation model "one-to-many", reuse of the text, the non-linear and top-down approach to translation, and the use of technologies. Such a detailed analysis of the features of localisation will provide a better perception of the phenomenon.

Authors who support the view that localisation is a more complicated phenomenon, of which translation is a mere subset or "even a language problem" (Pym 2008:2), mention the size, scope and complexity of the process of localisation. Software is usually composed of many elements: windows, help menus, hot keys, commands, interfaces and online help which all have to be translated, often without knowing any particular context. The size, scope and complexity would also involve various tasks that are performed in addition to translation. These would generally include software engineering, testing, project management, user training and product maintenance after the process of localisation is completed. Such features are characteristic only of software localisation. Such size, scope and complexity cannot be attributed to the translation of a book, for example, at least in the traditional sense, as books are usually written by an author and then translated by a translator.[1] During the process of translation, a decision about what to culturalise or localise (the names of persons, places, etc.) has to be made. When the translation is completed, it is edited and corrected by

[1] However, this could be denied by saying that the translation of a book such as the Bible is also quite big in scope, size and complexity.

specialists of the target language,[2] then edited by an editor, not to mention the entire process of publishing. Another similar case of complexity, size and scope would be the subtitling or dubbing of a film where, first of all, the entire creation of a product takes place with script writers, directors, a team of actors, camera men and other staff members, without mentioning the entire industry of dubbing or subtitling where the same project management and testing, similar to software localisation, is involved. This proves that in terms of size, scope and complexity, localisation is not something new, as these features are sometimes attributed to other types of translation (literary, audiovisual).

Another feature of localisation would be software internationalisation, which is defined as the preparation and generalisation of a product "so that it can handle multiple languages and cultural conventions without the need for re-design" during the process of product engineering (LISA 1998:4). Internationalisation means "writing for translation" (Esselink 2000:3), or developing "an intermediary version" of a text to be translated (Pym 2010:122). This process ensures the possibility of writing the correct date formats, referencing local currencies, and using the correct linguistic characters within a particular alphabet. The process of internationalisation is a new concept offered for Translation Studies and is characteristic only of localisation (ibid.:123-127). Internationalisation takes place during the time of product design. The product is prepared by neutralising culture- or language-specific items (colours, date formats, etc.); only then is it translated. Here, Pym (ibid.:124-125) proposes the "one-to-many" model of translation, since after internationalisation, the product can be translated into many target languages at the same time. Such a model is not characteristic of the previously discussed translation of a book, which does not need to be internationalised like software. However, several examples that are related to my personal experience will be provided here.

A certain type of product preparation was typical of Lithuania and other countries of the Soviet Union. Any book that was translated from English into Russian, Lithuanian or any other language of the Soviet Union countries had to be prepared in such a way that the translations could be handled in multiple languages and cultural norms, without any manifestations of free

2 For example, if a book is translated from English into Lithuanian, the translated text is reviewed by a specialist of the Lithuanian language and then returned to the translator(s) for review once again.

will, independence or freedom. Negative remarks about communism were not allowed, and collectivism had to be glorified against dark and wild capitalism. Thus, before translation, books were read and adapted by the deletion of certain places or the provision of some explanations. For example, the translation of Hemingway's novel *For Whom the Bell Tolls*, which was published in Lithuania in 1972, contains an article about the novel that characterises both Hemingway and Robert Jordan (the main character) as fighters for folk ideas, revolution, communism and a brighter tomorrow (Simonovas 1972:570). The subtitles from the Lithuanian film *Nut Bread* (1978) also serve as a good illustration of such neutralisation: one of the characters states that he wants to perform a piece of music entitled *Ir blogi laikai taps gerais, kai vėl tave pamatysiu* (original English title: *Bad Times Will Become Good When I See You Again),* while the subtitles indicate that the character wants to play the song "The sun'll shine when I see you again". The metaphor of *Bad Times* symbolising Soviet times and their change to good times (a symbol of Lithuania regaining its independence) is completely neutralised. Of course, this is more related to the rigorous censorship of the Soviet regime and is not directly related to internationalisation as defined by LISA. The preparation of this type of product (a poem, song, book or film) took place prior to the translation. However, such preparation is similar to the neutralisation carried out during internationalisation, as culture- or language-specific items were removed. The book was neutralised and after its release, one could see comments about the author and the book/novel in the preface or foreword that used to manifest certain propaganda.

Subtitling and dubbing also undergo similar processes of internationalisation, as the films to be translated/subtitled or dubbed must often provide certain explanations necessary to adapt the film to a specific country, culture and language. This preparation also takes place during the development of the film. As with localisation, films are also released into many languages at the same time, so the model "one-to-many" is not limited to the localisation industry.

In addition, product (brand) launching is also quite similar to product preparation and culturalisation. Brands, though they are the property of a company, must also be adapted to specific cultures and consumers to avoid the kinds of misunderstandings that are often quoted in handbooks on marketing. For example, Estée Lauder's moisturiser *Country Mist* was not purchased in Germany as the noun *Mist* means *manure* in German. Similarly, advertisements for *Schick* razors are not shown in Lithuania, as the pronunciation of *Schick* sounds like the Lithuanian verb *šik*, which is the imperative mood of the vulgar verb *to shit*. These examples are not the only ones that prove the process of internationalisation to be characteristic not only of localisation – though that is where internationalisation is most visible.

One more feature that is ascribed to localisation would be the non-linear, top-down, de-contextualised translation approach (Pym 2010:132). When localising, software texts (if they can be called texts) are not translated like sentences in a book. Software texts are quite rare (with the exception of error messages, which can be rather long) since there are no coherent texts within software like the ones in books or articles, and translators/localisers usually deal with individual words. The words are translated in a linear manner, presenting an equivalent of the original word in the target language; at the same time, however, the same word might be linked to some other information (hypertext) which can be seen by clicking the word. The entire picture is displayed within tree architecture with the possibility to go deeper and deeper, so the top-down method of translation pertains to the digital medium. Moreover, the feature of de-contextualisation is also quite obvious in software translation, because the context is rather vague despite the fact that certain file extensions or special programming sentences give a clue as to the purpose of various commands, hot keys, fields or menu items and components. For example, translating the field name *search* into Lithuanian is quite tricky, as it could be translated as *paieška* (noun form of the verb *to search*), *ieškoti* (infinitive of the verb *to search*), *ieškok* (familiar imperative of the verb *to search*) and *ieškokite* (polite imperative of the verb *to search*). The non-linear and top-down approach, as well as de-contextualisation, could be the most distinctive features ascribed to localisation that are not found in "traditional" translation (e.g. the translation of any book, article, etc.).

The reuse of previously localised versions is also attributed to localisation, as software development proceeds rapidly and new updates are released every year (if not more often). So the reuse of previously translated versions allows translators/localisers to save some time and money by translating only the new parts within a new release. Technologies (localisation tools) help to identify the missing parts. Reusability is usually applicable only to software and website localisation; however, in this age of technologies, it could also be ascribed to translations of any other type of text. For example, there are many texts, novels and books that are retranslated, i.e. new translations of the Bible keep appearing in the market. Moreover, translators are keen to use translation technologies that allow them to reuse any texts or passages that have been translated before. Thus, reusability could be attributed to any translations as technologies have become inseparable from a modern translator, whose picture has changed from that of a person armed with a pencil, paper and many dictionaries to one of a person armed with powerful information communication technologies (ICT), Internet access and other high-tech tools. However, the constant reuse of already translated texts might lead to problems of the authorship of translations, as translation tools allow the sharing of translated texts among translators. This would be an interesting issue for another study.

The Lithuanian context and perception of localisation

If the first attempts to localise software were observed in the 1980s, 1996 saw the first such attempt in Lithuania. IBM initiated a project with the aim to localise OS/2 (Operating System 2) for secondary schools in Lithuania. Microsoft introduced its two localised products only in 2001. This late appearance of the localisation phenomenon in Lithuania can presumably be explained by demographic data. Lithuania is a small country with a small locale, a nation of about three million and a market that does not provide big opportunities for localisation companies. In addition to this, Lithuanian, in comparison with "big languages" such as English, Chinese or Spanish, falls into the category of "small languages".

Moreover, the Lithuanian language is not particularly easy to localise. Being a representative of the Baltic branch of the Indo-European group of languages, Lithuanian is the most archaic of all the living Indo-European languages and has preserved an archaic grammatical structure and patterns of word building (Miliūnaitė 2006). The French linguist Antoine Meillet (1866-1936) suggested that "anyone wishing to hear how Indo-Europeans spoke should come and listen to a Lithuanian peasant". This quotation has become so deeply rooted and often used when describing the Lithuanian language in documents and websites that references to the original source are impossible to be traced and are never given.

Not only the glorious past of the language, but also the history of the country[3] have long led both average Lithuanians and the professional body of the State Commission of the Lithuanian Language to try to preserve the native tongue; the latter institution is obsessed with the idea of cleaning the language from the barbarisms and jargon words coming from Russian and, currently, English. In addition to this, the need to Lithuanise is rigorously governed by the Law on the State Language (31 January 1995, No. I-779) that regulates "the use of the state language in public life of Lithuania, protection and control of the state language, and the responsibility for violations of the Law on the State Language". This law underlies the language policy and requires all transactions, establishments and organisations, various public events, courts, signs and information to function and comply with the norms of the state language. The law is rather strict and even triggered an international scandal in July 2010, as the Polish minority in Lithuania cannot write their personal names in Polish (due to their use of Polish letters that do not appear in the Lithuanian alphabet) and are forced to Lithuanise them.

Even though the phenomenon of localisation has been recently observed within the Lithuanian market, the tradition to Lithuanise is quite embedded within Lithuanian culture and was characteristic of the entire twentieth century, described as the age of Lithuanisation (Matuzevičius/Valionis 1980). Lithuanisation and the tradition to Lithuanise thrived during Soviet times. The Soviet government claimed that all art is for the people and aimed to educate society and provide access to the cultural heritage of other nations. Thus, names, songs, books, films and operas were Lithuanised. For instance, the well-known song "Do Re Mi" from the musical *The Sound of Music* is a good example of localisation. The only resemblance to the original song is the melody and the references to "a female deer" or a "drop of golden sun" have been Lithuanised: *Do – tai saulė danguje* (*the sun in the sky*)/*Rė – švelnus jos spindulys* (*its tender ray*). Moreover, the tradition to Lithuanise names is still alive and deeply entrenched within the Lithuanian language. For example, Shakespeare would never recognise his own name, as in Lithuanian, William Shakespeare is *Viljamas Šekspyras* or *Shakespeare'as*, Antoine Meillet is *Antuanas/Antanas Mejė,* Margaret Thatcher is *Margaret/*

[3] The Lithuanian language and its press were banned by the Russian Tsar during the period 1864-1904, when it was also required that the Cyrillic alphabet be used instead of the Latin and that the press be released in Russian; Lithuania underwent a second period of Russification during Soviet times.

Margarita Tečer, and Anthony Pym is *Antoni Antonis/Antanas Pim/Pimas/Pym'as.*

In addition to this, with reference to the process/term *localisation* itself, the verb *to localise* and the noun *localisation* have localised Lithuanian versions that are more commonly used, for international words are frequently Lithuanised. For example, *linguistics* can be translated as *lingvistika* or *kalbotyra* (Eng. *language research*), while *jury* will be either *žiuri* or *komisija* (Eng. *board/committee*). As for the term *localisation*, the noun *lietuvinimas* (Eng. *making Lithuanian/Lithuanisation*) is applied instead. The term "Lithuanisation" is perceived as the localisation of software to the particular environment that is named after the term denominating the environment. As a result, the adaptation of products to the Lithuanian language and culture is called Lithuanisation, while adaptation, for example, for the Arabic language and culture would be called Arabisation (Dagienė 2004). Similarly, the verb *to localise* is replaced by the Lithuanian verb *su/lietuvinti* (Eng. *to Lithuanise/make Lithuanian*). Thus, the definition of localisation could be changed in that Lithuanisation is not restricted only to linguistic modification and is perceived as a process of adapting a particular product to the Lithuanian language and culture.

Despite the fact that the tradition to Lithuanise is quite anchored in both the Lithuanian language and culture, the advent of high-tech processes and technologies (new ICT words and the absence of their equivalents in Lithuanian) is conceived of as a potential threat to the Lithuanian language. The impact of English has intensified after the fall of the iron curtain and Lithuanian is being strongly anglicised. The majority of ICT products are US-based, which means that most ICT words are English. And if there are no Lithuanian counterparts, and the terminologists do not manage to provide Lithuanian words promptly enough, English words begin to take root in Lithuanian. The nouns *pozicionavimas* (Eng. *positioning*) and *rūteris* (Eng. *router*) could serve as an illustration. Hence, it has been stated that software has to be exploited as a means of preserving and cherishing the Lithuanian language (Telksnys 1998:25). The UNESCO chair in Informatics for Humanities, Laimutis Telksnys (ibid.), expressed the idea of exhausting software possibilities for maintaining the native tongue and culture.

Although it is perceived as a challenge, localisation and its impact on Lithuanian have not been studied by translation or language scholars in Lithuania. Research in the area of localisation and its relationship with translation is still in its infancy. In examining localisation, Lithuanian scientists follow Western tradition and rely on the works of Western theorists and practitioners. Much has been done by Dagienė, Gintautas and Jevsikova (2011), the leading professors and researchers of Mathematics and Computer Science and Informatics who have been acknowledged as the pioneers in localisation research in Lithuania. They are looked to as authorities by linguists, translation theorists and professionals alike. Localisation has been considered an important turn in Translation Studies and in 2006; it was included in the Master's programme of technical translation and localisation at Kaunas University of Technology. However, studies of localisation as part of Translation Studies have just begun, and translation theorists in Lithuania follow the works of the Lithuanian scientists of Mathematics and Computer Science mentioned above. They define *localisation* as adaptation that cannot be regarded as translation. Researchers agree that translation is just a subset of localisation. Yet when talking about the process of localisation and providing some statistics on the localisation industry in Lithuania, scientists synonymously use words related to translation such as *to translate, translated software, a need to translate software* (Dagienė 2004; Dagienė/Grigas 2006).

Conclusion

Localisation can be perceived as a multifaceted phenomenon where language, culture and technologies come together with the goal to present some creative content of a product (book, film, software or website) to a target audience. Since localisation is the offspring of language and technologies, it shares some linguistic aspects that become palpable when examining the understanding of the phenomenon, exploring its linguistic grounds (mainly translation theories) and studying localisation practices in particular contexts. The analysis of localisation practises in Lithuania has revealed the fact that the tradition to Lithuanise is firmly embedded within the Lithuanian language and culture, and localisation within the Lithuanian context is defined as Lithuanisation which is used as a tool to preserve the Lithuanian language (the oldest living Indo-European language). The diverse conceptions of localisation as the consequence of the merger of language and technologies allows highlighting linguistic aspects of localisation that make the grounds for localisation be treated as a paradigm within Translation Studies. Moreover, this reveals new trends within Translation Studies and emphasises the need to widen the scope of Translation Studies by integrating the phenomenon of localisation into both the research of translation and translator training curricula while appreciating the significance of translation as a profession. Taking this into consideration, it is possible to predict that within the scope of Translation Studies, localisation could evolve into a separate field of translation, alongside audiovisual translation – another offspring of language and technologies.

References

Austermühl, Frank (2001) *Electronic Tools for Translators.* Manchester: St Jerome.

Brooks, David (2000) "What Price Globalization? Managing Costs at Microsoft". In Sprung, Robert C. (ed.) *Translating into Success: Cutting-edge Strategies for Going Multilingual in a Global Age.* Amsterdam-Philadelphia: John Benjamins, 43-57.

Charalampidou, Parthena (2007) "Website localization". In Mus, Francis (ed.) *Selected Papers of the CETRA Research Seminar in Translation Studies 2006*, http://www2.arts.kuleuven.be/info/bestanden-div/CHARALAMPIDOU.pdf [3 July 2012].

Cronin, Michael (2003) *Translation and Globalization.* London-New York: Routledge.

Dagienė, Valentina (2004) Report on the Research Work "Atviras kodas švietime", www.ipc.lt/wp-content/uploads/2009/11/atvirasKodasSvietime_ataskaita.pdf [3 July 2012].

Dagienė,Valentina/Grigas, Gintas (2006) "Quantitative Evaluation of the Process of Open Source Software Localization". *Informatica* 17:1, 3-12.

Dagienė, Valentina/Gintautas, Grigas/Jevsikova, Tatjana (2011). *Programinės įrangos lokalizavimo pagrindai.*Vilnius: Vilniaus universitetas.

Esselink, Bert (2000) *A Practical Guide to Localization.* Amsterdam-Philadelphia: John Benjamins.

Esselink, Bert (2006) "The Evolution of Localization". In Pym, Anthony/Perekrestenko, Alexander/Starink, Bram (eds.) *Translation Technology and its Teaching (With Much Mention of Localization).* Tarragona: Intercultural Studies Group, 22-29.

Fernández Costales, Alberto (2009) "Translation 2.0. The Localization of Institutional Websites Under The Scope of Functionalist Approaches". In: De Crom, Dries (ed.) *Translation and the (Trans)formation of Identities, Selected Papers of the CETRA Research Seminar in Translation Studies 2008*, http://www2.arts.kuleuven.be/info/bestanden-div/Fernandez%20Costales.pdf [3 July 2012].

Gil, José Ramón B./Pym, Anthony (2006) "Technology and Translation: A Pedagogical Overview". In Pym, Anthony/Perekrestenko, Alexander/Starink, Bram (eds.) *Translation Technology and its Teaching (With Much Mention of Localization).* Tarragona: Intercultural Studies Group, 5-19.

Gouadec, Daniel (2007) *Translation as a Profession.* Amsterdam-Philadelphia: John Benjamins.

Kade, Otto (1968) *Zufall und Gesetzmäßigkeit in der Übersetzung*. Leipzig: VEB Verlag Enzyklopädie.

Lakoff, George/Johnson, Mark (2003) *Metaphors We Live By*. Chicago: The University of Chicago Press.

Law on the State Language (1995), http://www3.lrs.lt/pls/inter3/dokpaieska.showdoc_l?p_id=275246 [3 July 2012].

LISA (1998) "Report of the Education Initiative Taskforce of the Localization Industries Standards Association", leit.lisa.org/pubs/public.pdf [1 June 2010].

Matuzevičius, Eugenijus/Valionis, Arvydas (1980) *Meninio vertimo problemos: Straipsnių rinkinys*. Vilnius: Vaga.

Miliūnaitė, Rita (2006) *Apie Kalbą ir Mus*. Vilnius: Lietuvių kablos institutas.

Munday, Jeremy (2008) *Introducing Translation Studies: Theories and Applications*. London-New York: Routledge.

Nida, Eugene A. (1964) *Towards a Science of Translating*. Leiden: Brill.

O'Hagan, Minako/Ashworth, David (2002) *Translation-mediated Communication in a Digital World: Facing the Challenges of Globalization and Localization*. Bristol: Multilingual Matters.

O'Hagan, Minako (2006) "Training for Localization (Replies to a Questionnaire)". In Pym, Anthony/Perekrestenko, Alexander/Starink, Bram (eds.) *Translation Technology and its Teaching (With Much Mention of Localization)*. Tarragona: Intercultural Studies Group, 39-44.

Pym, Anthony (2004) *The Moving Text: Localization, Translation and Distribution*. Amsterdam-Philadelphia: John Benjamins.

Pym, Anthony (2008) "Localization from the Perspective of Translation Studies: Overlaps in the Digital Divide?", http://www.elda.org/en/proj/scalla/SCALLA2004/Pymv2.pdf [3 July 2012].

Pym, Anthony (2010) *Exploring Translation Theories*. London-New York: Routledge.

Schleiermacher, Friedrich (1813/2004). "On Different Methods of Translating". In Venuti, Lawrence (ed.) *The Translation Studies Reader*. London-New York: Routledge, 43-63.

Simonovas, Konstantinas (1972) "Ispanijos tema Hemingvėjaus kūryboje". In Hemingway, Ernest, *Kam Skambina Varpai*. Vilnius: Vaga, 564-574.

Sprung, Robert C. (2000a) "Introduction". In Sprung, Robert C. (ed.). *Translating into Success: Cutting-edge Strategies for Going Multilingual in a Global Age*. Amsterdam-Philadelphia: John Benjamins, ix-xxii.

Sprung, Robert C. (ed.) (2000b) *Translating into Success: Cutting-edge Strategies for Going Multilingual in a Global Age*. Amsterdam-Philadelphia: John Benjamins.

Telksnys, Laimutis (1998) "Informatika lietuvių kalbai ir kultūrai". *Veidrodis* 8:51, 23-29.

Venuti, Lawrence (1995) *The Translator's Invisibility: A History of Translation*. London-New York: Routledge.

Vinay, Jean Paul/Darbelnet, Jean (1958) *Stylistique Comparée du Français et de l'Anglais: Méthode de traduction*. Paris: Didier.

Vinay, Jean Paul/Darbelnet, Jean (1995) *Comparative Stylistics of French and English: A Methodology for Translation*. Translated by Juan C. Sager and M. J. Hamel. Amsterdam-Philadelphia: John Benjamins.

Zeller, Irma (2006) "Lokalizacijos iššūkiai vertėjams". *Darbai ir Dienos* 45, 79-69.

ANA ISABEL FOULQUIÉ RUBIO

University of Murcia, Spain

The Lawyer and the Interpreter in Police Settings

Interpreting in police settings can be considered as part of either legal interpreting services or public service interpreting, but in any case, legal consequences arise when someone is arrested by the police. Most studies within the field of Interpreting Studies focus on the work of interpreters from their own perspective, and few studies take into account the perspective of other people involved in the proceedings. In police interpreting, one of the people who is involved in the questioning, apart from the detainee and the police officer, is the lawyer. The lawyer must make sure that all the rights to which the detainee is entitled, among them the right to an interpreter, are protected. Therefore, the lawyer becomes a cornerstone in the provision of adequate interpreting services within police settings. This research, conducting in 2005, aims to investigate the perspective of lawyers working with foreign detainees in the Spanish context, and the problems they experience when communicating with these detainees.

Keywords: public service interpreting, interpreter's tasks, lawyers, police, human rights

Introduction

The right to access an interpreter for a foreign detainee has long been granted when the detainee does not speak or understand the language. As stated by Glegg already in 1984 "the provision of appropriate interpreting and translation is absolutely fundamental from any sort of anti-racist or equity based perspective" (Glegg, qtd. in Longley 1984:179). However, the problem arises when trying to define "appropriateness" if we look at the existing legislation and the way in which interpreting services are provided in Spain.

The main aim of this research is to investigate the perspective of lawyers working with foreign detainees and the problems they experience when communicating with them within a Spanish context. To start with, I shall provide an overview of the legislation that governs police interpreting in Spain. Then, I will discuss the current situation of police interpreting in Spain. I will report some of the results of a survey carried out in 2005 among a sample of lawyers working with foreign detainees in the province of Granada, Spain, in which they were asked about their expectations regarding the tasks of the interpreter. The aim of the study was to know the expectations of lawyers, as well as to give lawyers awareness of the interpreter's work. This study focuses on only one category of users who benefit from interpreting in police stations, that of lawyers. There have been previous studies which have assessed the perspective of interpreters with regard to the job they do (e.g. Fox 2001; Ortega Herráez 2004, 2011), and there has been some research showing the perspective of service providers (e.g. Martin 2004). Also, a study by Kadrić (2010) examines the perspective of the users of interpreting services by focusing on police stations in Austria and compares the answers from interpreters and police officers.

The right to be assisted by an interpreter

In Spain, as in many European countries, there are two types of detention: criminal and administrative. Criminal detention would involve anything having to do with criminal acts, and the administrative version would include detention of a foreigner for breaking a provision of the immigration law.

Apart from the situations where the foreigner is the detainee, there are also other situations in which a foreigner needs to communicate with police officers, for instance asylum seekers who already are in Spain, as they have the possibility to initiate proceedings at police stations.

In Spain, the provision of interpreting services is well protected by international conventions, as it is in many other European countries (Foulquié Rubio 2002a, b). Within the Spanish national legislation, the right to be assisted by an interpreter is also recognised, although most of the existing provisions do not specify the level of qualification or training necessary to act as an interpreter. Therefore, in daily practice, virtually anyone can serve as an interpreter within the legal sphere without infringing upon the law. Together with this Spanish legislation, the provision of interpreters is also regulated by other European legislation.[1] However, I am going to outline only the main pieces of Spanish legislation regulating the provision of interpreting services in Spain.

---

[1] 14552/1/09 REV 1 Proposal for a Council Framework Decision on the right to interpretation and translation in criminal proceedings.

Within the scope of criminal law, there are different acts. Criminal law is crucial as it states the cases where the person is granted free access to an interpreter. The main act is the Spanish Criminal Procedure Act.[2] According to this act, the court is free to choose anyone to act as an interpreter. Therefore, most of the time, the training and qualification of the interpreter is left to the preference of the court. The same situation occurs in police stations where the interpreter is chosen according to the preferences of the police officer in charge of the case, without giving any importance to this person being a qualified interpreter or not. Another act to be applied within criminal law is Judiciary Act 6/1985, article 231. According to this act, the court or judge has the full power to appoint anyone as an interpreter during a case, and in the case of police stations, the police officer has the full power to appoint the interpreter (Alonso Pérez 1997:25). Therefore, police officers can choose anyone they think will do the interpreting job properly during the police interview. The problem is that there are no guidelines for assessing when the interpreter is doing the job properly, nor agreement about how the term "properly" should be understood.

The final piece of legislation pertaining to criminal law is the Passive Extradition Act 4/1985, of 21 March, specifically articles 12 and 14. This act requires the presence of an interpreter for the extradition of anyone who does not understand or speak Spanish when a person is detained as a result of a request from the police or court in another country. Most of these acts refer to the right to be assisted by an interpreter in court, but they have to be extended to also include the moment the person is first detained by the police (Alonso Pérez 1999:65).

Within the administrative law, there are acts that regulate only the actions to be taken related to foreigners who come to and live in Spain. They include the Immigration Act 4/2000 of 11 January.[3] This act requires the presence of an interpreter whenever removal proceedings are initiated, that is to say, when a foreigner enters or lives illegally in Spain and is asked to leave the country or is expelled from it. This is to ensure that a non-Spanish speaker understands at all times the reasons for his/her removal for being in Spain illegally. The right of a non-Spanish speaker to be assisted by an interpreter free of charge is granted for the duration of the proceedings,

---

2 Articles 440, 441, 443, 520 par. e) and 785.

3 This act was amended by Act 8/2000 of 22 December, Act 11/2003 of 29 September and Act 14/2003 of 20 November. Articles 22, 26 par. 2, 62*bis* par. h) and 63 par. 2.

from the moment the proceedings are initiated until the moment the removal order is issued.

In order to facilitate the above-mentioned act, lawmakers passed Royal Decree No. 864/2001 of 10 July, approving the regulations enabling Act No 4/2000 of 11 January on the Rights and Freedoms of Aliens in Spain and their Social Integration. These regulations put into effect Act No. 8/2000 of 22 December,[4] and they explain the way proceedings are to be initiated. They refer mainly to the point at which non-Spanish speakers are denied entrance into Spain or, once they are in Spain, when they are detained and proceedings to remove them are initiated. In this case, and as well as it was shown in the Salduz case,[5] the assistance of the interpreter is very important for a lawyer, as detained persons, like any other detainee, have the right to know why they have been detained and this information is given mainly at the police station.

The problem with most of the legislation is that it does not define what kind of qualifications the person acting as interpreter should possess. This is mostly because some of the acts are very old, and they have not been amended with respect to the paragraphs relating to the interpreter since they were first enacted. Also, and most importantly, this situation might be the result of the authorities' lack of knowledge about the nature and importance of the work performed by interpreters in the legal system.

Interpreting in police settings

On some occasions, in police interpreting, the situation is similar to that of court interpreting in Spain. Most of the interpreters do not have a qualification as interpreters and the profiles of the people who undertake this work are very diverse. In police interpreting, there are different types of contracts (in house, temporary, freelance) which is also true in court interpreting (Feria García 1999; Arróniz 2000; Mayoral 2000; Ortega Herráez 2011).

However, few police stations have interpreters as permanent staff, although such services are starting to be implemented. In most cases, acceptance or entry requirements for working as an interpreter are still minimal. The main system used when recruiting interpreters for the police is that of

[4] Articles 30, 110 par. 2, 116 par. b), 127 par. 7, 137 and 138 par. 2

[5] The Salduz case decided by the European Court of Human Rights in Strasbourg requesting the presence of a lawyer from the moment of arrest to protect detainee's rights.

temporary staff interpreters, where interpreters are hired for a set period of time, usually summer due to the increase in the number of tourists, and the requirements to be eligible are minimal. Usually, being able to speak two languages and being unemployed for a long time constitute the main requirements, without any reference to holding a degree in translation and interpreting. In some cases, an interview is held in order to choose the best candidate. However, in many cases, especially outside the summer period, interpreting services in police stations are outsourced to private translation and interpreting companies who are then in charge of looking for interpreters to interpret in police stations. Sometimes, as reported in one newspaper article (*El País* 2002), police will also use immigrants to act as *ad hoc* interpreters.

The lawyer's view

In order to know the expectations of the lawyers, a survey was conducted among them.[6] The results of this study were obtained through a questionnaire distributed among the lawyers attending a specific course on immigration law. The sample was made up of 84 practising lawyers who work with non-Spanish speakers in the province of Granada. This course provided a good opportunity to question a significant number of lawyers who were likely to be interested in addressing the issue of the work of the interpreter in police stations, as many of them have to work with interpreters.

We chose this sample because, from our point of view, it is very important that the lawyer, as the main guarantor that the rights of the detainee are respected, knows the work of the different people involved in the detention process. It is also important that those acting as interpreters know what the work they have to carry out is and how to act in this type of situations (public service interpreting). According to Pöchhacker (2000), the lack of a code of ethics leads to people performing their work without knowing the expectations of the user and without knowing what they should or should not do since they are not professional interpreters. The interpreter and the users must know that there are some limits to the work that the interpreter

[6] This research was conducted by the GRETI research group, which is based at the University of Granada, Spain, and funded by the Andalusian Regional Authorities. Therefore, "we" refers to the GRETI research group.

has to do (Martin/Abril 2002:57), such as omitting, changing and adding information.

This is one of the reasons for why not only interpreters should be trained for their work, but also users working with interpreters (Sanders 1992; Corsellis 1997, 2000, 2002). In our study, the user is the lawyer. From my own experience, I am aware that there are cases where police officers ask the interpreter to inform the detainee about his/her rights. The lawyer has to be aware that this, in fact, is not the job of the interpreter and, as the guarantor of the detainee's rights, the lawyer should make this clear if the interpreter does not already know it.

As already mentioned above, it is crucial that the detainee understands the reasons for his/her detention, either under the criminal or administrative law, and that such a provision is included in the list of rights read to the detainee. When the person does not speak or understand Spanish, this provision implies that he/she has the right to be assisted by an interpreter. However, the question remains: what kind of interpreter? All too often, when reviewing cases published by the press or in case law, it becomes clear that the interpreter does not have the qualification or training to act in such a capacity. Under these circumstances, the lawyer is the guarantor who makes sure that the right to be assisted by an interpreter is indeed implemented by insisting upon the use of a trained or qualified interpreter.

In some cases, lawyers think that it is better to have a "bad" interpreter and conclude the case as soon as possible rather than wait for a qualified interpreter.[7] Therefore, a further aim of the study was to make lawyers realise that sometimes it is not difficult to find a qualified interpreter and to make them aware of the importance of their cooperation in providing appropriate interpreting services.

All too often, the authorities excuse the need for using untrained interpreters by saying that there were problems finding a qualified interpreter for particular languages. This can be understood when talking about minority languages such as Moroccan or Wolof, but there are also many cases in which obviously no effort has been made to finding a qualified interpreter (e.g. for English, Arabic or French), as Spain has around 20 universities offering degrees in translation and interpreting and some universities also offer postgraduate courses in translation and interpreting. At this point, it

---

[7] Interview with lawyers who work with foreign detainees.

seems necessary to add that, obviously, most universities offer training in majority languages, such as English, French, German and Arabic, but not in minority ones, as language demand changes from one year to the next. This is important in the field of public service interpreting, because most of the people who use these services do not speak the so-called "majority" languages. This may lead to different levels of quality depending on the language of the detainee or to the use of English or French as the *lingua franca.*

Methodology and questionnaire design

The questionnaires were designed using a model described by Oppenheim (1996), which allows us to measure the different variables in our survey and which has also been used by other researchers in Translation and Interpreting Studies at the University of Granada (Calvo Encinas 2001; Way 2003; Ortega Herráez 2004) and, thus, can be validated. Most questions were closed questions, where the interviewee was offered different options to choose from. However, we also included an open question, where the lawyers could add any additional information relevant to the question.

The questionnaires did not include any kind of information that could identify the respondents. We divided the questions into two sections, the first being a general one, where we asked the lawyers to answer nine questions related to expectations about the interpreter's work, while the second part of the questionnaire was to be answered only by those lawyers who have defended a foreign detainee.

Results of the study

Differences between translation and interpreting

The first question concerned the differences between translation and interpreting. The question was as follows: *Do you know the differences between translation and interpreting?* Respondents could answer by choosing *Yes/No.* They were also asked to name any differences they were aware of between the two. We included this question because the term interpreting has different meanings depending on the field in which it is used. The problem with recognising both terms was demonstrated through a series of interviews done by GRETI, in which the researchers realised that the problems were caused by the use on our part of the term interpreting. When we refer to interpreting, one of the main differences is the oral factor included in the interpreting, as stated by Gentile (1996) and Pöchhacker (2004). So, when analysing our questionnaire, we considered this to be the correct answer. The purpose of this question was to know if lawyers know what we are referring to when talking about interpreting, as it has a different meaning in the legal context, which will be mentioned below.

In total, 84 lawyers out of 400 answered the questionnaires. In terms of the results, for this first question concerning knowledge about difference between translation and interpreting, 75% of them answered "yes" and 25% of them answered "no". The problem appeared when stating the differences between these two terms. When analysing the results, in this case, 14.8% gave a correct answer, 60.7% gave an incorrect answer and 24.6% did not give any answer, although they had answered "yes" to the first question. This is an example of an answer considered to be correct: "*Translation is written and interpreting is spoken*". This is an example of an answer considered to be incorrect: *"Translation: literal, interpreting: understanding"*. This is a common misconception, particularly among lawyers, probably resulting from the meaning of "interpreting" within the field of Law, where it means to understand something as having a particular meaning or significance (*Diccionario de la Lengua Española* 2001). Therefore, as shown by their answers, some lawyers want the interpreter to translate following a "literal translation model" (Valero Garcés/Gauthier Blasi 2010), which will not work in many cases and may create misunderstandings and communication problems.

Characteristics of the interpreter

As there is not a code of ethics, many interpreters do not know how to act and what is expected from them, and therefore, they can exceed the limits of their work. So, the questionnaire included a question related to the characteristics that lawyers thought an interpreter should have: *Besides speaking the language, what characteristics do you think an interpreter working in police settings should have?*

The question included four different characteristics based on a literature review. These characteristics were as follows: *impartiality, efficiency, secrecy* and *fidelity*. We also offered the possibility of "adding any other characteristic" that they considered important. In this context, impartiality is understood as a case in which the interpreter must remain impartial to each party, no matter who has hired him/her (Hale 2005). Efficiency is understood as enabling communication in an efficient way, without delays and misunderstandings. Secrecy is usually included within the code of ethics of any profession, and it is understood as being able to keep the information secret and not give the information to third parties (Code of Conduct of the NRPSI 2011). Fidelity should be understood as being able to convey the message in a faithful way (Lázaro 2007).

Looking at the literature (Gentile 1996; Garber 2000; Mesa 2000), the interpreter should always be impartial regardless of the party that has hired him/her. Furthermore, it is very important that every party sees the interpreter as an impartial person who is there to enable communication. As for efficiency, the interpreter must carry out the work efficiently and effectively. The interpreter must obviously also be fluent in both languages in order to be understood by both parties and to understand both parties. As for secrecy, the interpreting has to be done with due observance of the confidential nature of what is said in every situation where an interpreter is required. This is a major feature of interpreting in police settings, as what is said in that situation could be very important for the development of the case.

According to the answers obtained, the characteristic that most lawyers thought was important was impartiality, but a large number of lawyers also considered fidelity, secrecy and efficiency necessary. As for any other characteristic, some lawyers added that the interpreter should have some knowledge of international law.

Main criteria when choosing an interpreter

We asked the lawyers to think about what the main criteria would be if they were the ones choosing an interpreter for their client, even though they do not, in fact, choose the interpreter when involved in police settings. Nevertheless, it would be an interesting issue to know whom they would choose if they had the chance to do so. Therefore, we asked them the following question: *If you had to choose an interpreter for your client, what would be your main criteria?*

Here again, the question included the possibility to choose from among the people who usually act as interpreters in the Spanish system, according to a study carried out by Foulquié Rubio (2002a, b) and by other members of GRETI. The given criteria were as follows: *just language knowledge, a degree in Translation and Interpreting, a degree in Languages and Literature, and a native speaker of the language of the detainee who also knows some Spanish or any other criteria.*

The reason for the distinction between a degree in Translation and Interpreting and a degree in Languages and Literature is the existence in Spanish universities of these two qualifications as different degrees, which are taught separately and with different learning outcomes and contents.

According to the answers given by the lawyers, the most important criteria would be that the person would hold a degree in Translation and Interpreting (50%) whenever possible and the second choice would be a person who knows both languages in question, Spanish and the language of the detainee (23.8%), with the other criteria obtaining a very low percentage of responses.

Interpreter's tasks

Interpreting in public service and court interpreting has long been considered a non-professional activity. As Pochhäcker (2000:50) states, referring to Harris (1990) and Gentile (1996), "in the absence of any code of practice of professional authority, these untrained community interpreters presumably shape their task according to some implicit norms of translational behaviour as well as expectations on the part of their client". Therefore the interpreter may exceed the limits of his/her tasks.

Some of the most controversial aspects among researchers in community interpreting are the problems deriving from the limits of the interpreter's role, as stated by Martin and Abril (2002). In interpreting within police settings, besides the lack of professionalisation and the qualifications of the interpreter, there are no codes of ethics and the interpreters do not have any guidelines as to their role.

In order to know more specific information about lawyers' expectations, the questionnaire included the following three questions:

1. *Do you think the interpreter should explain any terminology whenever he/she thinks that it might be unclear for the foreign detainee?*

There is an ongoing debate with regard to the limit between interpreting for the foreign detainee and explaining some terms that may not be clear to him/her; however, such terms are probably not clear to a Spanish detainee either. In this case, and according to Cambridge (2002:123), "they [the interpreters] do not give personal advice or opinions" as it is the task of the lawyer and not the interpreter to explain to the detainee any unclear terminology. It may be argued that in receiving an explanation from an interpreter who is not an expert in the law, the detainee may become confused and the interpreter may exceed his/her tasks.

However, a high percentage of our sample (62%) considered it appropriate that the interpreter should explain any terminology that may be unclear to the foreign detainee. This could be due to the fact that they realise that some terms can be very difficult to understand for a foreigner who does not know the Spanish legal system.

2. *Do you think the interpreter should explain cultural references to both parties at her/his own initiative?*

During the interpreting situation, cultural differences might arise and these can cause difficulties in communication. The aim of this question was thus to find out what the lawyers expect interpreters to do: either stop communication and make this cultural reference clear or let the parties to the conversation realise it and ask for clarification. Interpreting and translation is sometimes considered as an activity in which culture is involved, rejecting the notion that interpreting is just a matter of two languages where the cultures do not have any influence.

As for cultural references, the number of respondents who answered "yes" (50%) and answered "no" (46%) shows that the respondents do not agree whether or not the interpreter should explain cultural references to both parties. This is probably due to the lack of information they might have about the work an interpreter does and the fact that many lawyers have the notion that an interpreter interprets languages but not cultures, even though culture is one of the main competences for public service interpreters, as stated by Abril (2006).

Sometimes, the lawyer may consider that the information is not correctly given if it is summarised or if something is added, therefore a question about this was included.

3. *Do you think the interpreter should extend or summarise information at his/her own initiative?*

As the discourse during a police interview is spontaneous, the interpreter may find that some parties repeat certain expressions and may not reproduce this repetition; at other times, the interpreter might think he/she should add some information which was said at some point of the statement but that the party has not repeated in this intervention.

According to the questionnaires, most lawyers (81%) think that the interpreter should not add or summarise information. Probably this comes from the idea that the interpreter has to "translate" word for word everything that is said.

When given the possibility to add their own comments, some lawyers complained about the difficulties they had when trying to contact professional interpreters and about the influence of time pressure. Here are two examples of the comments:

"There is a lack of information on how to contact qualified interpreters."

"Time pressure is important when looking for an interpreter."

These two comments added by the lawyers show that some of them are starting to be aware of the problems when finding an interpreter and that, as guarantors of the detainee's rights, they are starting to worry about problems such as the importance of having qualified interpreters and the problems derived from the time pressure, as the detainee cannot be detained for more than 72 hours in police cells.

Conclusion

It seems that the use of the term interpreting may pose some problems when it is used outside the field of Translation and Interpreting Studies. The reason for arguing that it might pose problems is that it may lead to misunderstandings about the work carried out by the interpreter by other parties in the interpreting situation such as the lawyer.

Furthermore, and looking at the results analysed here, it can be concluded that lawyers think that impartiality is the main characteristic that an interpreter should possess, which coincides with the views of several scholars (Mesa 2000; Hale 2005; Abril 2006), among others. However, in Spain, codes of ethics exist for interpreters in more recognised and professionalised fields, such as conference interpreting, but not for public service interpreting. Therefore, it is interesting that lawyers consider this characteristic to be most important. Another point analysed in this paper was the training and qualification of the interpreter: the lawyers thought the interpreter should have a degree in Translation and Interpreting. As stated before, this is applicable for majority languages such as English, German, French and Arabic. For future studies, though, possible solutions for training interpreters for the other languages should be considered. However, some universities are starting to implement new postgraduate courses, such as the one offered by the University of Alcalá de Henares, in other languages, such as Chinese and other minority languages.[8] Based on the analysis of the question about training and also some of the comments in the open questions, it seems that some lawyers find it difficult to understand why interpreting in police stations is not carried out by professional interpreters, which is something they take for granted, since, for their part, lawyers must be registered in the Professional Association and meet the requirements established by it before being allowed to try a case or defend a detainee in police settings. The importance given to the interpreter being a professional and having a qualification coincides with the fact that the Spanish press has begun reporting on miscarriages of justice or unsatisfactory situations caused by the use of unqualified interpreters, mainly in the courts. So, in some way, one of the objectives of the research project was achieved: some lawyers (50%) were aware that it is important that the interpreter has a degree in Translation and Interpreting.

As for the results concerning the interpreter's task, a high percentage of lawyers think that the interpreter should explain some terminology to the detainee and this may contradict the limits of the work of the interpreter and may cause the interpreter to act in the role of a mediator who helps the detainee rather than just interpret for him/her.

Furthermore, and as commented on by some lawyers in the open question, there is much to do on the part of authorities to facilitate access to qualified interpreters, as laywers complain that sometimes they do not know how to contact professional interpreters. Time pressure also appeared in the open question as a way to justify the use of non-professional interpreters. According to some of the lawyers, time pressure has an influence when trying to contact an interpreter, as the detainee cannot be detained for more than 72 hours. However, this time pressure may sometimes be used as an excuse because currently, there are more than 20 Spanish universities training translators and interpreters. Therefore, and for some languages such as English, French and even Arabic, it should not be difficult to find qualified interpreters. Furthermore, it seems necessary that lawyers are aware of the importance of having an accurate interpretation in order to defend a

---

[8] The University of Alcalá de Henares offers a postgraduate course for people who work or want to work as a public service interpreter. In addition to English, German and French, the languages offered are Polish, Bulgarian, Russian and Chinese.

foreign detainee and this accurate interpretation may be easier to reach with a qualified interpreter. So, this kind of research project may contribute to raise this awareness among lawyers and other users of public service interpreting.

References

Abril, María Isabel (2006) *La interpretación en los servicios públicos: Caracterización como género, contextualización y modelos de formación. Hacia unas bases para el diseño curricular.* University of Granada: PhD Dissertation.

Alonso Pérez, Fernando (1997) *La policía judicial.* Madrid: Dykinson.

Alonso Pérez, Fernando (1999) *Intervención del abogado ante la Policía Judicial.* Madrid: Dykinson.

Arróniz, Pilar (2000) "La traducción y la interpretación en la Administración de Justicia". In Kelly, Dorothy (ed.) *La traducción y la interpretación en España hoy: perspectivas profesionales.* Granada: Comares, 157-169.

Calvo Encinas, Elisa (2001) *La evaluación diagnóstica en la didáctica de la traducción jurídica: diseño de un instrumento de medida.* University of Granada: PhD Dissertation.

Cambridge, Jan (2002) "Interlocutor Roles and the Pressures on the Interpreters". In Valero Garcés, Carmen/Mancho Bares, Guzmán (eds.) *Community Translation and Interpreting: New Needs for New Realities.* Alcalá de Henares: Servicio de Publicaciones Universidad de Alcalá, 121-126.

Code of Conduct of the NRPSI (2011), http://www.nrpsi.co.uk/pdf/CodeofConduct 07.pdf [3 July 2012].

Corsellis, Ann (1997) "Turning Needs of Public Personnel Working with Interpreters". In Carr, Silvana E./Roberts, Roda P./Dufour, Aideen/Steyin, Dini (eds.) *The Critical Link: Interpreters in the Community.* Amsterdam-Philadelphia: John Benjamins, 77-89.

Corsellis, Ann (2000) "Turning Good Intentions into Good Practice". In Roberts, Roda P./Carr, Silvana E./Abraham, Diana/Dufour, Aideen (eds.) *The Critical Link 2: Interpreters in the Community.* Amsterdam-Philadelphia: John Benjamins, 89-102.

Corsellis, Ann (2002) "Creating a Professional Context for Public Service Interpreters". In Valero Garcés, Carmen/Mancho Bares, Guzmán (eds.) *Community Translation and Interpreting: New Needs for New Realities.* Alcalá de Henares: Servicio de Publicaciones Universidad de Alcalá, 31-38.

Diccionario de la Lengua Española (2001), http://www.rae.es/drae/ [3 July 2012].

El País (2002) "El sueldo del gorrilla Ioan", http://www.elpais.com/articulo/ andalucia/sueldo/gorrilla/Ioan/elpepiautand/20020425elpand_45/Tes [3 July 2012].

Feria García, Manuel (1999) "El traductor-intérprete en la Administración de Justicia". In Feria García, Manuel (ed.) *Traducir para la Justicia.* Granada: Comares, 87-108.

Foulquié Rubio, Ana Isabel (2002a) "Interpretación social: la interpretación en la policía en Granada y Málaga". In Padilla, Presentación/Kelly, Dorothy/Martin, Anne (eds.) *Puentes.* Granada: Comares, 107-115.

Foulquié Rubio, Ana Isabel (2002b) "La interpretación en la policía: ¿un derecho o un privilegio?" In Valero Garcés, Carmen/Mancho Bares, Guzmán (eds.) *Community Translation and Interpreting: New Needs for New Realities.* Alcalá de Henares: Servicio de Publicaciones Universidad de Alcalá, 93-98.

Fox, Annemarie (2001) "An Interpreter's Perspective". *Context. The Magazine for Family Therapy and Systemic Practice* 54, 19-20.

Garber, Nathan (2000) "Community Interpretation: A Personal View". In Roberts, Roda P./Carr, Silvana E./Abraham, Diana/Dufour, Aideen (eds.) *The Critical Link 2: Interpreters in the Community.* Amsterdam-Philadelphia: John Benjamins, 9-20.

Gentile, Adolfo (1996) *Liaison Interpreting.* Melbourne: Melbourne University Press.

Hale, Sandra (2005) "Controversies Over the Role of Court Interpreter". Plenary speech presented at the Conference Translation as Mediation between Languages and Cultures, April 2005. University of Alcalá de Henares, Madrid.

Harris, Brian (1990) "Norms in Interpretation". *Target* 2:1, 115-119.

Kadrić, Mira (2010) "The Trouble With Police Interpreting – An Empirical Study on Practices in Austria". Paper presented at the Critical Link Conference 6, 26-30 July 2010. Birmingham, UK.

Lázaro, Raquel (2007) "Dilemas éticos del traductor/intérprete en los servicios públicos", http://www.translationactivism.com/articles/Raquel_Lazaro.pdf [3 July 2012].

Longley, Pat (1984) "What is a Community Interpreter? Some Thoughts After the First Experimental Course in Peterborough". *The Linguist* 23:2, 178-181.

Martin, Anne/Abril, María Isabel (2002) "Los límites difusos del papel de intérprete social". In Valero Garcés, Carmen/Mancho Bares, Guzmán (eds.) *Community Translation and Interpreting: New Needs for New Realities.* Alcalá de Henares: Servicio de Publicaciones Universidad de Alcalá, 57-62.

Martin, Anne (2004) "Community Interpreting in Spain: The Service Provider's Perspective". Unpublished poster presented at the Critical Link Conference 4, 20-23 May 2004. Stockholm, Sweden.

Mayoral, Roberto (2000) "Consideraciones sobre la profesión de traductor jurado". In Kelly, Dorothy (ed.) *La traducción y la interpretación en España hoy: perspectivas profesionales.* Granada: Comares, 117-144.

Mesa, Anne Marie (2000) "The Cultural Interpreter: An Appreciated Professional. Results of a Study on Interpreting Services: Client, Healthcare Worker and Interpreter Points of View". In Roberts, Roda P./Carr, Silvana E./Abraham, Diana/Dufour, Aideen (eds.) *The Critical Link 2: Interpreters in the Community.* Amsterdam-Philadelphia: John Benjamins, 67-82.

Oppenheim, Abraham Naftali (1996) *Questionnaire Design, Interviewing and Attitude Measurement.* London: Pinter Publishers.

Ortega Herráez, Juan Miguel (2004) *Panorámica de la interpretación judicial en España: un análisis de la profesión.* University of Granada: Unpublished Research Project.

Ortega Herráez, Juan Miguel (2011) *Interpretar para la Justicia.* Granada: Comares.

Pöchhacker, Franz (2000) "The Community Interpreter's Task: Self Perception and Provider Views". In Roberts, Roda P./Carr, Silvana E./Abraham, Diana/Dufour, Aideen (eds.) *The Critical Link 2: Interpreters in the Community*. Amsterdam-Philadelphia: John Benjamins, 49-65.

Pöchhacker, Franz (2004) *Introducing Interpreting Studies*. London-New York: Routledge.

Sanders, Marsha (1992) "Training Community for Interpreters". In Picken, Catriona (ed.) *ITI Conference 6. Proceedings*. London: Aslib, 45-50.

Valero Garcés, Carmen/Gauthier Blasi, Laura (2010) "Bourdieu and Public Service Interpreting and Translation. Towards a Social Theory in PSIT". In Díaz Fauces, Oscar/Monxó, Esther (eds.) *Monti: Monografías de Traducción e Interpretación*. Alicante: Universidad de Alicante, 97-117.

Way, Catherine (2003) *La traducción como acción social. El caso de los documentos académicos (español-inglés)*. University of Granada: PhD Dissertation.

Constraints in multimodal translation

ELISA MORONI

Bologna University, Italy

The Representation of Orality in the Translation of Russian Epics

In this paper, I will discuss the way orality is rendered in translation. I will consider the question of orality in relation to Russian epic poetry, which was orally transmitted by generations of storytellers and systematically transcribed between the nineteenth and twentieth century. Russian oral epics are a specific genre of national folklore and carry a number of cultural elements referring to an ancient oral tradition. Mythological motifs are hidden behind archaic formulas. Style thus becomes a relevant medium to convey content and to provide a framework within which the poems are recognised as epics. When epic poetry is first written down and then translated, the orality embedded in it turns into a kind of frozen orality. Through an analysis of the Italian translations of Russian epics, based on the transcriptions of the actual performances, I will try to describe how oral features are represented in translation.

Keywords: orality, epics, folklore, Russian, Italian

The status of oral epics in the Russian polysystem

In this paper, I will consider the question of orality and its consequences for translation, with specific reference to Russian oral epics, known in Russian as *былины* (*byliny*).[1] These epic folk songs, usually of three hundred to four hundred lines, were performed orally, but survived only through ethnographers' transcriptions. The poems probably originated in southern Russia and Ukraine (Terras 1985:66) between the ninth and tenth century (Lipets 1969:10), but were transmitted in variants until the twentieth century mainly in Northern European Russia. Although the first texts date back to the seventeenth century, these were "prose paraphrases made for the purpose

[1] A term derived from the *Tale of Igor's campaign* (*Slovo o polku Igoreve*), the Russian epic poem dating back to the late twelfth century. *Был-* (*byl-*) comes from the past participial form of *быть* (*byt'*) "to be". Peasants knew epic songs as *старины* (*stariny*), singular *старина* (*starina*), "old stories". The term *былина* (*bylina*), plural *былины* (*byliny*), was introduced in the 1830s as a scholarly designation of Russian epics (Chadwick/Chadwick 1936/1986:3).

of providing interesting reading material" (Oinas 1978:236), and the most renowned collections appeared between the nineteenth and twentieth century.[2]

Until the eighteenth century, Russian culture was dominated by religious art, and written literature was under the Church's control and subject to censorship (Jakobson 1946:632-633). Thus, for a long time folklore was the only medium of verbal creation for most of the population (Chadwick/ Chadwick 1936/1986:xiv). Traditional oral poetry, therefore, had played an important role in the shaping of a national literature, and "had aroused a certain amount of interest in the west before the Russian Revolution of 1917, and a number of collections had found their way into English libraries" (ibid.:3).

Oral narrative poetry has always drawn the attention of scholars and received a special status in the Russian cultural polysystem. With the Romantic revival of folklore, a certain emphasis was given to the epics, and several expeditions were organised to the areas where oral poetry was still alive. Indeed, "folklore has always been popular among all strata of Russian society" (Terras 1985:139), but Russian folklore studies officially began only in the 1860s, following Western trends, and "the discovery of a flourishing bylina tradition in northern Russia by Rybnikov and Gil'ferding in the 1860s and 1870s resulted in an increase of interest in folklore which lasted unabated until World War I" (ibid.).

In Soviet times, folklorists saw their freedom extremely limited, especially in 1932, when the Union of Soviet Writers was created to control literature and folklore. A great emphasis, though, was given to folklore, used for ideological purposes to serve a political agenda, and viewed as "a powerful force to advance communism" (ibid.:140). Thus, on the one hand, the regime "politicised" folklore, making it, in some cases, into a propaganda vehicle. On the other hand, it was considered a "safer" area of intellectual endeavour than modern literature, and so it attracted some great minds that did important research, while skirting politically sensitive issues.

Byliny ceased to be a living genre of folk verbal art towards the first half of the twentieth century, and they became a cultivated tradition and an object of academic research in the USSR. Throughout the twentieth cen-

---

[2] Some of the most relevant collections were published by Danilov (1804/1958); Kireevskiy (1860-74); Rybnikov (1861-67); Gil'ferding (1873/1949-51); Grigor'ev (1899-1901/2002-03); Markov (1901); Astakhova (1938-51).

tury, byliny, together with the folklore of the other peoples of the USSR, were seen as one of the most genuine products of Russian and Soviet culture but after the fall of the Soviet Union, they gradually lost their popularity. Thus, they now occupy a less prominent position in the Russian polysystem, being an élite kind of literature mainly accessible to specialists. Their status obviously changed: until the first half of the twentieth century, they were recited for the peasants, who shared with the singers that tradition, whereas soon after dying out, they gradually became an object of study, and now they are only read by students and folklorists. Hence, the marginality of the Russian epics may influence translation strategies, determining their position in the target systems (Moroni 2010:7).

Nevertheless, folklore is still considered and studied as a relevant part of the Russian cultural polysystem. In consequence, various translations of byliny and folk tales were published in most European languages, showing a certain interest in Russian epic poetry. Such translations, though, are still in need of scholarly attention (Ivanova 1993:313). This is one of the reasons why I believe Russian epics might be an important subject of study, especially from the viewpoint of translation.

Folk culture and style

Since byliny have been collected among peasants/storytellers from different parts of Russia, they present peculiarities of the Russian dialects and linguistic varieties spoken in those regions, together with realia, i.e. culture-bound terms referring to different epochs and places. The language of byliny thus shows several common traits with oral speech, but at the same time, it differs from it: the use of specific terminologies is conditioned by the stylistic constraints of the epic genre. Tradition sets up the right compositional parameters and patterns for each genre (Foley 1995:xiii), while performance provides the "interpretive frame" necessary for the audience to acknowledge the text as the expression of a particular genre (Muhawi 2006:366). Thus byliny have a precise structure based on three main parts, "the introduction, the narrative portion, and the epilogue" (Oinas 1978:247).

Moreover, the epics carry concepts, symbols and motifs of various ages: archaic folklore elements, dating back a thousand of years, coexist with realia from contemporary Russian daily life (Lipets 1969:10). Realia therefore play a relevant role in the poetic system of Russian byliny, since, being the product of an ancient oral tradition, they contribute substantially to create the peculiar reality represented in the oral epics. In this view, realia, often conveying ancient meanings, can be considered as essential features of the specific oral nature of byliny. Like realia, proper names also have a significant role in the compositional structure of the epics, and they may refer to real historical characters or mythological figures.

The numerous historical references present in byliny are a combination of real and invented facts: "They frequently distort historical fact", and "they also introduce elements manifestly unhistorical" (Chadwick/ Chadwick 1936/1986:101). A historical event might serve as the first kernel for the plot, but then other factors would also play a significant role in transforming that realistic surface according to the needs of the poetic composition (Skaftymov 1924:3, 100-101). Aspects of reality are depicted only in general traits, and although certain images may refer to concrete and existing objects and facts, after all, they are only ideal representations of life, reflecting people's hopes (ibid.:124-125).

Russian epics display linguistic and stylistic elements peculiar to oral poetry and folklore, such as repetition and parallelism, fixed formulas, epithets and themes or commonplaces (*loci communes*), regarded by scholars as the main features of oral verbal art, especially poetry (Lord 1960/2003; Ong 1982/1988). Repetition in particular is evident at all levels, becoming one of the traits that distinguish oral from written literature. Webster (2008:445) claims that "the exact repetition of a line [...] is the maximal form of parallelism: it is repetition without variation. Other forms of repetition that nearly match but vary in some ways are examples of poetic parallelism". Repetition and parallelism are thus substantial to byliny poetics.

Parallelism is a special device relating linguistic elements of the oral epic to one another and linking them through constant correspondences at the syntactic, semantic and phonological level. Grammatical parallelism pervades the whole epic text, playing with grammatical forms and structures (Jakobson 1966:424). The basic units of the poems are the lines, which have a precise cohesion with each other, and employ several types of meters.[3] These formal aspects of the texts are rich in cultural and symbolic references that are hard to translate into a foreign language imbued with rather different cultural implications. Furthermore, linguistic and diachronic bor-

---

[3] The most common epic meter consists of three stresses per line and "a varying number (one to three) of unstressed syllables between stresses. Usually the ending is dactylic" (Oinas 1978:250).

ders distance the source from the target text. Thus, oral features may have specific consequences for translation. In the following chapters, I will describe such oral features more in detail, and I will examine how orality may affect the translation process.

For a definition of orality

In the context of translation, orality may acquire particular connotations due to the many challenges represented by oral poetry and its highly formulaic style. In the previous section, I referred to specific traits of orality, such as parallelism, repetition, realia and formulas that characterise byliny and help identify them as oral texts. Now, I should specify what I understand here by the concept of orality, and what specific kind of orality is involved in the context of Russian epics.

With their emphasis on writing and written texts, Western chirographic cultures have tended to see orality mainly as opposed and subordinate to literacy; language, in fact, is based on orality, and all verbal communication originates from oral speech. Language is thus made up of sound units first, and then of letters composing the written speech (Ong 1982/1988:5). Since its introduction, writing has gradually transformed and enhanced the potentiality of language, exerting a strong and innovative power on all cultural phenomena. Nevertheless, orality should not be considered less significant than literacy in the development of cultures.

Ong (ibid.:6) identifies two different types of orality, primary and secondary: the first is that of "cultures untouched by literacy", while the second is that of people familiar with writing. In this paper, I will specifically refer to the latter, since Russian storytellers were not always illiterate, and it was not so uncommon for them to know collections of folk epics and tales.

Oral creation, regardless of whether it is prose or poetry, is often classified as "oral literature". According to Ong (ibid.:11), the term *literature* is not completely correct, since it inevitably reminds one of writing, revealing the prejudice on which our idea of orality is based. However, this is a widely accepted term to designate traditional poetry (Finnegan 1977/1992:16-17), and as such I will refer to it with regard to byliny.

Oral verbal art is performed, sung or recited, and based on a vital and dynamic interrelation between kinesics, sound and speech. However, the orality conveyed in the transcribed Russian epics is of a special kind, since it no longer belongs to a dynamic, living, spontaneous phenomenon but is the result of a scholarly transcription, which is never a neutral act.[4]

Even though all renderings of oral tales in writing diminish certain key characteristics of the performance of oral cultural artefacts, features and elements of Russian folk poetry, such as realia, proper names, formulas and formal stylistic devices, can be rendered in transcription, building a bridge between oral and written elements. Nonetheless, transposing performance elements into print remains one of the most controversial problems in folklore studies.

The process of writing down oral texts can be explained as an example of what Roman Jakobson referred to as "intersemiotic translation" (Jakobson 1959/2004:139), where several changes occur from the act of performance. For instance, the purpose of the oral features is different: in the performance, they had a practical mnemonic function, while in the fixed transcribed text, they acquire a literary facet. In this process, the orality of byliny is thus converted into a sort of fictitious orality. Translators have now access only to the written texts, where they have to cope with such *frozen* orality.[5] The *freezing* that first takes place in the process of writing down the epics is redoubled and enhanced in the translation phase. Hence, such oral texts undergo two levels of transcription: the first when they are transcribed into written Russian, and the second when they are translated into the target language.

The influence exerted by ideology on these texts is also a complex aspect to consider. Ideology first shapes the original transcription of the oral text into written form (of the source language) and then shapes the translations of these transcriptions, making the translations doubly mediated. Hence, in such translations, orality and literacy are intertwined, thus creating a hybrid dimension where oral and literary features coexist.

The nature of folklore texts

Russian oral epics belong to a domain suspended between orality and literacy: they were originally oral, but now they only exist in transcription. However, although these poems can now only be read, they cannot be considered as written poetry, because originally they were meant to be per-

[4] On the transcription process as an ideological act, see Bucholtz (2000).

[5] The term "frozen orality" is a term coined by the author.

formed. They involve thus a series of elements not present in writing but related to the specific act of performance and characteristic of the oral style. According to Muhawi (2006:365), folkloric texts are "culturally saturated forms of verbal art", since they carry semantic connotations closely connected with mythology, folk culture, beliefs and traditions.

Translating folkloric texts, therefore, is a complex task: the folk cultural elements they are imbued with are not intelligible to the readers of the target text. For this reason, translations of such texts often include additional metatextual information, explaining cultural and linguistic elements obscure to the target audience (Tymoczko 1995:17).

Since every text inevitably refers to other texts, as every utterance reminds us of other utterances (see Todorov 1984), every telling should be regarded as a sort of retelling (Tymoczko 1999:41). In this view, oral narratives are also a retelling of other tales: "It is agreed that the content, form, and performance techniques of any given traditional song or tale, for example, derive from established patterns that the teller or singer inherits and in turn passes on to those who succeed him" (ibid.).

Furthermore, "any writing is a rewriting" (Tymoczko 1995:16), and translation is also a sort of rewriting. The translation of traditional texts is thus a special kind of rewriting, since translators *rewrite* oral tellings that evoke metonymically other tellings of the source oral tradition within the parameters of the target culture, and reify "the entire tradition that the audience and teller share" (Tymoczko 1999:43). Translators therefore may decide to adapt those tellings to the target culture or instead bring the readers to that tradition. Moreover, as we have seen, the translation of oral texts such as Russian byliny is based on transcriptions, where the dimension of performance can be only partially recaptured.

As I mentioned earlier, this process involves a sort of double *intersemiotic* transfer, a passage from orality to literacy, which helps create an foreignising combination of oral and literary modes of expression (O'Sullivan 2006:390). Thus, oral devices in translation no longer have a mnemonic function; they now have a literary one. At the same time, literary patterns carry an oral component, and are not always conducive to an extremely fluent writing. Hence, translation becomes a virtual space where the source and target culture meet, creating a new dimension which does not efface the cultural other but keeps its difference.

The Italian translations of byliny

Russian epics belong to the domain of folklore, which may exert a certain influence on translation strategies and solutions. Unlike translations (generally accomplished by a single person), these texts were not the work of a single author, being instead the product of a community of people; this, too, may somewhat condition the translation process. Here, I will consider this and other issues by analysing the Italian translations of byliny, and I will try to find out which ideologies and principles may have determined their solutions.

There are five Italian translations of byliny all grouped in different anthologies. The first translation, dating back to 1911, was accomplished by Domenico Ciampoli, an academic, who was mainly a populariser of Slavic cultures in Italy. The second one was comprised in an anthology of Russian literature published in 1957 by Ettore Lo Gatto, a prominent scholar of Slavic literature. The third one was published in 1974 by the Slavist Bruno Meriggi, and the fourth and fifth ones were accomplished by Edgardo Tito Saronne and Kamilla Fedorovna Danil'chenko in 1997, and Edgardo Tito Saronne and Elisa Moroni in 2010, respectively. All these translations remained isolated attempts to popularise byliny among Italian readers, and they did not receive great attention from the public. Russian epics have been represented as élite literature rather than folkloric texts, even when translators had declared different intentions, stressing the role of the collective dimension in which epics were composed and transmitted.

Moreover, the translations of byliny were shaped by Italy's relationship with Russia and Russian culture, and this relationship changed over time under the influence of historical/ideological circumstances. Between the nineteenth and twentieth centuries, the interest in Russian literature grew rapidly in Italy, and consequently, the number of translations increased. Nonetheless, contacts between Russian and Italian literature had been already developing since the end of the eighteenth century through translations and reviews (Scandura 2002:13). Ciampoli was Professor in Slavic literatures at the University of Catania, and he translated the works of several major Russian authors, such as Gogol', Pushkin, Lermontov, Dostoevskiy, Turgenev and Tolstoy.

Lo Gatto is considered the father of Italian Slavic studies, and he was also a prominent translator, who created a sort of canon for the translation of Russian literature based on philological accuracy (ibid.:18). In the Soviet era, the relationships between Russia and Italy intensified through the Italian communist party, and this encouraged new translation attempts from Russian.

Meriggi was also a philologist particularly interested in Slavic folklore. Saronne, Professor in Slavic philology, accomplished a first translation of byliny together with the Russian dialectologist Danil'chenko, and a second one with the author of this article.[6]

Hence, it is interesting to note that the Italian translations of Russian epics were all accomplished by scholars. Except for Ciampoli's and Lo Gatto's versions, which only include the Italian translation without mentioning the Russian original, the remaining anthologies are annotated translations with commentaries, notes and parallel texts. Hence, they could be all somehow described as philological translations, although sometimes, they seem to follow different principles.

According to Tymoczko (1995:18), there are mainly two types of translations of traditional marginalised texts, namely popular and scholarly, but both use strategies which could seem to contradict the main scope of the translation:

> In a scholarly translation the text is embedded in a shell of paratextual devices that serve to explain the metonymies of the source text, providing a set of contexts for the translation. In the case of a popular translation, by contrast, the translator typically focuses on a few aspects of the literary text which are brought to a broad segment of the target audience.

Following this statement, we may identify Ciampoli's, Lo Gatto's, Meriggi's, Saronne and Danil'chenko's, and Saronne and Moroni's versions as scholarly translations, although Ciampoli's and Lo Gatto's display elements that are sometimes more typical of popular translations. Now, we shall see how in some instances, these texts may differ from each other or adopt similar approaches.

Oral features in translation

In the previous sections, I have tried to point out how oral features can be relevant to the translation of traditional epics. Archaisms, culture-bound

---

[6] In this case, mixing the roles of the researcher and the researched has not represented an obstacle. The role of the researcher, in fact, has been useful to reflect upon and understand better the role of the translator.

terms, fixed formulas, repetition, and an extensive use of hypocoristic nouns, i.e. diminutives, are some of the devices that represent the highest challenge to translation: how were they rendered in different translations? Are there similar tendencies or patterns relating the target texts one to another? We shall now see some examples from the Italian translations of byliny that should display the translators' choices about the abovementioned traits of orality. In particular, I will focus on the following features: 1) realia; 2) proper nouns; 3) hypochoristics; 4) formulas; 5) repetition; 6) punctuation.

Realia

I have already mentioned the relevance of realia within byliny poetics. Culture-bound terms such as *богатырь* (*bogatyr'*),[7] byliny epic heroes, are often left untranslated, since they are believed to convey meanings that have no direct equivalents in other languages. Ciampoli, on the contrary, in some of his translations, uses the word *paladino*, "paladin", which clearly refers to Italian and ancient Romance epic poetry:

> Nel rosso tramonto del sole: erano sette *paladini* russi[8]
>
> [In the red sunset of the sun: they were seven Russian paladins][9]

By referring to the written Romance epic tradition, the use of the term *paladino* helps create a familiar context for the reader, thus enhancing the frozenness of orality and the combination of oral and literary references that I mentioned earlier. However, this is one of the few attempts to translate such words into Italian. Later translators established a sort of tradition in the rendering of similar culture-bound terms: realia are thus generally left in Russian, as in the following examples from Lo Gatto, Saronne and Danil'chenko, Meriggi, and Saronne and Moroni, respectively:

---

[7] *Богатырь* (*bogatyr'*), plural *богатыри* (*bogatyri*) probably derives from the Tartar words *bogatur*, *batur*, *batyr'*, *bator*, *bagadur*, which referred to valiant warriors.

[8] "Come i paladini sparvero dalla santa Russia" (Ciampoli 1911:48). Ciampoli and Lo Gatto do not give information about the source texts. (All the titles in inverted commas given in the footnotes refer to different byliny).

[9] All passages in the examples given in squared brackets are interlinear translations from Italian by the author.

Con la sua coraggiosa *druzhina*[10]
[With his brave druzhina][11]

In tre anni raccolse la *druzhina*[12]
[In three years he gathered the *druzhina*]

Tiene il *bogatyr'* questo discorso[13]
[Delivers the *bogatyr'* such speech]

Nell'alto *terem* sta rinchiusa[14]
[In the high *terem* she is locked up][15]

In this way, as we see in examples (2), (3), (4) and (5), a certain distance is created between the target readers and the source text in order to maintain the cultural specificity of the latter. Such terms recur frequently in byliny as part of the ancient Russian oral tradition to which epics belong. Choosing not to translate these terms displays a pattern defined by a precise ideology hidden behind the translations. Words such as *bogatyr'* and *druzhina* (to cite only a few) were totally understandable and familiar to the source audience, whereas to a foreign reader unacquainted with Russian epics, they may appear odd. Orality is thus employed in translation to insert a queer and foreignising element (Moroni 2010:6). In this way, it becomes a frozen orality, where realia are used to recreate the cultural atmosphere of the original.

Proper nouns

As Tymoczko (1999:223) points out, "names are [...] dense with information", and "are rich in semantic and semiotic significance". In addition, the semantics of names is strictly interrelated to their phonology and orthography. Byliny abound with proper names referred to heroes, enemies, brides, heroes' parents, and often related to real historical or mythological charac-

[10] "Vol'ga Svyatoslavich e Mikula Selyaninovich" (Lo Gatto 1957:79).

[11] From *друг* (*drug*), "friend", it designated warriors faithful to the prince.

[12] "Volkh Vseslav'evich" (Saronne/Danil'chenko 1997:119), from Danilov (1804/1958).

[13] "Svyatogor" (Meriggi 1974:131), from Parilova and Soymonov (1941).

[14] "Choten Bludovich, marito ricco per forza" (Saronne/Moroni 2010:89), from Rybnikov (1861-67/1989-91).

[15] *Терем* (*terem*): the highest part of the princely house, or tower.

ters. These proper names frequently acquire precise connotations and meanings within the compositional structure of the poems, and they are often used as hypocoristics, suggesting the singer's affection for his heroes and stories. Moreover, as Tymoczko (ibid.) suggests:

> Even when names are meaningless in a semantic sense, they are unsupported by the normal redundancies of language and, therefore, are loci of information in the technical sense of unpredictability. This may be one function of the formulaic epithets and patronymics in the Homeric texts and other oral epics: to add redundancy to names and, hence, predictability in oral performance.

Translating names, especially in the case of oral epics, is thus a complex and controversial task, and translators have two different choices: retaining the original phonology of the names, or adapting them to the target culture (ibid.:224). In the Italian translations of byliny, we can notice the same tendencies outlined by Tymoczko regarding the translation of proper names.

In some cases, for instance, Ciampoli translates proper names, by using Italian equivalents, as this was a common translation habit of his time:

(1) Usciva *Alessio* Popovich, il giovinetto[16]
[Went out Alessio Popovich, the lad]

Example (6), where the Russian name *Alesha* is rendered with the Italian equivalent *Alessio*, displays a strategy revealing a particular translation norm. However, it is interesting to notice that Ciampoli translates *Alesha* but retains in Russian the patronymic *Popovich*. This shows that opposite strategies are used to translate similar items.

(2) Mikhaylushka *rigiuoca la sua testa da bravo giovane*[17]
[Mikhaylushka *replays his head of brave young man*]

(3) Grazie a te Ilyushen'ka di Murom[18]
[Thanks to you Ilyushen'ka from Murom]

In examples (7) and (8), both translators retain the Russian hypocoristics of the original *Mikhaylushka* and *Ilyushen'ka* (the corresponding simple proper names are Mikhaylo and Il'ya), which links these two translations one to another, displaying an established convention in the translation of Russian

---

[16] "Come i paladini sparvero dalla santa Russia" (Ciampoli 1911:48).

[17] "Mikhaylo Potyk" (Meriggi 1974:65), from Gil'ferding (1873/1949-51).

[18] "Svyatogor e la bara" (Saronne/Danil'chenko 1997:99), from Sokolov and Chicherov (1948).

epics. This is again an attempt to preserve the frozen orality of the transcription by keeping features typical of the colloquial register. However, the effect produced in the target language of course is different, since the hypocoristics might not be immediately recognised as such by every reader. Thus the orality recreated in the target text is even more fictitious and frozen.

When the translator is especially concerned to render the meaning of proper names, then he usually translates them into Italian, as we can see in the following example from Lo Gatto:

(4) E cadde Usignolo il Brigante sull'umida terra[19]
[And fell down Nightingale the Robber on the damp earth]

In example (9), Lo Gatto translates the name of the epic monster *Solovey-razboynik* in a literal way in order to make its semantics more explicit. On the contrary, Meriggi (1974:159), for example, preserves this name in Russian. On the one hand, by translating the proper name, Lo Gatto aims at making the meaning of the text more accessible to the target reader. On the other hand, he moves away from the original orality of the source text producing an foreignising effect in the peculiar intertwining of orality and literacy.

Other translators, such as Saronne and Moroni, make an attempt to render the meaning of proper names more intelligible through the use of explicitation:

(5) Tu Kostya-Lostya di Novyi Torzhok[20]
[You Kostya-Lostya from Novyi Torzhok]

(6) Ecco arrivar Potyanushka lo Zoppo[21]
[And here he comes Potyanushka the Cripple]

In example (10), where "Kostya-Lostya from Novyi Torzhok" is the equivalent for the name of the epic character *Kostya-Lostya Novotorshchenik*, Saronne and Moroni explicitate the epithet *Novotorshchenik*, meaning literally "born in the city of Novyi Torzhok", and used also for rhythmical reasons in the original. The same happens in example (11), where the translators explicitate the epithet *Khromen'ka*, "the Cripple", which is referred to the

---

[19] Il'ya Muromets e Usignolo-Brigante" (Lo Gatto 1957:85).

[20] "Avventure e morte di Vasilii Buslaevich" (Saronne/Moroni 2010:123), from Astakhova (1938).

[21] "Avventure e morte di Vasilii Buslaevich" (Saronne/Moroni 2010:103), from Astakhova (1938).

proper name *Potyanushka*. On the one hand, in both cases, the translators retain the Russian proper names. On the other hand, they adapt to the target culture the epithet referred to the name. Thus we can notice the use of different and sometimes opposite strategies that create a peculiar combination of orality and literacy and tend to produce a frozen orality.

Hypochoristics

Hypocoristics are commonly used in Russian, and their function is immediately acknowledged by the audience, whereas in Italian they create an foreignising effect, since the reader does not possess the key to access that information. Even when the overt aim of the translators is to keep oral features, what results is always a different kind of orality, which becomes frozen, as we can see in the following examples:

(7) Marinka graziosa figlia di Ignat[22]
[Marinka the nice daughter of Ignat]

(8) Un grande patto - non un patterello[23]
[A big deal, not a little deal]

(9) Le balie, le mammine e le cameriere rispondono[24]
Nannies, little mothers and maids answer]

(10) Cavalca un omaccio contadino[25]
[Rides a bad man of a farmer]

In example (12), the Russian name *Marinka* (hypochoristic of Marina) is preserved in the translation. Nonetheless, the suffix -ka, which here gives the name a pejorative connotation, cannot be directly perceived as negative by the target audience. Marinka is a witch, and the reader can only understand it further on from the context, while for the source audience this was already apparent from the pejorative suffix added to the name *Marina*. However, in the transcription, the effect of the hypochoristic is less immediate than it was during the performance act, and orality already turns into a frozen orality. The translator therefore tries to retain the frozen orality of the transcription, producing an even more foreignising and fictitious orality.

22 "Dobrynya e Marinka" (Meriggi 1974:103), from Gil'ferding (1873/1949-51).

23 "Dobrynya e il drago" (Saronne/Danil'chenko 1997: 199), from Gil'ferding (1873/1949-51).

24 "Solovey Rudimirovich" (Ciampoli 1911:42).

25 "Il'ya Muromets e Usignolo-Brigante" (Lo Gatto 1957:85).

Examples (13), (14), and (15) show an attempt to recreate the frozen orality of the original by using hypochoristic nouns, which are more common in oral than in written speech. However, in the written Italian translations these hypochoristic nouns produce a somewhat foreignising effect, thus leading to a *double-frozen* orality.

Formulas

As we have seen in the previous chapters, fixed recurring formulas (i.e. combinations of nouns and epithets) are one of the most prominent characteristics of oral poetry, especially epics. They had a precise function in the performance, since they helped singers tell their stories without losing control on the narration. In translation, formulas are used with totally different purposes. Saronne and Danil'chenko, for instance, through formulas convey poetic connotations that create intertextual references to Italian epic poetry. Meriggi, on the contrary, translates formulas in a more literal way, thus adopting foreignising solutions, as in the following examples:

(11) Balenante falco[26]
[Shining hawk]

(12) Marmoree stanze[27]
[Marble rooms]

(13) Campo aperto[28]
[Open field]

(14) Le bianche mani[29]
[White hands]

Examples (16) and (17) show an attempt to create a literary image: in Russian, formulas are phrases of a less high register, respectively *ясные соколы* (*yasnye sokoly*), "bright hawks", and *палаты белокаменные* (*palaty belokamennye*), "white-stone palace", while in Italian, the epithets belong to a high literary register. However, in the Russian transcription, these formulas are already the product of a frozen orality caught from the performance act.

---

[26] "Volkh Vseslav'evich" (Saronne/Danil'chenko 1997:123), from Danilov (1804/1958).

[27] "Dobrynya e il drago" (Saronne/Danil'chenko 1997:191), from Gil'ferding (1873/1949-51).

[28] "I bogatyri di scolta. Duello di Il'ya Muromets col figlio" (Meriggi 1974:177), from Grigor'ev (1899-1901/2002-03).

[29] "Il primo viaggio di Il'ya Muromets. Il'ya e Solovey-razboynik" (Meriggi 1974:165), from Bazanov (1940).

Examples (18) and (19) are instead very close to the original. The method used in all these examples reveals then different aims: literal translation is Meriggi's aim, while reaching a literary aesthetic effect is Saronne and Danil'chenko's intention. Both retain formulas as relevant features of the epic, but what they obtain is a *literary double-frozen* orality. In the original, formulas convey symbolic meanings representing the essential link with tradition. They evoke "metonymically all previous tellings of the tale that the audience has participated in and, further, the telling instantiates and reifies metonymically the entire tradition that the audience and teller share" (Tymoczko 1995:14). These metonymies inevitably disappear in the translations, and the frozen formulas of the transcription turn into literary features used to create an image of the epic in the target culture.

Repetition

The use of special formulaic expressions that helped shape the text in performance made the oral epic recognisable by the audience as a specific genre of verbal art. Repetition, which is used extensively in oral poetry, is an essential part of the formulaic structure of the Russian epics. We shall now see how Italian translators have tried to render repetition.

(15) Venendo dal mare, dal mare azzurro[30]
Coming from the sea, from the blue sea]

(16) Verso quelle tane - quelle tane di drago[31]
[Towards those burrows - those dragon's burrows]

(17) E tu figlio, figlio diletto[32]
[And you son, dear son]

In example (20), *quelle tane - quelle tane*, "those burrows - those burrows", shows an attempt to reproduce repetition, which in the original reads as follows: *Ко тым норам да ко змеиным* (*Ko tym noram da ko zmeinym*), "towards those burrows, toward the dragon [ones]". In Russian, syntactic repetition is employed, using ellipsis to represent the noun, and only the preposition *ко* (*ko*), "to", is repeated. In the translated passage, the translator is forced to repeat the noun *quelle tane*, "those burrows", twice, by means of compensation, since the ellipsis present in Russian is not possible in Italian.

[30] "Solovey Rudimirovich" (Ciampoli 1911:39).

[31] "Dobrynya e il drago" (Saronne/Danil'chenko 1997:191), from Gil'ferding (1873/1949-51).

[32] "La guarigione di Il'ya Muromets"(Meriggi 1974:141), from Sokolov and Chicherov (1948).

The same happens in example (21), where the translator repeats *dal mare, dal mare*, "from the sea, from the sea", using a similar strategy. In these cases, repetition is used as a means to preserve the frozen orality of the transcribed Russian text.

In example (22), repetition is used differently: in the original it reads: *А уж ты, чадо, чадо милое* (*a uzh ty, chado, chado miloe*), "and you son, dear son". Meriggi chooses literalness to convey orality.

Punctuation

Punctuation is a good example to observe the double frozenness of orality that occurs in the translation of oral texts. As I have already pointed out, the Italian translations of byliny are based on transcriptions, where the orality of the performance has already undergone a process of freezing. This is particularly obvious in the use of punctuation, which is regularly employed in the transcriptions as these were common written texts. Translators thus might decide to introduce punctuation, or to omit it, as in the following examples:

(18) Ma egli è vissuto, è vissuto; è invecchiato, invecchiato;[33]
[But he lived, he lived; he grew old, he grew old]

(19) "Ah, tu, fratello mio, Ekim Ivanovich!"[34]
["Ah you my brother, Ekim Ivanovich!"]

(20) Cavalca, il giovane, si diverte:[35]
[The young man rides, has fun]

(21) Verso quei monti di Sorochin gloriosi[36]
[Towards those Sorochin mountains]

(22) Ma un giorno a un gran banchetto non chiamano Sadke[37]
[But one day at a great feast they do not invite Sadke]

In examples (23), (24) and (25), punctuation is retained and used extensively to make the text more fluent and acceptable in writing, whereas in examples (26) and (27), punctuation is absent. In the first case, the frozenness of the

---

33 "Dobrynya" (Ciampoli 1911:29).

34 "Alesha Popovich" (Lo Gatto 1957:89).

35 "I bogatyri di scolta. Duello di Il'ya Muromets col figlio" (Meriggi 1974:175), from Grigor'ev (1899-1901/2002-03).

36 "Dobrynya e il drago" (Saronne/Danil'chenko 1997:207), from Gil'ferding (1873/1949-51).

37 "Sadke e il Re del mare" (Saronne/Moroni 2010:59), from Rybnikov (1861-67/1989-91).

transcription is enhanced, and a double passage from orality to literacy occurs in the translation, since the punctuation of the original transcribed text is kept thus stressing the literary function of the translation. In the second case, translators strive instead to reproduce the original orality of the performance partially lost in the transcription. Nevertheless, the effect created by the absence of punctuation in writing is foreignising, and orality is recaptured and frozen in the written text.

Double-frozen orality: a conclusion

The Italian translations of byliny examined above were accomplished with different aims and employing different strategies. Ciampoli and Lo Gatto intended to popularise byliny; Meriggi translated several variants for a comparative study, whereas Saronne and Danil'chenko, and Saronne and Moroni represented byliny as élite epic poetry. In all these translations, we have seen how in the double passage from oral into written text, following the sequence performance - transcription - translation, orality changes its facet, becoming a double-frozen orality. Several elements might display this phenomenon, such as the use of punctuation, as we have seen in the previous section. Ciampoli, Lo Gatto and Meriggi, for instance, preserve the punctuation of the original, while Saronne and Danil'chenko, and Saronne and Moroni almost completely ignore it. This is a way of manipulating the text according to precise aims. The aim of Meriggi's version, for instance, is obviously the compositional structure of the source text, whereas that of Saronne and Danil'chenko's, and Saronne and Moroni is the rendering of oral features with aesthetic purposes, but within a familiar context for the reader. The result in both cases is a foreignising translation, where orality is used for literary purposes.

Ciampoli's version seems to be an attempt to popularise byliny, rendering them accessible and somewhat acceptable to the readers. He keeps oral features, such as repetition, but adapts certain folk motifs and stylistic patterns to the target culture. His text displays literary conventions prevailing at the time it was published, such as the use of a highly literary register. Ciampoli's translation was not very successful, though, and subsequent translators did not even mention it in their work. Although he probably wished to reach a broader audience, he often introduced foreignising elements which might create a distance between the readers and his text. Meriggi's translation, instead, follows a philological approach, keeping close to the original: it seems to serve as a complement to his introductory chapters on the meanings of byliny. Oral features are all rendered accurately, even when this might create an awkward effect.

By virtue of their reciprocal links, translations are a collective phenomenon (Lambert 1979:9); thus, Saronne and Danil'chenko's version establishes a sort of intertextual relation with Meriggi's: the authors mention the scholar's translation in few passages of their introduction in order to criticise some of his solutions. They clearly strive to distance themselves from this previous version, addressing their text to a wider public. However, they also make an effort to preserve oral devices such as formulas and repetitions. These, though, are rendered with different purposes: Saronne and Danil'chenko, and Saronne and Moroni use repetition even when this does not show up in the original, trying to insert the frozen orality of the transcription in a literary dimension. Meriggi retains this feature only when it appears in the source text.

Marginalised oral transcribed texts such as byliny encourage foreignising translations, since their intertextual framework is not accessible to the target audience, and translators may adapt the frozen orality of the transcription within the framework of a literary written text. Thus, the frozenness of orality is still more apparent in the translation. In conclusion, although the main aim is to preserve oral features, one has to be conscious that this orality will be always different from the original performance, turning into a double-frozen orality, where an encounter of oral and written dimension occurs.

References

Astakhova, Anna Mikhaylovna (1938-1951) *Byliny Severa.* Moscow-Leningrad: AN SSSR.

Bazanov, Vasilii Grigor'evich (1940) *Byliny P. I. Ryabinina-Andreeva.* Petrozavodsk: Kargosizdat.

Bucholtz, Mary (2000) "The Politics of Transcription". *Journal of Pragmatics* 32:10, 1439-1465.

Chadwick, Hector Munro/Chadwick, Norah Kershaw (1936/1986) *The Growth of Literature.* Vol. 2. Cambridge: Cambridge University Press.

Ciampoli, Domenico (1911) *Poesia Russa: Byline, Canti Storici, Canto d'Igor.* Lanciano: Carabba Editore.

Danilov, Kirsha (1804/1958) *Drevnye rossiyskie stikhotvoreniya sobrannye Kirsheyu Danilovym.* Moscow-Leningrad: Literaturnye pamyatniki.

Finnegan, Ruth (1977/1992) *Oral Poetry. Its Nature, Significance and Social Context.* Bloomington: Indiana University Press.

Foley, John Miles (1995) *The Singer of Tales in Performance.* Bloomington: Indiana University Press.

Gil'ferding, Aleksandr Fedorovich (1873/1949-1951) *Onezhskie Byliny, Zapisannye A. F. Gil'ferdingom Letom 1871 goda.* Moscow-Leningrad: AN SSSR.

Grigor'ev, Aleksandr Dmitrievich (1899-1901/2002-03) *Arkhangel'skie Byliny i Istoricheskie Pesni, Sobrannye A. D. Grigor'evym v 1899-1901 gg. s Napevami, Zapisannymi Posredstvom Fonografom.* St. Petersburg: Tropa Troyanova.

Ivanova, Tat'yana Grigor'evna (1993) "Russkie Byliny v Angliyskikh Perevodakh". *Russkiy Fol'klor* 27, 313-323.

Jakobson, Roman (1946) "On Russian Fairy Tales". In Guterman, Norbert (ed.) *Russian Fairy Tales (Selected from Afanas'ev's Collection).* London-New York: Routledge, 631-651.

Jakobson, Roman (1959/2004) "On Linguistic Aspects of Translation". In Venuti, Lawrence (ed.) *The Translation Studies Reader.* London-New York: Routledge, 138-143.

Jakobson, Roman (1966) "Grammatical Parallelism and its Russian Facet". *Language* 42:2, 399-429.

Kireevskiy, Petr Vasil'evich (1860-1874) *Pesni, Sobrannye P. V. Kireevskim.* Moscow: Obshchestvo lyubiteley rossiyskoy slovesnosti.

Lambert, José (1979) "Introduction". In Hoffmann, Ernst Theodor Amadeus, *Contes fantastiques.* Vol. 1. Paris: Garnier-Flammarion, 7-25.

Lipets, Rakhil' Solomonovna (1969) *Epos i Drevnyaya Rus'.* Moscow: Nauka.

Lo Gatto, Ettore (1957) *Le più belle pagine della letteratura russa.* Milano: Nuova Accademia Editrice.

Lord, Albert Bates (1960/2003) *The Singer of Tales.* Cambridge: Harvard University Press.

Markov, Aleksey Vladimirovich (1901) *Belomorskie Byliny, Zapisannye A. Markovym.* Moscow: A. Levenson.

Meriggi, Bruno (1974) *Le byline: Canti popolari russi.* Milano: Accademia.

Moroni, Elisa (2010) "Between Orality and Literacy: Parallelism and Repetition in Russian Folk Epics and Their Challenge to Translation". In *Bergen Language and Linguistic Studies* 1, 1-28.

Muhawi, Ibrahim (2006) "Towards a Folkloristic Theory of Translation". In Hermans, Theo (ed.) *Translating Others.* Vol. 2. Manchester: St Jerome, 365-379.

Oinas, Felix J. (1978) "Russian Byliny". In Oinas, Felix J. (eds.) *Heroic Epic and Saga: An Introduction to the World's Great Folk Epics.* Bloomington: Indiana University Press, 236-256.

Ong, Walter J. (1982/1988) *Orality and Literacy. The Technologizing of the Word.* London-New York: Routledge.

O'Sullivan, Carol (2006) "Retranslating Ireland". In Hermans, Theo (ed.) *Translating Others.* Vol. 2. Manchester: St Jerome, 380-391.

Parilova, G. N./Soymonov, Aleksey Dmitrievich (1941) *Byliny Pudozhskogo Kraya.* Petrozavodsk: Gosizdat K-F SSR.

Rybnikov, Pavel Nikolaevich (1861-1867/1989-1991). *Pesni, Sobrannye P. N. Rybnikovym.* Petrozavodsk: Kareliya.

Saronne, Edgardo Tito/Danil'chenko, Kamilla Fedorovna (1997) *Giganti, incantatori e draghi.* Milano: Luni editrice.

Saronne, Edgardo Tito/Moroni, Elisa (2010) *L'epos dei mercanti. Byline russe del ciclo di Novgorod.* Roma: Carocci.

Scandura, Claudia (2002) *Letteratura russa in Italia. Un secolo di traduzioni.* Roma: Bulzoni editore.

Skaftymov, Aleksandr Pavlovich (1924) *Poetika i Genezis Bylin. Ocherki.* Moscow-Saratov: V. Z. Yaksanov.

Sokolov, Yurii Matveevich/Chicherov, Vladimir Ivanovich (1948) *Onezhskie Byliny.* Moscow: Gosudarstvennyy literaturnyy muzey.

Terras, Victor (1985) *Handbook of Russian Literature.* New Haven: Yale University Press.

Todorov, Tzvetan (1984) *Mikhail Bakhtin. The Dialogical Principle.* Minneapolis: The University of Minnesota Press.

Tymoczko, Maria (1995) "The Metonymics of Translating Marginalized Texts". *Comparative Literature* 47:1, 11-24.

Tymoczko, Maria (1999) *Translation in a Postcolonial Context. Early Irish Literature in English Translation.* Manchester: St Jerome.

Webster, Anthony K. (2008) "Running Again, Roasting Again, Touching Again: on Repetition, Heightened Affective Expressivity, and the Utility of the Notion of Linguaculture in Navajo and Beyond". *Journal of American Folklore* 121:482, 441-472.

Giovanna Di Pietro

University of Bari 'Aldo Moro', Italy

More Than Words: A Study of Paralinguistic and Kinesic Features of Humour in Dubbed Sitcoms

This paper presents the status of my ongoing research work, whose main objective is to analyse the interplay between verbal and nonverbal communication in the creation of humour within the field of audiovisual translation from English into Italian. The paper will report on the preliminary findings obtained from the multimodal analysis of the first episode of the contemporary US sitcom *How I Met Your Mother (HIMYM)* and its dubbed Italian translations, in order to investigate the elusive link between what is said and how it is said: not only the words uttered, but the way in which they are pronounced, the sounds and images accompanying them and the facial and bodily movements emphasising them.

Keywords: audiovisual translation, dubbing, nonverbal communication, humour, English to Italian

Introduction

This paper draws on the author's ongoing research into the multimodal analysis of three contemporary US sitcoms (*Scrubs*, *How I Met Your Mother*, *The Big Bang Theory*) and their dubbed Italian versions (*Scrubs – Medici Ai Primi Ferri*, *… E Alla Fine Arriva Mamma*, *The Big Bang Theory*). Such analysis pursues the aim of studying the interplay between verbal and nonverbal communication in the creation of original and translated humour. This paper will focus only on the *How I Met Your Mother* (*HIMYM*) pilot episode and its dubbed Italian version.

Situation comedies abound with humorous discourse whose verbal and visual features co-pattern to produce meaning multiplicatively with sound effects, music and camera action. Multimodal analysis tools (Kress/van Leeuwen 1996; van Leeuwen 1999; Taylor 2003; Baldry/Thibault 2005) and prosodic transcription models (Bonsignori 2009) are extremely useful in the attempt to study the dynamics of verbally- and nonverbally-expressed humour as they allow us to integrate incongruity[1] and superiority theories.[2] By employing such methodology, we can explore the ways in which humour is globally achieved in audiovisual texts through the interrelation between verbal and nonverbal meaning-making resources. Nonverbal Communication Studies (Ekman/Friesen 1969, 1972; McNeill 1992; Kendon 2004; Poyatos 2002a, b, c, 2008) acquire a paramount relevance when analysing audiovisual texts, which are characterised by a complex semiotic unit where multi-channel and multi-code communication types intertwine (Delabastita 1989).

The acoustic and visual channels convey their messages in an audiovisual text by means of verbal and nonverbal codes. Most research works concerning the study of humour within the field of audiovisual translation focus on the former and are usually based on the analysis of the written transcript of the film/TV series involved (e.g. Franco 1991; Goris 1991, 1993; Chiaro 1992, 2000; Baccolini/Bollettieri Bosinelli/Gavioli 1994; Heiss/Bollettieri Bosinelli 1996; Bollettieri Bosinelli et al. 2000; Pérez-Gonzalez 2007; Freddi/Pavesi 2009; Martínez Sierra 2009). The author's intention is to reach a broader understanding of the mechanisms underlying the production of humour beyond the verbal level by means of a multimodal analysis seeing the verbal and the nonverbal code in their indissoluble interaction.

Humour in original and dubbed sitcoms

Situation comedy is produced with the intent of creating laughter and amusing the audience. The blend of visual and acoustic data, which characterises it, succeeds in the purpose of entertaining the viewers via a series of humorous situations depicting a rather fixed scenario: the narration of real people's lives in real situations and as portraying everyday routine in realistic settings that are familiar to the audience. The fortune of a sitcom depends on the possibility for its viewers to relate to the stories it depicts:

---

1 According to Attardo (1994), for a text to be humorous, there must be a "script opposition", i.e. a contrast between two overlapping semantic scripts producing an effect of incongruity or contradicting what is expected in some given circumstances.

2 Superiority can be defined as a "happiness increment" and a "heightened self-esteem" (La Fave/Haddad/Maesen 1976:86, qtd. in Vandaele 2002:224). Differently from incongruity, which is a cognitive process, superiority has a social dimension, since "being superior is always being superior to someone" (Vandaele 2002:225). See Vandaele for an integrated approach to incongruity and superiority theories of humour (ibid.:221).

> most situation comedy is realist in characters, settings, stories, and language. By looking at the ways in which sit-com presents us with 'real' people in 'real' situations we can begin to see how they fit into our picture of the society we live in. (Bowes 1990:128)

A sitcom also owes its success to the focal role of characters, the way they react to each other in the ongoing interaction between them and in the humorous situation that said interaction produces. Wolfe (2003:29) places more emphasis on the overall situation than on the mere verbal component: "it is not a half-hour of one-liners and gags strung together. The laughs should come from the situation and the way the characters behave in that situation". Such context necessarily entails an interplay between verbal and nonverbal communication, whose humorous intent is sustained by the use of canned laughter,[3] an extradiegetic paralinguistic feature which prompts the viewer to laugh, thus spurring his/her positive reaction and making him/her feel included in the scene.

> Since canned laughter signals the intended humorous moments of a programme, it can be interpreted as an objective humour-spotting device:
> US television sitcoms tend to be based on an attempt to establish a regularity of humorous illocutionary effects emphasised by the subsequent emission of canned laughter, and it is quite common to come across the use of this punning resource when watching an episode. (Sanderson 2009:127)

Humour in sitcoms seems to reside in a precarious balance between the written and the oral pole, a gray area which crosses the boundaries between planned discourse and the illusion of spontaneity. Like all fictional audiovisual texts "written to be spoken as if not written" (Gregory 1967:192), sitcoms stand on a fine line between realism and fiction, and their success is largely determined by the "suspension of disbelief" they aim at provoking in their audience. The tighter the link between words and actions, the more realistic a sitcom will be, and the more enjoyable. What happens when a sitcom is dubbed, then? Is this balance retained or modified, or even broken?

The language-paralanguage-kinesics triad cannot be translated in each of its parts during the dubbing process. While language and paralanguage can cross linguistic borders, kinesics remains unaltered, as the original images of the audiovisual product cannot undergo any modifications. The aim of this

---

[3] Also known as "laugh track" or "added laughter", and indicated as "CL" in the multimodal analysis (see "Nonverbal communication: a multimodal analysis" section and Appendix).

paper is to discuss if and how the cohesion between (translated) language, (translated) paralanguage and (original) kinesics in the TT is in any way similar or different from the original cohesion between language, paralanguage and kinesics in the ST, and what consequences a potential difference may bring to the vehiculation of humour in the sitcom.

On the basis of the author's multimodal analysis of the sitcom episode in its original and dubbed version, this paper identifies three dominant tendencies shaping the interplay between verbal and nonverbal codes in the creation of humour at an interlinguistic level:

1. kinesics and paralanguage *reinforcing* verbal language;
2. kinesics and paralanguage *contradicting* verbal language;
3. kinesics *contradicting* paralanguage.

It also points out the tendency of the dubbed version to bring about modifications concerning:

1 the original paralinguistic features;
2. the original meanings expressed by the verbal language;
3. the interplay between paralinguistic and kinesic features.

As a consequence of such modifications, the dubbed sitcom will present some differences in the rendition of humour at a verbal and nonverbal level.

How I Met Your Mother: an overview

HIMYM is an US-American sitcom created by Craig Thomas and Carter Bays that premiered on CBS in 2005. In Italy, its dubbed version aired on Italia 1 and Joi in 2008. The framing device is construed as a retrospective narration; in 2030, Ted Mosby (Josh Radnor), a middle-aged man whose face is never shown throughout the series, recounts to his teenage son and daughter the events that led him to meet their mother (whose face is never shown either).

The pilot episode gives the narration a start in 2005 with Ted, a single, 27-year-old architect living with his two best friends from college, Marshall Eriksen (Jason Segel), a law student, and Lily Aldrin (Alyson Hannigan), a kindergarten teacher, who have been dating for nine years when Marshall proposes. Their engagement causes Ted to think about finding his soulmate, much to the disapproval of his self-appointed best friend and cynical womaniser Barney Stinson (Neil Patrick Harris), who invites him to enjoy life by having random liaisons. After a failed attempt on Ted's part to ask out Yasmine, a Lebanese girl who is already dating Carl, bartender at Mac Laren's, Ted falls victim of a *coup de foudre* for a young Canadian reporter, Robin Scherbatsky (Cobie Smulders), to whom he inadvertently discloses his feelings twice that very night, thus scaring her away. Throughout the episode, Future Ted lets his children think that Robin is the "mother" by avoiding mentioning her name until the end of the episode, when he unexpectedly reveals that she is not the one after referring to her as their "Aunt Robin".

The following sections will analyse the verbal and nonverbal communication features of the original and translated *HIMYM* episode, with a focus on humour.

Nonverbal communication: a multimodal analysis

Following Poyatos's terminology, we distinguish between language and nonverbal communication, the latter being composed of paralanguage, which is strictly acoustic (Ladd 1996; Brazil 1997; Crystal 1997; Halliday 2000), and kinesics, which is mainly visual, but can sometimes be visual-acoustic, as in the case of phonokinesics (Poyatos 2002b:211), visual-acoustic-tactile, as in the case of haptics (Poyatos 2002a:198-225), or kinaesthetic.

My multimodal analysis of the *HIMYM* episode is based on an integrated methodological approach deriving from Poyatos's (2002a, b, c) paralinguistic taxonomy, which consists of primary features (pitch, loudness, rhythm, tempo, syllabic duration, resonance, timbre and intonation), qualifiers (laryngeal/pharyngeal control), alternants (onomatopoeias, hesitators, etc.) and differentiators (laughing, shouting, crying, etc.). Unlike Poyatos, who does not account for canned laughter, we include the canned laughter in the latter category, since we consider it as a paralinguistic feature in its own right and, as such, worth analysing. As for kinesics, we follow Ekman and Friesen's (1969; 1972) taxonomy, which identifies five categories of kinesic gestures: emblems, illustrators (beat gestures, deictics, kinetographs, ideographs, pictographs, rhythmic movements, emblematic movements), affect displays, regulators and adaptors.

The orthographic transcription[4] of both kinesics and paralanguage is adapted from Bonsignori (2009) and AIDAC's transcription notes,[5] with the addition of kinesic descriptions and screenshots of the episode indicating kinesic action and eye gaze orientation by means of vectorial arrows.

The language-paralanguage-kinesics triad and humour

Figure 1 shows an emblem[6] used as a greeting gesture with humorous results. In this scene, Ted has just learnt that Yasmine, the girl he is interested in, has a boyfriend, Carl, the bartender. Camera action shifts to get a close-up of Carl, who immediately confirms the bad news by giving Ted a very eloquent look which works as a nonverbal face-threatening act serving the purpose of triggering a humorous effect. Ted, the butt of the joke, therefore attempts a face-saving act: he tries to conceal his embarrassment and "play cool" by waving at Carl, but his speaking face reveals what his body language tries to conceal; his embarrassment shows as he tilts his head down and smiles awkwardly with a disengaged gaze in order to avoid further eye contact with Yasmine and Carl, which proves Ted's feeling of inferiority. The paralinguistic features of the ST and the TT in Table 1 co-pattern with kinesics to create such embarrassing situation. Nevertheless, ST and TT seem to diverge in terms of paralanguage, since the former shows a sincerely sorry Yasmine – whose sympathy is conveyed by hesitators and by a surprised tone, while the latter depicts a more assertive and even aggressive behaviour on her part, thus modifying the social relationship between her and Ted in an unequal way, the former becoming superior to the latter. Ted, in turn, is more assertive in the ST, since he tries to dissimulate his

---

[4] See Appendix for a list of conventions in the prosodic transcription.

[5] AIDAC (Associazione Italiana Dialoghisti-Adattatori Cinetelevisivi) is the Italian Association of Dialogue Adapters for Dubbed Audiovisual Products.

[6] Emblems are culture-specific gestures with a direct verbal translation, e.g. the Okay hand signal, made by connecting the thumb and forefinger in a circle and holding the other fingers straight. Problems may arise when emblems appear in an audiovisual product that has to be dubbed in a foreign language, especially if the specific meanings they convey in the source language/culture are not expressed by the same gesture in the target language/culture. It suffices to think about the "loser" hand signal (made by extending the thumb and forefinger to resemble the letter L), of capital significance to any US-American viewer but incomprehensible to many Italian speakers. This aspect becomes of crucial importance when analysing visual humour in dubbed sitcoms, since the media-based constraint that leaves the visual channel unchanged through the translation process restricts the translator's freedom to circumvent the presence of potentially incomprehensible kinesic signs.

feeling of embarrassment via the greeting gesture accompanied by paralinguistic features conveying affected nonchalance, while the awkward laughter, the frightened gasp and the stuttering words in the TT declare Ted's weakness. In this case, kinesics and paralanguage reinforce verbal language in the ST, but they contradict it in the TT in virtue of a modified paralinguistic behaviour which does not co-pattern anymore with kinesics, with a consequent shift in the rendition of humour that makes Ted seem (and sound) weaker than he is.

Figure 1: Ted's emblem (screenshot)

CHAR-ACTER	ST: VERBAL LANGUAGE	TT: VERBAL LANGUAGE	ST: PARA-LANGUAGE	TT: PARA-LANGUAGE	KINESICS
YAS.	I'm **sorry**… C-Carl's my **boyfriend**! //	Ah, mi dispiace… Carl è il mio ragazzo. //	Caught off guard: hesitations, staccato rhythm, slow tempo; surprise: rising tone	Less emotionally charged reply: calm tone, slightly defiant	Surprised, clueless about how to reply: frowns, lowers head and chest, points to bartender.
CARL					Gives him a sarcastic "surprise!" look
TED			(CL)	Uncomf. laughter (CL)	Ted mouths an ironic "ok" , embarrassed smile, waves at him

TED (to Carl)	'Sup, Carl?	Ah-ah--Va tutto bene, Carl?	Throaty voice: simulating nonchalance (CL)	Gasps (CL)	Emblem: snaps his fingers and points at him + open-mouthed smile, then disengaged gaze: head tilted down, embarrassed smile

Table 1: Ted's emblem (script)

Deictics[7] are an inexhaustible source of humour in HIMYM, as seen in Figure 2 and Table 2. In a flashback showing the first time Ted and Barney met, the latter interjects a conversation between Ted and two people, who are total strangers to him, and joins them. Humour stems from Barney's abrupt intrusion in Ted's proxemic space as well as in his private conversation, but also from the incongruity between the semantic content of information – the embarrassing circumstances of their first encounter, especially if recalled in front of other people – and the paralinguistic/kinesic cues – the nonchalant, referential tone of Barney's utterance "we met at the urinal" (which interestingly enough is translated with humorous intentions in a more vulgar way in Italian by the sentence "ci siamo visti al cesso", meaning "we saw each other in the can"), duplicated by the deictic gesture and paired with his self-confident and amicable manners. Barney's paralinguistic features (his assertive tone) and kinesics (his way of sitting comfortably with legs crossed resting on the booth, his arm around Ted, the intimate proxemic space between them) seem to suggest that the two are close friends while they hardly know each other, to the point that Barney has to remind Ted when and where they met. His crossed legs, his relaxed look reveal an exaggeratedly self-confident Barney who continues talking while resting his hand on Ted's shoulder and addresses him in a direct way, even calling him by his first name. It is Ted's puzzled face expression, accompanied by a moment of silence (/), which calls for Barney's explanation, making the viewers laugh at the incongruous situation. In this case, nonverbal communication contradicts verbal language in both ST and TT. The latter accentuates the incongruity by adding an extra dialogue cue ("E' quello che ho visto", meaning "that's what I saw") to clarify that Ted is talking to someone else before Barney steps in.

---

[7] By "deictics", I refer to pointing movements which indicate objects, people or events in the surrounding environment.

Figure 2: Barney's deictic (screenshot)

CHAR-ACTER	ST: VERBAL LANGUAGE	TT: VERBAL LANGUAGE	ST: PARA-LANGUAGE	TT: PARA-LANGUAGE	KINESICS
TED and BARN.					Ted is talking to another couple; Barney randomly joins them and interrupts
TED		TED: E' quello che ho visto!			
BARN.	Ted, I'm gonna **teach** you **how to live**. /	Ted, io ti insegnerò come fare a vivere. /	(CL) Declarative tone	(CL) declarative tone	Sits next to him, puts his legs on the booth in front of him and crosses them, pats him on the shoulder, rests his hand there
TED					Looks clueless about who his interlocutor is
BARN.	Barney. We… met at the urinal.	Barney. Ci siamo visti al cesso.	(CL)	(CL)	Nods + points at bathroom offscreen with hand holding a bottle of beer. Frowns, as if he were surprised at Ted not recognising him
TED	Oh, right. Hi.	Oh, giusto. +Ciao*.	Slow tempo, staccato rhythm: confused	Slow tempo, staccato rhythm: confused	Looks at Barney, nods along, stares at void in front of him + frowns, puzzled.

Table 2: Barney's deictic (script)

Impressions are a common source of humour in *HIMYM*, as showed in Figure 3, where Marshall is moving and talking like a robot to cheer about

Ted's date with his newfound "future wife" Robin. Marshall's utterance, pronounced with a metallic voice in a monotonous intonation and with a staccato rhythm (see Table 3), is strengthened by his jerky kinetographs.[8] Nonverbal communication reinforces verbal language here; nonetheless, the TT presents a modification in the rendition of the verbal dialogue (which becomes "Oh, she's the one! I give you my little robot's word", thus making the reference to the robot explicit while eliminating the rhyme) and of the paralinguistic features, which humanise Marshall's voice and alter the rhythm and tempo of the sentence by eliminating its co-deployment with the staccato kinesic movements, with significant reverberations on the humorous effect. The canned laughter, however, has been intensified in length and frequency in the TT; this is a recurring translational behaviour in *HIMYM*, probably used as a compensation strategy whenever a humorous moment has diminished its original efficacy in the passage from SL to TT in order to make up for this loss by stimulating the audience to laugh harder about something that is not so funny *per se* anymore.

Figure 3: Marshall's kinetographs (screenshot)

CHAR-ACTER	**ST: VERBAL LANGUAGE**	**TT: VERBAL LANGUAGE**	**ST: PARA-LANGUAGE**	**TT: PARA-LANGUAGE**	**KINESICS**
MARSH.	Oh, IT IS **ON**!	Oh, è quella **giusta**!	enthusiastic	enthusiastic	Triumphant smile.
	It is **on-till-the-break-of-dawn**.	E' quella giusta… parola di robottino!*****.	(CL) imitates robot: metallic voice, level tone	(CL)+ Enthusiastic voice: high pitch, trembling voice, falling tone	Imitates robot: stiff movements, hands and arms moving slowly up and down with alternating movements

Table 3: Marshall's kinetographs (script)

8 Kinetographs are gestures depicting a body movement.

Ideographic movements[9] showing thought process can produce humour, as Figure 4 and Table 4 prove. In this scene, Ted has rushed into declaring his feelings for Robin twice and, after being politely rejected by her, reacts by being self-ironic about his failed attempt to win her heart. His utterance is a face-saving act emphasised by an ideographic movement (Ted's disengaged gaze) and accompanied by a paralinguistic feature (a pause in his flow of speech) which aim at giving him some time to ponder his next move and create the suspense before his "eccentric" jab line, which serves the purpose of attenuating his inferior position and switching from the "laughed at" to the one "laughing with", as a nonverbal bonding agent with Robin making up for his verbal *défaillance*. Interestingly, the TT eliminates the presence of the canned laughter, a choice which, if coupled with a more emotively charged utterance expressing fear and embarrassment, seems to suggest an intention on the translator's part to reinterpret the whole scene in a more serious key, thus annihilating any trace of humour. In this case, nonverbal communication reinforces verbal language, but canned laughter undergoes a radical change in the TT.

Figure 4: Ted's ideographs (screenshot)

CHAR-ACTER	ST: VERBAL LANGUAGE	TT: VERBAL LANGUAGE	ST: PARA-LANGUAGE	TT: PARA-LANGUAGE	KINESICS
TED	So, when you tell this story to your friends, could you avoid the word…"**psycho**"? I prefer… "**eccentric**".	Se racconterai questa storia ai tuoi amici, potrai evitare la parola "psico… **patico**"? Preferirei… "**eccentrico**".	Self-ironic: pretending nonchalance (CL)	Higher pitch than in ST, trembling voice No(CL)	Self-ironic: looks seriously at her Disengaged gaze, squints: mental process Tilts head towards Robin + up, arches eyebrows + half-smile

Table 4: Ted's ideographs (script)

[9] Ideographic movements are "[m]ovements which sketch a path or direction of thought, tracing the itinerary of a logical journey" (Ekman/Friesen 1969:68).

A particular example of rhythmic movements[10] with humorous purposes is given in Figure 5 and Table 5 by Barney, who attempts a face-threatening act to Ted's detriment by mocking him after his brief encounter with Robin because he thinks that she refused his attentions. The rhythm of his sarcastic utterance is modulated visually and acoustically by means of a converging kinesic and paralinguistic behaviour aiming at emphasising his voluntary double pause to better savour the incoming mockery directed at Ted, who retorts with an equally successful face-saving kinesic behaviour expressed via a deictic gesture showing him Robin's business card, as if to imply that she is interested in seeing him again. Barney's verbal aggression is supported by diverging, but equally effective paralinguistic features in the ST and the TT: the rough voice becomes trembling in the translated text, with no substantial change in the humorous effect.

Figure 5: Barney's rhythmic gestures (screenshot)

CHAR-ACTER	ST: VERBAL LANGUAGE	TT: VERBAL LANGUAGE	ST: PARA-LANGUAGE	TT: PARA-LANGUAGE	KINESICS
BARN.	(starts OS) **Dee**—wait for it—**niiied**!	(starts OS) **Ri**-piccola pausa-**fiutato**!	Rough voice on focus words + drawling syllabic duration laughter	High pitch + trembling voice on focus words +Laughing*	makes a halt signal with his hands as to say "wait for it", then moves them forward in a wavy way

[10] Rhythmic movements are movements depicting the rhythm of an event.

	Deniiied!	+**Rifiutaaato***!	(CL) Laughter	(CL) Laughter	points twice at him + mocking smile
TED	We're going **out** tomorrow night.	Usciamo insieme domani sera.	Higher pitch on focus word, assertive tone	Singsong intonation: mocking tone	shows Robin's business card with an amused smile

Table 5: Barney's rhythmic gestures (script)

Finally, Figure 6 and Table 6 show another face-threatening attempt (this time a successful one) via an emblematic gesture[11] made by Barney, who mocks Ted's lack of courage as he delayed action with Robin while waiting in vain for "the signal" by means of a particularly bitter sarcastic remark, which is made even more poignant by the joint use of *ad hoc* paralinguistic and kinesic behaviour: his eyelashes batting intermittently and his words, uttered with a drawling syllabic duration and with a staccato rhythm voiced monotonously, add to the overall humorous effect. In the TT, the aggressive charge in Barney's words is strengthened by the use of a more assertive tone (with no hesitations and repetitions) and by a longer articulation of the syllables, as if to further indulge in his ruthless mockery.

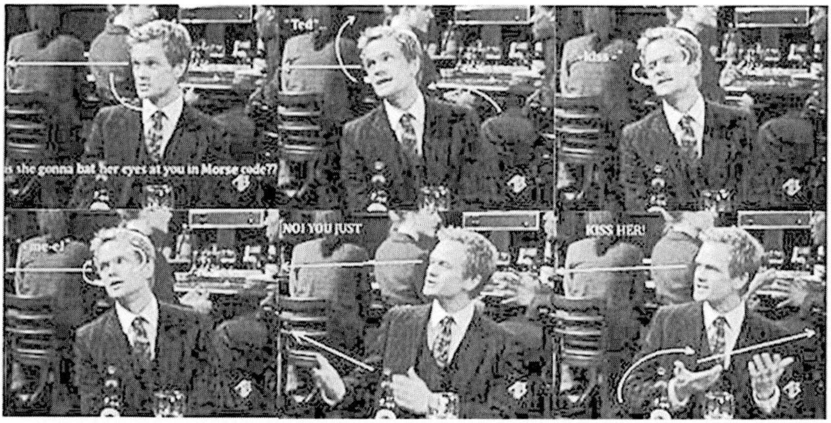

Figure 6: Barney's emblematic gestures (screenshot)

[11] Emblematic gestures "illustrate a verbal statement, either repeating or substituting for a word or phrase" (Ekman/Friesen 1972:360).

CHARACTER	ST: VERBAL LANGUAGE	TT: VERBAL LANGUAGE	ST: PARA-LANGUAGE	TT: PARA-LANGUAGE	KINESICS
BARN.	What, is she gonna--is she gonna **bat** her eyes at you in **Morse** code??	Ma cosa doveva fare? Sbattere gli occhi facendo l'alfabeto Morse??	Unbelieving + amused, stutters	Reproachful	
	"**TED**…"				
	"**Kiss mee**!"	"**Teed**…"			
		"**Baa-cia-mii**!"	Ridiculous voice with monotonous intonation	Ridiculous voice with monotonous intonation, drawling syllabic duration	bats eyes bats eyes again
	—**NO**! YOU JUST **KISS** HER!	—**NO**! **TU** dovevi baciare lei!	Mocking (CL)	Reproachful (CL)	mocking smile, deictics: points to him and outwards

Table 6: Barney's emblematic gestures (script)

An example of a regulator[12] employed with a humorous intent is showed in Figure 7 and Table 7, where Barney is deliberately ignoring Ted as he rambles on in an endless stream of whiny words about him being almost thirty and still unmarried, but pretends to be listening to him by nodding along, while all he is really interested in is trying to understand how the bartender could get together with a Lebanese girl, an aim he has not reached yet despite his elegant (and, according to him, irresistible) suits. Two parallel discourses intermingle, each one brought about by a single interlocutor living, talking and acting in his own little bubble. In this scene, nonverbal communication contradicts verbal language with humorous results; in the TT, Ted and Barney's mutual indifference is accentuated by the latter cutting off the former twice, the first time ignoring him completely, the second time pretending to keep the conversation going by nodding, although his disinterest transpires from the fast tempo and the level tone of his "exactly", which functions as a mere backchannel.

[12] Regulators are movements "which maintain and regulate the back-and-forth nature of speaking and listening between the interactants" (Ekman/Friesen 1969:82).

Figure 7: Barney's regulator (screenshot)

CHAR-ACTER	ST: VERBAL LANGUAGE	TT: VERBAL LANGUAGE	ST: PARA-LANGUAGE	TT: PARA-LANGUAGE	KINESICS
TED	Why am I +freaking out* all of a sudden? This is crazy! I'm not ready to settle down!	Chissà perchè mi faccio di questi problemi! E' assurdo! Io non sono pronto ad +accasarmi*!	+laughing nervously*	Serious tone	Nervous smile, emphatic beat gestures, eyes wide open + arched eyebrows on focus words
BARN.	How does Carl land a **Lebanese** girl?	+Dove* l'ha **trovata** Carl una ragazza egiziana?	Pondering: falling tone (CL)	Skeptical: falling-rising tone (CL)	Ignoring Ted. Looks at Carl, frowns, shakes head
TED	Plan has always been… "don't even **think** about it till you're thirty."	Io al matrimonio non dovevo pensarci fino ai +**trenta***!	Staccato rhythm, higher pitch and loudness on focus word for emphasis	Angry	Wide open eyes + arched eyebrows on focus word + hand moving horizontally from left to right (kinetograph to sweep that thought away)
BARN.	Exactly!	+Proprio* così!	fast tempo, level tone	fast tempo, level tone	turns his head towards Ted to pretend he is listening, but still with his back facing him,

	The guy doesn't even own a **suit**!	E non porta nemmeno la **giacca**!	irritated: rising pitch and loudness (CL)	clueless (CL)	turning his head again to look at Carl, frowning

Table 7: Barney's regulator (script)

A similar situation occurs in Figure 8 and Table 8, where Lily reproaches Ted for not making a move on Robin: while her kinesic behaviour seems to suggest sincere sympathy (with the pity smile and the head-bobble), her sarcasm transpires from the words uttered and the paralinguistic features emphasising their aggressive force. In this case, kinesics and paralanguage contradict one another, both in the ST and in the TT, although the latter employs a euphemistic paraphrase ("te la facevi sotto e hai rifiutato", meaning "you soiled your pants and called it quits") to avoid the expletive "b…h", with a consequent diminution in the face-threatening charge of Lily's utterance. An overtly sarcastic tone is used to compensate for the minced verbal aggression.

Figure 8: Lily's regulator (screenshot)

CHAR-ACTER	ST: VERBAL LANGUAGE	TT: VERBAL LANGUAGE	ST: PARA-LANGUAGE	TT: PARA-LANGUAGE	KINESICS
TED	Look, this woman could be my future **wife**; I want our first kiss to be **amazing**.	Potrebbe essere la mia futura **moglie**! Il primo bacio dovrebbe essere **indimenticabi-le**!	Emphatic: fast tempo	Emphatic: fast tempo	Engaged gaze, serious face

LILY	Aww, Ted, that is so **sweet**! So you **chickened out** like a little **b…h**!	Ooh, Ted, ma quanto sei stato **cariiino**! Quindi tu te la facevi sotto e hai rinunciato!	in a falsely soft, cuddly voice (CL)	in an overtly contemptuous, sarcastic voice (CL)	Smiles + nods nods rhythmically + bobbles head back, arches eyebrows

Table 8: Lily's regulator (script)

Adaptors[13] vehiculate humour on several occasions in *HIMYM*, as showed in Figure 9 and Table 9. In this scene, humour stems from baffled expectations created in the viewers thanks to a joint effort of camera action, paralinguistic features and kinesic behaviour. First, we see Marshall on his knees, opening a ring box and proposing – which makes us expect his fiancée to be in front of him; but immediately after, camera action moves to Ted, whose enthusiastic face and paralanguage make us understand that they are just rehearsing Marshall's proposal. The canned laughter prompts the audience's positive reaction, thus making the viewers' role shift from the butt of the joke to in-group members. As shown by the paralinguistic analysis, primary features undergo some changes during the translation process as a consequence of the dubbing actors' personal reinterpretation of their respective characters, which may diverge remarkably from the original actors' choices or natural dispositions. This may be due to various factors ranging from the dubbing director/actor's individual sensitivity, as "the director and his players have given their own perception of the characters' peculiarities of speech" (Poyatos 2008:180), to interlinguistic divergences in paralinguistically-expressed meaning. The dubbing actors are "adding from their own paralinguistic repertoires" (ibid.:181) deriving from the language/culture they belong to, which may result in different performances and convey new messages. As a result, Marshall's trembling voice and rising-falling tone in the TT express a higher degree of emotion than in the ST; at the same time, Ted's primary features in the ST – which co-pattern with kinesic action clearly showing embarrassment and disappointment – suggest that the realisation of the uncomfortable implicatures in his "you have sex on the kitchen floor" utterance backfires on him, much to his displeasure, by making him the butt of his own joke, as showed by a self-

[13] Adaptors are haptic movements where individuals touch objects (object-adaptors), their body (self-adaptors) or other people (alter-adaptors).

adaptor (Ted clapping hands as a self-ironic comment to his mental process).

In the TT, however, Ted's reaction seems to be the opposite: that laughter interrupting his flow of speech makes him become the one "laughing with", thus modifying considerably his social role within the humorous situation at issue. In this scene, kinesics and paralanguage reinforce verbal language, but the paralinguistic behaviour in the TT diverges – and eventually vehiculates different messages from – the ST, with a consequent shift in the overall rendering of humour and a mismatch between kinesics (suggesting embarrassment) and paralanguage (suggesting merriment).

Figure 9: Marshall's object-adaptor, Ted's self-adaptor (screenshot)

CHAR-ACTER	ST: VERBAL-LANGUAGE	TT: VERBAL-LANGUAGE	ST: PARA-LANGUAGE	TT: PARA-LANGUAGE	KINESICS
MARSH.	Will you **marry** me.	Vorresti sposarmi?	Falling tone (as in a statement) (CL)	trembling voice, rising-falling tone (CL)	Opens jewellery box

TED	YES, **PERFECT**! And then you're **engaged**, you pop the **champagne**! You drink a **toast**! You have sex on the kitchen **floor**…	Sì, **perfetto**! Così sarai fidanzato, stapperai lo champagne, farai un brindisi e farai sesso sul pavimento!	Fast tempo, high loudness and pitch, rising tone: enthusiasm	Fast tempo, high loudness and pitch, trembling voice: enthusiasm	Enthusiastic face, walks happily to the kitchen, points at the floor Pause: freezes with a shocked face expression imploring him with his eyes
	Don't have sex on our kitchen floor.	+No, non farlo sul pavimento*.	lower loudness and pitch, fast tempo, falling tone, throaty voice: realising (CL)	+Laughing* (CL)	

Table 9: Marshall's object-adaptor, Ted's self-adaptor (script)

Conclusion

The multimodal analysis of the *HIMYM* pilot episode revealed that kinesics (K) and paralanguage (P) can reinforce verbal language (VL) or contradict it; also, kinesics can contradict paralanguage. Of the nine examples examined, six showed the tendency of kinesics and paralanguage to reinforce verbal language (see Figures/Tables 1, 3, 4, 5, 6, 9), two showed the tendency of kinesics and paralanguage to contradict verbal language (Figures/Tables 2, 7), one showed how kinesics can contradict paralanguage (Figure/Table 8) in the ST, while four showed the first tendency (Figures/Tables 3, 4, 5, 6), three the second (Figures/Tables 1, 2, 7), three the third (Figures/Tables 1, 8, 9) in the TT. Figure 10 shows graphically the changes in such tendencies between ST and TT.

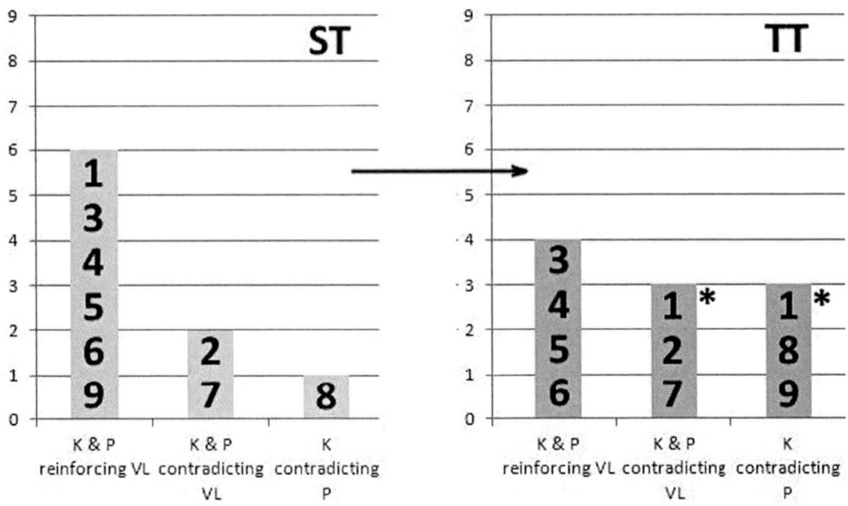

* multiple occurrences

Figure 10: Interplay between language, paralanguage and kinesics in ST and TT

The results of the analysis reveal paralanguage as the linguistic category undergoing the most radical changes during the translation process, probably as a consequence of the Italian dubbing actors' penchant for reinterpreting their roles in a creative way. More *pathos* occasionally leads to an over-expressive acting style which modifies the original balance between kinesics, paralanguage and verbal language as it was intended in the ST. Such alteration of cohesion in the TT has inevitable reverberations on the humorous effect, which tends to weaken or even collapse in some cases (e.g. Figure/Table 3). When this happens, a repair strategy is employed; humour is restored *ab externo* through the intensification of the canned laughter.

A tendency of the dubbed version to bring about modifications concerning paralinguistic features, verbal content and the interplay between paralinguistic and kinesic features was also pointed out. Of the nine examples examined, eight showed the first tendency (Figures/Tables 1, 3, 4, 5, 6, 7, 8, 9), three the second (Figures/Tables 2, 3, 8), two the third (Figures/Tables 1, 9). Figure 11 shows graphically such tendencies.

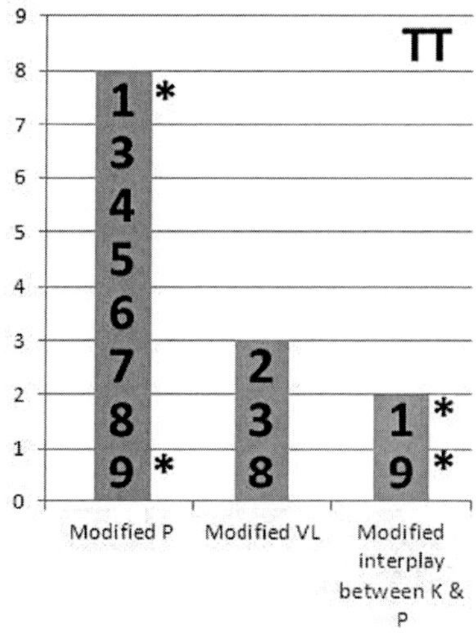

* multiple occurrences

Figure 11: Modifications concerning paralanguage, verbal language and interplay between paralanguage and kinesics in the TT

The Italian adaptation of the episode seems to have produced mixed results, with a marked tendency towards the alteration of paralinguistic features. In particular, the presence and intensity of alternants and differentiators seems to be more frequent in the TT, probably as a compensatory strategy to make up for the overall foreignness of the actors' kinesic behaviour, which is culture-specific and may consequently be unfamiliar to the target audience,[14] but also as a reflection of the different ways in which the SL and the TL express feelings and emotions. US-English tends to be a concise and elliptic language, unlike Italian, whose prolixity and expressiveness are self-evident; while for US-American speakers actions (and movements) speak for themselves in various circumstances, which leads them to use kinesics only (e.g. the reaction to a joke or some shocking news is often expressed solely through facial gestures and/or eye gaze), Italians need to voice their

[14] There are innumerable examples of culture-bound kinesic signs in this sitcom. In *HIMYM* season 1, episode 8, for instance, Barney makes a sly joke, then smiles while touching the tip of his nose with his index finger and pointing at his interlocutor with his other hand's index finger, meaning "you got it". This gesture, easily understandable to any US-American viewer, is doomed to remain a visual enigma to the Italian audience unless explained verbally or paralinguistically.

thoughts, feelings and emotions via paralanguage. For this reason, the Italian dubbing actors often add paralinguistic cues to originally silent reactions.

Primary features undergo considerable changes throughout the episode, as a consequence of the Italian dubbing actors' more emphatic interpretations of their respective roles, with significant consequences for the overall rendition of humour at an interlinguistic level, which results to be slanted towards the verbal/paralinguistic pole and less oriented towards a synchronic rendition of nonverbal action.

References

Attardo, Salvatore (1994) *Linguistic Theories of Humor.* Berlin-New York: Mouton de Gruyter.

Baccolini, Raffaella/Bollettieri Bosinelli, Rosa M./Gavioli, Laura (eds.) (1994) *Il doppiaggio. Trasposizioni linguistiche e culturali.* Bologna: CLUEB.

Baldry, Anthony/Thibault, Paul J. (2005) *Multimodal Transcription and Text Analysis: A Multimedia Toolkit and Coursebook.* London-New York: Equinox.

Bollettieri Bosinelli, Rosa M./Heiss, Christine/Soffritti, Marcello/Bernardini, Silvia (eds.) (2000) *La traduzione multimediale: quale traduzione per quale testo?* Bologna: CLUEB.

Bonsignori, Veronica (2009) "Transcribing Film Dialogue: From Orthographic to Prosodic Transcription". In Freddi, Maria/Pavesi, Maria (eds.) *Analysing Audiovisual Dialogue. Linguistic and Translational Insights.* Bologna: CLUEB, 185-200.

Bowes, Mick (1990) "Only When I Laugh". In Goodwin, Andrew/Whannel, Garry (eds.) *Understanding Television.* London: Routledge, 128-140.

Brazil, David (1997) *The Communicative Value of Intonation in English.* Cambridge: Cambridge University Press.

Chiaro, Delia (1992) *The Language of Jokes. Analysing Verbal Play.* London: Routledge.

Chiaro, Delia (2000) "The British Will Use Tags, Won't They? The Case of *Four Weddings and a Funeral*". In Soravia, Giulio/Taylor, Christopher (eds.) *Tradurre il cinema.* Trieste: Università degli Studi di Trieste, 27-39.

Crystal, David (1997) *The Cambridge Encyclopedia of the English Language.* Cambridge: Cambridge University Press.

Delabastita, Dirk (1989) "Translation and Mass Communication: Film and T.V. Translation as an Evidence of Cultural Dynamics". *Babel* 35:4, 193-218.

Ekman, Paul/Friesen, Wallace V. (1969) "The Repertoire of Nonverbal Behaviour. Categories, Origins, Usage and Coding". *Semiotica* 1, 49-98.

Ekman, Paul/Friesen, Wallace V. (1972) "Hand Movements". *The Journal of Communication* 22, 353-374.

Franco, Eliana P. C. (1991) *Everything You Wanted to Know About Film Translation (But Did Not Have The Chance to Ask).* Universidade Federal de Santa Catarina: Master's Dissertation.

Freddi, Maria/Pavesi, Maria (eds.) (2009) *Analysing Audiovisual Dialogue. Linguistic and Translational Insights.* Bologna: CLUEB.

Goris, Olivier (1991) *À la recherche de normes pour le doublage. État de la question et propositions pour une analyse descriptive.* Katholieke Universiteit Leuven: Master's Dissertation.

Goris, Olivier (1993) "Investigating French Dubbing". *Target* 5:2, 169-190.

Gregory, Michael (1967) "Aspects of Varieties Differentiation". *Journal of Linguistics* 3, 177-198.

Halliday, Michael A. K. (2000) *An Introduction to Functional Grammar.* London: Arnold.

Heiss, Christine/Bollettieri Bosinelli, Rosa M. (eds.) (1996) *Traduzione multimediale per il cinema, la televisione e la scena.* Bologna: CLUEB.

Kendon, Adam (2004) *Gesture. Visible Action as Utterance.* Cambridge: Cambridge University Press.

Kress, Gunther/van Leeuwen, Theo (1996) *Reading Images. The Grammar of Visual Design.* London-New York: Routledge.

Ladd, D. Robert (1996) *Intonational Phonology.* Cambridge: Cambridge University Press.

Martínez Sierra, Juan J. (2009) "The Challenge of Translating Humour for Dubbing. Some Problematical Issues". In Goldstein, Angelika/Golubović, Biljana (eds.) *Foreign Language Movies – Dubbing vs. Subtitling.* Hamburg: Verlag Dr. Kovac, 129-149.

McNeill, David (1992) *Hand and Mind. What Gestures Reveal About Thought.* Chicago: The University of Chicago Press.

Pérez-Gonzalez, Luis (2007) "Appraising Dubbed Conversation. Systemic Functional Insights Into the Construal of Naturalness in Translated Film Dialogue". *The Translator* 13:1, 1-38.

Poyatos, Fernando (2002a) *Nonverbal Communication Across Disciplines.* Vol. I: Culture, Sensory Interaction, Speech, Conversation. Amsterdam-Philadelphia: John Benjamins.

Poyatos, Fernando (2002b) *Nonverbal Communication Across Disciplines.* Vol. II: Paralanguage, Kinesics, Silence, Personal and Environmental Interaction. Amsterdam-Philadelphia: John Benjamins.

Poyatos, Fernando (2002c) *Nonverbal Communication Across Disciplines.* Vol. III: Narrative Literature, Theater, Cinema, Translation. Amsterdam-Philadelphia: John Benjamins.

Poyatos, Fernando (2008) *Textual Translation and Live Translation. The Total Experience of Nonverbal Communication in Literature, Theater and Cinema.* Amsterdam-Philadelphia: John Benjamins.

Sanderson, John D. (2009) "Strategies For the Dubbing of Puns With One Visual Semantic Layer". In Díaz-Cintas, Jorge (ed.) *New Trends in Audiovisual Translation*. Bristol: Multilingual Matters, 123-132.

Taylor, Christopher (2003) "Multimodal Transcription in the Analysis, Translation and Subtitling in Italian Films". *The Translator* 9:2, 191-205.

Vandaele, Jeroen (2002) "Humor Mechanisms in Film Comedy: Incongruity and Superiority". *Poetics Today* 23:2, 221-249.

van Leeuwen, Theo (1999) *Speech, Music, Sound*. Macmillan: London.

Wolfe, Richard (2003) *Writing Comedy. A Guide to Scriptwriting for TV, Radio, Film and Stage*. Robert Hale: London.

Appendix

CAPITALS:	characters, high loudness level (e.g. screaming)
Boldface:	focus (stressed syllables, words, parts of utterances)
[some]:	paratextual information
(OS):	off screen
(OnS):	on screen
(starts OS):	starts off screen
(ends OS):	ends off screen
(starts OnS):	starts on screen
(ends OnS):	ends on screen
(CL):	canned laughter
(CL)+:	more intense canned laughter
(CL)-:	less intense canned laughter
(No CL):	eliminated canned laughter
(Yes CL):	added canned laughter
=:	latching (Bonsignori 2009:200)
+some*:	overlapping (Bonsignori 2009:200)
(laughter):	alternants/differentiators (adapted from Bonsignori 2009:200)
(laughing) +some*:	alternants and differentiators preceding a part of the utterance (adapted from Bonsignori 2009:200)
(kinesic action) + (kinesic action):	simultaneous kinesic actions
(kinesic action), (kinesic action):	consecutive kinesic actions
"some":	reported speech (Bonsignori 2009:200)
…:	short pause (see AIDAC's transcription notes, available at www.aidac.it)
/:	medium pause (AIDAC's transcription notes)
//:	long pause (AIDAC's transcription notes)
?:	interrogative tone
!:	exclamatory tone
!?:	interrogative-exclamatory tone
--:	hesitation, interrupted speech (Bonsignori 2009:200)
-:	false start, self-correction (Bonsignori 2009:200)

Nicole Nolette

McGill University, Montreal, Canada

Introducing Playful Translation: Some Notes from Backstage

The domains of Translation Studies, Theatre Studies and multilingualism may be linked with the question of how heterolingual plays can be translated. The study of the contemporary French/English Canadian play *Sex, lies et les Franco-Manitobains* and its subsequent translation yielded a number of linguistic and performance games. These games of translation in language(s) and in the *mise en scène* establish a link of "playful translation" from the original heterolingual performance to its translated (even more heterolingual) counterpart. These playful winks to translation contribute to a supplementary value to the play for its bilingual audience members.

Keywords: theatre translation, heterolingualism, playful translation, wordplay, Canada

Introduction

Montreal, says 2010 CETRA professor Sherry Simon, is a locus of creative multilingualism, a city divided and multiplied by its linguistic affiliations to English and French, "a site of tensions that are both divisive and fruitful" (Simon 2006:27). In the cramped geographical and imaginary quarters of Montreal, "the pulsing of languages shapes literary culture" (ibid.:16) and translation becomes the city's main mode of linguistic crossing, maintenance, hybridisation and deviance. Echoing Simon's concern for modes of living and speaking in small spaces such as the city, Michael Cronin argues for a micro-cosmopolitanism based on the idea of *fractal differentialism*, as "the same degree of diversity is to be found at the level of entities judged to be small or insignificant as at the level of large entities" (Cronin 2006:15). My own research invites us to such small, yet infinitely diverse, spaces of Canada: minority francophone theatres sprinkled across a continent where heterolingual plays are produced, performed and translated. Unlike Simon's Montreal, where there are two strong languages contesting each other, the setting for these theatres is an overwhelmingly English-language civic terrain – albeit one of varying degrees of individual bilingualism and multilingualism. Heterolingual plays, then, as they incorporate English, French and other languages in their literary and performance undertakings, travel and settle across different geographies and audiences.

Heterolingualism and translation

Rainier Grutman coined the term "hétérolinguisme" (heterolingualism in English) in his work on nineteenth century Québec novels, to describe "the use of foreign languages or social, regional and historical varieties *in* literary texts" (Meylaerts 2006:4; see also Grutman 1997: 37). This insistence on the *literary* dimension of heterolingualism serves to distinguish this concept from other sociolinguistic terms such as multilingualism and bilingualism, whose real-world manifestations are studied. Most research on heterolingualism, since 1994, has adopted a functionalist approach, focusing on the *effects* of heterolingualism. These effects have often had much to do with the links between identity politics and language use in literary texts.[1] As such, these identity politics have been marked by anxiety over the linguistic and cultural loss associated with sharing a textual space in the context of the unequal exchange of languages. In Canada, and in the texts and performances of my corpus in particular, this unequal exchange occurs between French as minority and English as majority languages. Yet more and more, the use of heterolingualism in these contexts could be said to be detaching itself from its strictly community-based identity politics. According to Canadian and Québécois theatre scholar Jane Moss,

> [à] Moncton, à Ottawa, à Sudbury, à Toronto, à Saint-Boniface et à Vancouver, de nombreux dramaturges ont réussi à transcender la dramaturgie identitaire et régionaliste qui a aidé les communautés minoritaires à préserver leur mémoire collective et leur culture traditionnelle. Sans oublier le rôle du théâtre dans la vie culturelle de leurs communautés, ces auteurs ont osé renouveler l'écriture et la production théâtrales pour leur public de plus en plus urbain et éduqué. (Moss 2005:63-64)
>
> [From the Canadian city of] Moncton [to] Vancouver, many playwrights have succeeded in transcending the regionalist identity-based dramaturgy that has helped these minority communities in preserving their collective memory and traditional culture. Without forgetting the role of theatre in the

[1] Millán-Varela points out that due to the "contextual (over)determination of minority contexts, translated texts can also become a space in which language and identity conflicts become textualized" (2004:52).

> cultural life of their communities, these authors have dared to renew theatrical writing and production for their ever more urban and educated audiences. (My translation)

As authors from Canada's minority language milieus make the transition to "post-identity" dramaturgy (Moss: "théâtre post-identitaire"), they also renew the ways in which heterolingualism is used. Far from taking on a purely mimetic function, heterolingualism in post-identity drama can, among other modes of operation, adopt parody or creativity.[2] For the playwrights involved to gain recognition and legitimacy beyond their own communities, however, their plays must travel, often in translation, to larger centres where the languages they put on stage are questioned and often misunderstood. My main interest lies in how heterolingualism and translation intersect: how do we translate heterolingual texts and/or performances? How have such objects gone through translation already?

Rainier Grutman discusses two possible solutions to translating heterolingualism: preserving the foreign elements or erasing the linguistic difference by translating into a single language (2001:160). In the first case, only the main language of the text is translated, whereas in the second, the entire text is adapted to a target language and culture considered as unilingual. These solutions, however, apply with great difficulty to cases where one of the source languages of the text is also the target language. The translation towards one of the languages comprising the heterolingual text calls for new questionings. In her introduction to the "Heterolingualism in/and Translation" special issue of *Target*, Reine Meylaerts tackles these theoretical and practical questions:

> How heterolingual can (or should) a translation be in a given context? What are the modalities and identity functions of language plurality in translation? And how are they related (or not) to modalities and identity functions of heterolingualism in "original" (source and target culture) texts, to discursive practices oriented towards the "Other", to the doxa on translation in particular contexts, etc. (Meylaerts 2006:5)

Meylaerts underscores that the translation of heterolingual texts troubles the premise of transposing fully from one (complete) language to another for monolingual model readers. First of all, they recall the non-monologic character of discourse and that "rather than just reflecting social polyglossia,

---

[2] Chantal Richard developed these three categories in her quantitative research on heterolingualism in the twentieth century francophone novel in North America (2003).

'original' and 'translated' discourses *select* certain (heterolingual) elements" (ibid.:5) for the function that they can hold. Secondly, heterolingual texts and their translations shed light on and question the presupposed monolingualism of "authors, critics, audiences, etc. in the source and target cultures" (ibid.) in a global context that we keep celebrating as "multilingual".

Heterolingualism and theatre translation

In order to avoid erasing all traces of heterolingualism, Kathy Mezei suggests that translators make use of "textual devices such as italics, parentheses, translator's notes, additions, conscious alterations and explanatory phrases" (Mezei 1995:145) to denote the presence of the target language in the original text. At the theatre, however, it is difficult to imagine that this textual difference would easily translate into a stage performance, into the mouths of actors.[3] For Phyllis Zatlin, theatre translation practitioner and theorist, the wide variety of multilingual dramatic writing methods demands equally diverse and creative translation strategies:

> At one end of the spectrum are scripts with characters who ostensibly speak different languages although the texts are written entirely in the language of the spectators. At the other end are works written in two languages without any expectation that spectators will understand both. Between these two extremes, which may require relatively little modification on the translator's part, there are numerous levels of *linguistic games* that the potential translator needs to address with imagination. (Zatlin 2005:103, emphasis added)

Even more recently, US-American theatre scholar Marvin Carlson (2006) explored at great lengths multilingual texts and theatrical performances in their multicultural, dialectical, postcolonial and postmodern manifestations. He suggested that the translator and translation could take on major and subversive roles in theatrical performance; moreover, side texts such as supertitles and interpreters onstage can be modes of translation and creation in multilingual theatre. According to him, however, in contrast to Europe, North America has been lagging behind in the use of creative translation devices for heteroglossic theatre. The pathways of research undertaken here are fertile ground for our study of the various representations of multilingualism in Canadian theatre as well as of the innovative translation practices of this multilingualism. As such, my research will attempt to explore the

3 See Ladouceur (2008) and Bassnett (1985:87).

diverse translation strategies present in heterolingual plays and/or their translations, notably through *playful translation*, that is to say the double game of translation in language(s) and in the *mise en scène*.

Invitations to play in translation

My master's thesis, defended at the Campus Saint-Jean of the University of Alberta (Canada) in 2008, focused on the translation of heterolingual dramatic texts from Western Canadian francophone playwright Marc Prescott (Nolette 2008). His texts *Big*, *Bullshit* and *Sex, lies et les Franco-Manitobains*, published together in an anthology, show differing relationships to language, which can either double or hybridise, mixing French with English in a game where code-switching serves as a motor to the plot. In *Sex, lies et les Franco-Manitobains*, Prescott's most intensely bilingual play, as code-switching mobilises the characters' actions, so does the staging of translation in the intersections between these characters' language fluencies. The play portrays three characters: one young, bilingual woman who sticks to French and refuses to speak English (*Elle*/Nicole), one young, bilingual man who alternates between French and English (*Lui*/Jacques) and one young man who speaks only English (*Him*). Their encounters and the linguistic frictions and games that ensue provide the main lines of this play set during two subsequent robberies on Christmas Eve. In the following excerpt, for example, an Anglophone thief (*Him*) asks rope-bound bilingual character Jacques (*Lui*) to translate Nicole's (*Elle*'s) personal diary, which is written exclusively in French. The scene revolves around differing levels of bilingualism and makes explicit the need for and resistance to translation.

Him

Cool. Here. (Il ouvre le journal devant Lui.) Translate.

Elle

No! It's personal. Please! I'm begging. It's not even any good.

Him

I'll be the judge of that. (À Lui.) Here. Can you translate?

Elle

No!

Lui

Fais-moi confiance. *(Lui lit un passage.) Hang on here. (Lisant.)* « J'ai rêvé de Paul hier soir et nous étions à l'Hôtel *Fort Garry.* » Euh… *I dreamt of Paul last night.*

We were at the the Fort Garry Hotel… in the dining room. He was very… uh, very… handsome.

Elle

T'as pas besoin de l'embellir.

Lui

Come on. T'as jamais entendu parler de la licence poétique?

Him

What's the problem?

Elle

He's doing a shitty translation job. (Prescott 2001:72)

If, in this scene, *Elle* disapproves of *Lui*'s translation through embellishment, she is later relieved by his censorship of later, more intimate sections of her diary. This staging of translation parodies the interpreter role often attributed to bilinguals. If unilingual individuals take for granted that translators will recreate a perfectly faithful copy of the original, it is because he considers them to be invisible, and rarely takes into account their possible motivations (Venuti 1998). According to Lawrence Venuti, this invisibility originates in translation strategies currently popular in the Anglophone world – strategies that facilitate reading and domesticating foreign texts. Prescott's Anglophone thief (*Him*) expects Jacques/*Lui*, to be an "invisible" translator, to offer a faithful, readable version in his own language. Jacques/*Lui*, on the other hand, chooses to translate as he wishes, with an ounce of resistance, both embellishing and camouflaging, in a playful and strategic translation.[4] This representation of translation echoes Sherry Simon's descriptions of "perverse translation":

> The reader must agree to take roundabout routes, to beat about the bush, and to venture along detours where translation encounters the pleasures of perversion. Perversions are acts that do not respect the normative functions of objects or practices, that turn away from their expected goals. And so perverse translations are those that do not deliver the goods. Instead of ensuring the efficient transfer of a message to another, perverse translations take advantage of the situation. The translator turns away from the straight and narrow path, revealing an unsuspected capacity for playful creativity. (Simon 2006:119)

---

4 For a more detailed analysis of this play, see Nolette (2008, 2011).

If this representation of bilingualism and of its functions seems comprehensible for bilingual readers and audiences, the diffusion of these plays and, by extension, their legitimisation by the officially monolingual Canadian theatre centres will have to go through translation. Translation in this case, however, could be just as "perverse" as in *Sex, lies et les Franco- Manitobains*, setting the stage for a new take on heterolingual performance. The addition of surtitles projected above the stage could both accommodate and resist the need for translation. "Perversely", they would ensure that the spectator's experience would vary according to his/her linguistic resources, just like the characters' experiences themselves. As such, some parts of the text could remain untranslated in the surtitles, allowing the new production to take advantage of the play's ludic specificity to stage games of linguistic inclusion and exclusion (Nolette 2008:87).

Introducing playful translation

These suggestions for new heterolingual performances highlight gaps within theoretical models for translation while establishing promising headways to a *playful translation* that emphasises both the supplementary value of bilingualism and the theatrical potential of the works.

The supplementary value refers here to what reveals the lacks inherent to monolingualisms (Derrida 1996)[5] but also to Venuti's affirmation that translations can work as "supplements" to the originals by modes of compensation or replacement. Rather than being an "addition to" the "original", the translation is solicited by the original in order to fill a lack within the original itself (Venuti 1995:216). Though the expression *traduction ludique*, or playful [ludic] translation may recall the theory of game translation, there are some clear differences between the two approaches. Game translation, based on mathematician John von Neuman's game theory, postulates that an individual will seek to find the best action strategy in a given situation (Guidère 2008:74). As a "minimax" strategy, game translation seeks to optimise the process of translation and to minimise wasting time. There is no question, in my conception of playful translation, of optimising gains or of minimising losses. A frequent critique of game translation has, in fact, rested on the very absence of a "playful", or fun, aspect:

[5] Homi Bhabha also refers to this theory of supplementarity in his reflection on postcolonial translation (Bhabha 1994:87).

> Il est évident que la préoccupation stratégique rend illusoire le plaisir que le traducteur ou le lecteur peut tirer d'un éventuel "jeu de la traduction". (Guidère 2008:74-75)
>
> It is evident that strategic concerns make illusory any fun that the translator or reader may eventually get from "game translation". (My translation)

How may playful translation take into account the "fun" of playing, be it between languages or between the dramatic text and its theatrical representation? How are the "games" of translation linked to comedy or to humour? David Crystal argues that "[e]njoyment, rather than humour [associated with laughter] is what language play is chiefly about" (Crystal 2001:16).

Sex, lies et les Franco-Manitobains in playful translation

Different "side texts" (Carlson) may be enacted by "playful translation", including interpreters intervening in the new production, the redistribution of lines among actors in a bilingual performance and the ludic use of surtitles (Carlson's supertitles). For *Sex, lies et les Franco-Manitobains*, I suggested that the translation of this intensely heterolingual play should take place within a bilingual performance through subtly deviant surtitles. Two years after the completion of my Master's thesis (2008) and sixteen years after its first production (1993), *Sex, lies et les Franco-Manitobains* was staged once again, this time by the playwright himself. First presented at the Francophone Collège universitaire de Saint-Boniface in Manitoba, Canada, the cast and crew subsequently travelled to the Campus Saint-Jean, the Francophone campus of the Anglophone University of Alberta in Edmonton, Alberta, Canada. This performance, however, was accompanied by surtitles. Starting in 2005, some Canadian Francophone theatres started using surtitles as a way to access larger (Anglophone) audiences. The Théâtre français de Toronto, the Troupe du Jour in Saskatoon, L'Unithéâtre in Edmonton and the Théâtre de la Seizième in Vancouver, for example, all started to include English surtitles during one or two evenings of each of their productions. *Sex, lies et les Franco-Manitobains*'s surtitled presentation in Edmonton, therefore, could count on a budding tradition of translation in performance in a context where this practice would have seemed foreign a decade earlier. Marc Prescott's staging of the production foregrounded the play's ongoing process of translation, its surtitles as well as the agency of the person who had to orchestrate their timing in accordance with the actors' lines.

That person, Shavaun Liss, the graduate student who had translated the play for surtitling, was placed on stage by the director, who also asked that the actors interact both with her and with the text unfolding on the horizontal screen on top of them. In one instance, the surtitle acted as a prompter to remind *Lui* (in the French dialogue) of some names he had forgotten (listed in the English surtitle). Clearly bilingual, the actor/character benefited from the surtitle and shared this benefit with the bilingual members of the audience in a wink to a creative translation process. In another instance, another character asked the surtitler, who was on stage for the whole performance, to act as a character witness and as a playful testifier of unfolding events. The text of the surtitles, moreover, added extra commentary to the play. In one scene where the English slang was considered almost incomprehensible even to native speakers of English, the surtitle read as follows:

> *(If you don't understand what this guy is saying, don't worry – Neither does 50% of the rest of the audience.) (This message brought to you by your friendly neighbourhood surtitle)* (Prescott 2009, slide 602).

If the interventions of the surtitler remained framed by parentheses and italics in this surtitle, they gained visibility elsewhere, where fonts such as those used in cartoons translated a string of profanity used on stage. "Fuckduhduhfuckfuck-fuckfuck" (Prescott 2001:42) thus became "♪#💣*✈%💧# 🕿☎&☠^🛎@📌! 🖨$🐈!♫" (Prescott 2009, slide 298), calling forth both an intersemiotic and intralinguistic translation (from vulgar English to ideogram English) and an interlinguistic translation (from popular French, where "fuck" is less vulgar than in English, to censored English) – but even the censorship effect was parodied since, of course, the French "fuck" was also heard in English! This playful use of surtitles fits well with the playful manner by which the two bilingual characters approach bilingualism and its high political stakes.[6]

Playful winks to translation[7]

These concerns about surtitles may perhaps find an echo in Abé Mark Nornes's work on subtitling in film. In his article on the cultural and ideological issues involved in subtitling, he proposed two categories for subtitles.

---

[6] For more information on this performance, see Ladouceur (2010).

[7] I would like to thank Andrew Chesterman for the metaphor of the wink for playful translation from a personal communication, CETRA Summer School 2010.

Reminiscent of Venuti's "domesticating" and "foreignizing" translation strategies, Nornes's subtitles can take either the "corrupt" or "abusive" labels:

> Even the subtitles for the most nondescript, realist film tamper with language usage and freely ignore or change much of the source text; however, corrupt subtitlers *suppress the fact of this violence necessitated by the apparatus*, while the abusive translator enjoys *foregrounding* it, heightening its impact and testing its limits and possibilities. (Nornes 1992/2004:464, emphasis added)

Nornes's "abusive" subtitling highlights the "apparatus" of translation itself, "foregrounding" the "violent" but often invisible process through which subtitling integrates the subtitled film. Prescott's vision of the surtitled production of *Sex, lies et les Franco-Manitobains* is one of "heightened", visible translation – translation that points itself out. Yet whereas Nornes adopts combative adjectives such as "abusive" and "violent", Prescott's staging of translation may perhaps best be viewed through a more "playful" optic. This playfulness in foregrounding translation makes visible the ways in which the practice is deemed necessary – and in which resistance to this practice is deemed equally as necessary. The deliberate act to counter translation is, in a lot of cases, including the minority settings staged by Prescott, one that is tied to the very linguistic and cultural survival of those who are being translated:

> It is resistance to translation, not acceptance, that generates translation. If a group of individuals or a people agree to translate themselves into another language, that is if they accept translation unreservedly, then the need for translation soon disappears. For the *translated* there is no more *translation.* (Cronin 2000:95)

Prescott's staging of a surtitled heterolingual performance introduces winks to translation that remain visible for a particular audience: the bilingual French-English audience that the play catered to originally. While the surtitles may seem to accommodate Anglophone audience members whose patronage is invited by this gesture, these spectators may remain mystified or become slightly irritated while their bilingual counterparts smile or laugh at the subtle interplay between the actors, the surtitles and the surtitler. In this way, playful translation highlights the lacks inherent to monolingualisms as well as the supplementary value of bilingualism. Thus this process points to its own bias, its own partiality: a fondness for a particular bilingual/ multilingual ideal spectator.

Conclusion

Though heterolingual theatre until recently sought solutions for its translation, playful strategies are emerging, foregrounding the non-redundant presence of multiple languages on stage. In *Sex, lies et les Franco-Manitobains*, heterolingualism and translation intersected in ways that crossed both the so-called original and its translation, creating different versions of heterolingual performance texts that catered to specific audiences. While accommodating audience members whose presence was deemed necessary to their diffusion and legitimisation, the playful translation of this play was also a gesture of resistance to these same audience members. The playful winks to the apparatus of translation and to that of performance used by Prescott in his surtitled staging of *Sex, lies et les Franco-Manitobains* shed light on these processes and on the poetics and politics of translating in a country where levels of bilingualism vary widely and where languages always seem to be intermingled in high-stakes games.

References

Bassnett, Susan (1985) "Ways Through the Labyrinth, Strategies and Methods for Translating Theatre Texts". In Hermans, Theo (ed.) *The Manipulation of Literature, Studies in Literary Translation*. London: Croom Helm, 87-102.

Bhabha, Homi (1994) *The Location of Culture*. London-New York: Routledge.

Carlson, Marvin (2006) *Speaking in Tongues: Languages at Play in the Theatre*. Ann Arbor: University of Michigan Press.

Cronin, Michael (2000) *Across the Lines: Travel, Language, Translation*. Cork: Cork University Press.

Cronin, Michael (2006) *Translation and Identity*. London-New York: Routledge.

Crystal, David (2001) *Language Play*. Chicago: University of Chicago Press.

Derrida, Jacques (1996) *Le Monolinguisme de l'autre*. Paris: Galilée.

Grutman, Rainier (1997) *Des langues qui résonnent: l'hétérolinguisme au XIXe siècle québécois*. Québec: Fides.

Grutman, Rainier (2001) "Multilingualism and Translation". In Baker, Mona (ed.) *Routledge Encyclopedia of Translation Studies*. London-New York: Routledge, 157-160.

Guidère, Mathieu (2008) *Introduction à la traductologie: penser la traduction: hier, aujourd'hui, demain*. Bruxelles: de boeck.

Ladouceur, Louise (2008) "Bilinguisme et performance: traduire pour la scène la dualité linguistique des francophones de l'Ouest canadien". *Alternative francophone* 1:1, 46-56, http://ejournals.library.ualberta.ca/index.php/af/article/view/4136/3375 [3 July 2012].

Ladouceur, Louise (2010) "Unilinguisme, bilinguisme et esthétique interculturelle dans les dramaturgies francophones du Canada". *International Journal of Francophone Studies* 13:2, 183-200.

Meylaerts, Reine (2006) "Heterolingualism in/and Translation: How Legitimate are the Other and his/her Language?". *Target* 18:1, 1-16.

Mezei, Kathy (1995) "Speaking White: Literary Translation as a Vehicle of Assimilation in Quebec". In Simon, Sherry (ed.) *Culture in Transit: Translating the Literature of Quebec*. Montréal: Véhicule Press, 133-148.

Millán-Varela, Carmen (2004) "Hearing Voices: James Joyce, Narrative Voice and Minority Translation". *Language and Literature* 13:1, 37-54.

Moss, Jane (2005) "Les théâtres francophones post-identitaires: état des lieux". *Canadian Literature* 187: 57-71.

Nolette, Nicole (2008) *Traduire la dualité linguistique de l'Ouest canadien pour la scène anglophone*. University of Alberta, Campus Saint-Jean, Edmonton: Master's Dissertation.

Nornes, Abé Mark (1992/2004) "For an Abusive Subtitling". In Venuti, Lawrence (ed.) *The Translation Studies Reader*. London-New York: Routledge.

Prescott, Marc (2001) *Big; Bullshit; Sex, Lies et les Franco-Manitobains*. Saint-Boniface: Les Éditions du Blé.

Prescott, Marc (2009) *Sex, Lies et les Franco-Manitobains*, English surtitles by Shavaun Liss (Louise Ladouceur), Théâtre au Pluriel, Campus Saint-Jean, University of Alberta, November 5-6.

Richard, Chantal (2003) *L'Hétérolinguisme littéraire dans le roman francophone en Amérique du Nord à la fin du XXe siècle*. Moncton University: PhD Dissertation.

Simon, Sherry (2006) *Translating Montreal: Episodes in the Life of a Divided City*. Montreal: McGill-Queen's University Press.

Venuti, Lawrence (1995) *The Translator's Invisibility. A History of Translation*. London-New York: Routledge.

Venuti, Lawrence (1998) *The Scandals of Translation: Towards an Ethics of Difference*. London-New York: Routledge.

Zatlin, Phyllis (2005) *Theatrical Translation and Film Adaptation: A Practitioner's View*. Clevedon-Buffalo-Toronto: Multilingual Matters.

The role of translation in a globalised world

EDUARDA MELO CABRITA

University of Lisbon, Portugal

English as a *Lingua Franca* in Legal Translation: The Early Stages of a Research Project

This paper aims to describe the initial stages of an ongoing corpus-oriented research project on intercultural relations between Anglophone countries and Portugal by means of translation. Drawing on the concept of cultural interference (Even-Zohar 2005), this paper seeks to provide and discuss examples of exposure to English as a *lingua franca* in several domains in Portugal, and to show how it can lead to interference in translation. In line with Šarčević (2000) and Cao (2009), this paper will try to determine how far system-bound characteristics of legal language such as Common Law preciseness and Civil Law conciseness influence the translation of English-language contracts into Portuguese.

Keywords: legal translation, English as a *lingua franca*, interference, conciseness, preciseness

Introduction

This paper aims to describe the exposure to English as a *lingua franca* (ELF)[1] in the legal domain in Portugal as part of a wider research project on intercultural studies. In a contemporary global society where English is a *lingua franca*, my research sets out to study relations between the English-speaking and Portuguese-speaking worlds by discussing the influence ELF seems to have on the translation of contracts into European Portuguese.[2]

The choice of this research topic was highly influenced by my experience as a translator and a teacher of legal translation,[3] which gradually led to the

[1] I will use English as *lingua franca* and ELF in this paper not with the meaning commonly associated with the Lingua Franca movement (e.g. Jenkins 2005; Seidlhofer 2009), but to refer to the preferred vehicular language spoken by native speakers and non-native speakers used for international communication, as defined by the study published by the Directorate General for Translation (DGT) of the European Commission (2011:8).

[2] In this paper, I will use "Portuguese" to refer to the variety of European Portuguese.

[3] I have been a freelance translator of legal documents from 1990, and I have been teaching translation at the Faculty of Letters of the University of Lisbon from 1992.

realisation that although there is a vast bibliography focusing on the legal similarities and differences between contracts in Common Law and in Civil Law countries, to date there is to the best of my knowledge hardly any systematic study on the implications of such characteristics on the translation of contracts from English into Portuguese.[4] This came as a surprise to me since Portugal was a founder of the European Free Trade Association (EFTA) has been an EU country from 1986 and is nowadays "uma das economias mais abertas da Europa" (Barreto 2002:9), ("one the most open economies in Europe", my translation) which points to the need for the translation of contracts governing business relations carried out internationally.

The absence of an in-depth study on translation of contracts from English into European Portuguese to date was one of the reasons for undertaking my research. In this paper, I will try to determine whether my assumption that there is a dominant presence of English in Portugal is supported by already available data, and I will reflect upon the tolerance to legal terms and drafting styles imported from Common Law countries which may result from Portugal's exposure to ELF in everyday life activities (i.e. the cinema, television, newspapers, literature) and in a specialised domain such as law.

Exposure to ELF in Portugal

The term *lingua franca* originally meant *the language of the Franks* spoken by the Arabs at the time of the Crusades when in contact with Western Europeans. It was used to refer to a language that enabled communication between people who would otherwise not understand each other. This language was mainly characterised by the absence of inflection, the lack of person, gender and case for nouns and pronouns, the lack of concord between noun and adjective and by using the verb in the infinitive (DGT 2011:20).[5]

Another meaning of *lingua franca lato sensu* is used to describe the current role of English, which has gradually become a favoured instrument of

4 A PhD thesis on legal language in the courtroom was submitted in 2005 by Maria da Conceição Carapinha Rodrigues to the Faculty of Arts of the University of Coimbra. It does not, however, focus on contracts.

5 For a historical overview of the *lingua franca* concept, see DGT (2011:9-22); see also Barotchi (1994:2211), House (2003:557, 2010:11), Phillipson (2008:261), among others.

global communication for several reasons, among which feature the expansion of British colonial power and the emergence of the United States as a leading economic power in the aftermath of World War II. English has assumed economic, political and cultural relevance as the world's most widely used language spoken as a first, second or foreign language, with estimates that range between 1,500 million (Crystal 2001:14) and 4,000 million speakers (DGT 2011:28).

This meaning differs from the original concept in that in today's world, ELF is also spoken by native speakers, and it is characterised by its "functional flexibility and its spread across many different domains" (House 2003:557).

The spread of English worldwide was conceptualised in 1985 by Braj Kachru as a three-concentric-circle model (1992:356) with each circle representing the geographical areas where English is spoken either as a mother tongue (the norm-providing Inner Circle), as a second or one of the official languages (the norm-developing Outer Circle) or taught as a foreign language (the norm-dependent Expanding Circle).

In the mid-1980s, the Kachruvian model offered what was then a new geographical interpretation of the status of the English language worldwide, and even nowadays, it is widely regarded as an accurate description of the way English was spreading.[6] With time, however, the intensification of exchanges in a globalised world has lead to the adoption of other perspectives which challenge Kachru's model. Among reasons for challenging this model are its underlying notion of Inner Circle native-speaker centrality, and the way it describes the status of the language spoken in the three circles. Native-speaker centrality might be accepted when the model was first conceptualised, but it is controversial nowadays when Outer Circle varieties of English are "widely recognized [as constituting] different Englishes in their own right" (Seidlhofer/Berns 2009:190); furthermore, distinctions within the status of the language do not seem to hold in a world where native speakers of English are largely outnumbered by non-native speakers, with a ratio which varies between three and four to one (Graddol 2000:10-12; Crystal 2001:13; House 2003:557), and where English is increasingly used as the foreign language preferred for intercultural communication carried out between the three circles (Firth 1996:240; DGT 2011:27).

[6] For this view, see Crystal (1995:107); Graddol (2000); Berns (2009); Bolton (2006); Jenkins (2009); Seidlhofer (2009); DGT (2011).

These major changes have given rise to differing, sometimes controversial opinions about the role of English worldwide, with views which range from the highly critical to a more detached approach.[7] This controversy falls, however, beyond the scope of my paper, and so I will not elaborate on the subject any further. For the purposes of my paper, I will use ELF *lato sensu* in the sense of the preferred language for international exchange between native speakers and non-native speakers with different mother tongues (DGT 2011:8).

In this sense, Portugal may be seen as a case in point of a diglossic situation where ELF is used for various "pockets of expertise" and non-private communication, to use House's terminology (2003:561). This situation is directly linked to one of the questions I have set out to address: how far does exposure to ELF influence the translation of contracts from English into Portuguese? To that effect, I will first try to establish the degree of exposure to ELF in Portugal.

English is the first and dominant foreign language in Portugal[8] and this is expressly stated on the website of the *Ministério da Educação* (ME), the Portuguese Department for Education. The high sociosemiotic value of English, what de Swaan (2004:8) calls the communication value, or Q-value, and prestige of English are acknowledged when ME states that English is integrated into the national curriculum because it is "*a* língua de comunicação internacional" (my italics), *the* international communication language. This official statement confers prestige on English and helps consolidate its high-ranking position, which coupled with emphasis on early teaching (6-year-olds onwards) creates high expectations as regards competence in English. These expectations seem to be confirmed by a look at law-related websites and at a specialist newspaper.

---

7 A highly critical view sees English as a *lingua tyranossaura* (Swales 1997:334; Tardy 2004:251), a *lingua frankensteinia* (Phillipson 2008:251-253) leading up to *linguicide, linguistic cannibalism* (Barotchi 1994:2211), *epistemicide* (Bennett 2007:154, 2010:17) and gatekeeping practices (Bhatia 1997; Graddol 2000:38; Tardy 2004:250; Bennett 2007:154). A somewhat more detached perspective (e.g. House 2003:62; de Swaan 2004:8) suggests that English need not be a threat if it is seen as a language for communication and not as a language for identification. This distinction is used by de Swaan (2004:4-6) and Mufwene (2004:217, n.d.:10-12) to challenge the adequacy of concepts such as *language imperialism, language war, linguicide, killer language* and *language endangerment.*

8 English is a statutory subject of the national school curriculum in Portugal from the first to the eleventh or twelvth grades. See the official site of the Portuguese Department for Education.

Diário Jurídico (*Daily Legal Newspaper*) is a Portuguese online blog on legal matters addressed to Portuguese lawyers. Traffic statistics provided by Bravenet Free Counter indicate an average of 336 visitors per day and a total of 412,066 to date, which shows a wide readership. As expected, *Diário Jurídico* provides detailed information in Portuguese on recently enacted laws and other legal matters. It also includes several hyperlinks to lengthy articles in *The New York Times, The Wall Street Journal,* the OECD and the International Chamber of Commerce in English. A very brief summary, which consists mainly of the translation of the English headline, is given in Portuguese but no translation of the articles is provided. Visitors are apparently expected to be proficient in English.

Advocatus[9] is an online version of a Portuguese monthly newspaper on legal matters. Information (ads, feature articles, interviews and news) is provided in Portuguese, but a randomly chosen online monthly issue (April 2011) features seven hyperlinks to international blogs written in English (e.g. the EU Law Blog, the Law Blog, the Legal Ethics Forum, the Harvard Law School Forum, the International Economic Law and Policy Board and the New York Real Estate Lawyers' Blog) with no translation or summary in Portuguese. Again, visitors seem to be expected to read the texts in English.

A look at the websites of six law firms[10] randomly chosen among those carrying out international business in Portugal reveals an identical situation: all websites can be accessed in English and in Portuguese but *both* versions feature articles and/or publications on legal matters in English (with percentages ranging from 55.8% to 63.3% of all online publications); no translation of the English articles is provided in any of the Portuguese versions of the websites. *Diário Jurídico, Advocatus* and the above-mentioned law firm sites seem to indicate that information on legal matters is posted on the assumption that all addressees are highly proficient in English so as

[9] No information on traffic statistics is provided.

[10] The websites visited were run by the following law firms: A.M. Pereira, Saragga Leal, Oliveira Martins, Júdice e Associados, Sociedade de Advogados R.L.; Cuatrecasas, Gonçalves Pereira e Associados R.L.; Henrique Abecasis, Andresen Guimarães, Pedro Guerra e Álvaro Roquette Morais Sociedade de Advogados R.L.; Jardim, Sampaio, Magalhães e Silva e Associados; R. Pinto Duarte, M. Medeiros e Associados Sociedade de Advogados R.L.; Uría-Menendez-Proença de Carvalho & Associados. They have been selected at random from law firms located and carrying out international business in Portugal. All partners of these law firms are Portuguese, except for Uría-Menendez-Proença de Carvalho where there are 12 Portuguese partners and one Spanish partner.

to be able to read intricate legal texts and reveal a high exposure to the English language in this domain.

Another case in point is the Portuguese language periodical *Diário Económico*, one of the country's leading daily business newspapers with a daily average of 182,851 readers. A random choice of one of its issues (14th April 2011) shows at least one occurrence of English in 33 out of its 56 articles and feature articles (i.e. 58.94%), in 23 out of its 72 short news and highlights (i.e. 31.9%), and in 12 out of its 18 ads (i.e. 66.6%);[11] no other foreign language occurrences were noted. English acronyms such as CTO and CEO were used but no translation was provided although CTO appeared in English both as an acronym and in full ("chief technology officer"). 62.64% (i.e. 161) occurrences were marked as foreign words by using single inverted commas but were not translated, nor was their meaning otherwise explained in Portuguese. In the same issue, a one-page ad advertising an international brand of luxury beds was in English, except for the store address in Portugal and a sentence in very small font size at the bottom of the page reading: "*as camas Hästens são feitas à mão e são integralmente constituídas pelos melhores materiais naturais* (i.e. "Hästens beds are handmade and made up of the best natural materials", my translation). The caption ("as natural as breathing") in very large font size was, however, in English and no translation was provided. Another point worth noting is that some of the English words in *Diário Económico* were clearly from the (expected) field of economics (e.g. bailout, payback, payoff, spread, yields) and as such probably more likely to be easily understood by its readers. However, 68.3% (i.e. 151) were everyday English words (e.g. clip-on, clubhouse, design, download, gadget, marketing, outdoor, performance, resort, rookie, think-tank, timing, upgrade, etc.) which substantiates my assumption that ELF is

[11] My count of 257 occurrences of English words does not include names of people (e.g. Simon Tilford) and/or companies (e.g. Bloomberg), stock exchange listings and indices (e.g. Dow Jones index), international political parties (e.g. True Finns) and places (e.g. South Africa) in English, but includes acronyms like CTO and CEO. Some examples of occurrences are: asset management, bailout, banner, beneficial owner, clip-on, clubhouse, cluster, design, fiscal monitor, gadget, live streaming, manager, marketing, offshore, outdoor, payback, payoff, performance, ratings, research, resort, road-show, rookie, screensaver, set, setup, slim, software, spreads, stand, tablet, test drive, think-tank, timing, top pick, trader, utility, wind-float, yields.

widely used in Portugal.[12] Another point which illustrates the prestige of ELF is the fact that several Portuguese companies mentioned in *Diário Económico* have an English or English-sounding name (Automation Labs, Magpower, Oon Recycling Solutions, Record, Taguspark, Troia Eco Resort & Residences) and several projects designed by Portuguese companies are carried out under an English name, e.g. Inovcity, Inovgrid Young Lions Portugal. The examples above point towards a high semiotic value of ELF and to considerable exposure of Portuguese users to ELF, the foreign language taught to students from age 6 onwards; they also point to the expected proficiency in English of the community of readers of such specialised media, i.e. economists, business administration experts, and lawyers.

The impact of ELF on translation and on legal translation in Portugal

Against this general background, I will now discuss the impact ELF bears upon translation in general and legal translation in particular. Available data (Antonini 2007; ICA 2009; Rosa forthcoming, 2012) seem to indicate that English, in the sense of a vehicular language spoken by native and non-native speakers, is the dominant source language (SL) in various domains of translation in Portugal, as happens in three areas which usually impact highly on people's lives: cinema, TV and literature.

Figures provided by the film industry show that between 70% and 80% of all fiction aired in Europe are US productions or co-productions (Antonini 2007:154). Portugal is no exception to this reality. *Anuário Estatístico/2009 Facts & Figures*, a bilingual publication of ICA – Instituto do Cinema e do Audiovisual (i.e. the Institute for Cinema and Audiovisuals), published in 2009 provides figures illustrating the overwhelming (100%) use of English as an SL for the top 10 films viewed (and translated) in Portugal between 2004 and 2009.

Identically, another study reveals that 71.05% of all programmes shown on Portuguese television in November 2007 were translations and English was

---

[12] A fact which is worth further looking into is that the only translated article in this issue does not feature any word in English. The article is authored by European Central Bank executive board member Lorenzo Bini Smaghi and was published originally in English in the *Financial Times* on the same date (14th April 2011) under the title "Ireland's taxpayers must share the pain". The Portuguese title reads "Contribuintes Irlandeses têm de pagar parte da factura" (i.e. "Irish taxpayers must foot part of the bill", my translation).

by far (70%) the main SL (Rosa forthcoming). As regards book translation, available data show that after World War II (between 1950-1955), in line with the reasons briefly mentioned in section 2 above, English increasingly became the first SL of published translated books in Portugal with 32.4% (Rosa in press:219).

It seems, therefore, that widespread use of English as a SL for translation in Portugal seems to be corroborated with existing data and, in a country where subtitling is by far the most frequent modality of audiovisual translation (Rosa forthcoming), this results in a marked exposure to ELF. English is also the most used SL for translated books and this fact, in itself, provides familiarity with English-language cultures, predominantly of the US variety.

But more important for my research project is to try to determine how far this exposure to ELF, as a vehicular language of communication as well as its dominant use as an SL in translation may also condition legal translation and especially the translation of contracts[13] in Portugal. Translation of contracts is system-bound (Šarčević 1994:303, 2000:13; Cao 2009:24) and this becomes especially difficult when the SL is English and the target language (TL) is Portuguese since Portugal is a Continental Civil Law country and most Anglo-Saxon countries are Common Law countries. This major difference impacts on the styles used for drafting contracts: Portuguese contract style is *concise* and concentrated, because it relies on codes and statutes for further information. In Common Law countries, however, the style is *precise,* and information is given in great detail often in the form of lengthy definitions and specific exceptions, because contract law rules allow for different interpretations, and it is not always easy to determine which judicial precedent will be applied to a particular contract term. This difference is crucial for translation in that contracts drafted in English often include an excessive information load by Portuguese standards, featuring a long list of terms which appear to be similar in meaning but which are nevertheless included for the sake of preciseness. Example (1a) is taken

[13] Legal translation is a vast concept and several criteria may be used to define different types of legal translation. With a view to narrowing down the scope of my research, in this paper, I will use Cao's terminology to speak about legal translation as the "translation of texts used in law and legal settings" (2009:12) and will focus on the translation of contracts. Contracts are defined by Cao as private legal documents (ibid.:9). On the different documents which should be included in or left out from this classification, see Harvey (2002); Šarčević (2000); Alcaraz/Hughes (2002) and Cao (2009).

from the definition clause of a loan agreement in English; examples (1b) and (1c) are possible Portuguese translations where (1b) translates all words with synonyms and example (1c) omits redundant terms. Example (1a) illustrates the need for preciseness:

(1) a. "Statutes" means the charter, by-laws, articles of incorporation or other similar documents constituting the relevant Person.

b. "Estatutos" significa o contrato de sociedade, os regulamentos, estatutos ou outros documentos semelhantes constitutivos da Pessoa relevante.

By "Statutes" it is understood the company contract, the regulations, the statutes or other similar documents constituting the relevant Person. (My back-translation)

c. Por 'Estatutos' entenda-se os documentos constitutivos da Pessoa relevante.

By 'Statutes' it is understood the documents constituting the relevant Person. (My back-translation)

The translator is faced with two alternatives: (a) to translate all terms, word-for-word, as in (1b) thereby producing an SL-oriented documentary translation in Nord's terminology (1991); or (b) to provide a simplified version producing an instrumental translation, as in (1c), thereby choosing not to transfer three of the four expressions of apparently identical meaning used in the English version, in line with "the unstated conventions by which [legal] language operates" (White 1982:423) particularly relevant in this case when applied to a Civil Law code-based country like Portugal.

It should be noted that in his/her choice, the translator should consider that it is not the *meaning* of the ST but the *function*[14] of the target text (TT) as defined by the communicative situation that matters, in line with Nord (1991), Šarčević (2000) and Vermeer (1992). Functionalists argue that STs have lost their inviolability and are just a means to an end, which is determined by the initiator. A documentary translation of this excerpt might then be redundant in the case of a specialist, but advisable if the receiver of the TT is a lay client/initiator.[15] Nevertheless, and regardless of which alterna-

[14] Different translation strategies (target- or source-oriented) may produce different versions of a contract, depending on whether the translated text is "for use in practice" or as "court evidence" (Šarčević 2000:18).

[15] I am using Nord's definition of documentary and instrumental translation (1991). In her view, the customer is the initiator of the translation process and the function of the TT is pragmatically defined by the purpose of the communication. Reiss and Vermeer argue, however, that it is the translator who fixes the translation *skopos* (Nord 1991:9).

tive the translator chooses, it will reveal varying degrees of interference and cultural filtering, replacing the original (Common Law) *preciseness* with Civil Law *conciseness*, which only genre and procedural knowledge render possible.

Another feature of English contracts is lexis. With a view to determining whether the influence of ELF is felt in the translation of contractual lexical items, I will discuss two examples, one about an everyday word like *consideration*, which has acquired a specific legal meaning, and the other related to the legal concept of *joint venture*.

First example: "consideration"

Before the law enforces an agreement, there must be something which is promised or done by one party in return for the promise of the other party. This is one of the essential ingredients of any agreement to constitute a contract and it is called *consideration*. The online version of the *Oxford Advanced Learner's Dictionary* lists four different meanings for *consideration*: the act of thinking carefully about something; something that must be thought about when you are planning or deciding; the quality of being sensitive towards others and thinking about their wishes and feelings; and a reward or payment for a service. The first three translate into Portuguese as *consideração*. The same online dictionary also lists two idioms featuring *consideration: to take something into consideration* i.e. to think about and include a particular thing or fact when you are forming an opinion or making a decision, which again translates into Portuguese as *consideração*; and *in consideration of something*, i.e. as payment for something, which is the specific legal meaning mentioned before. The lexical false friend *consideração* for the legal meaning of *consideration* in contracts is void of meaning in the Portuguese legal context, although it is appropriate for all the other everyday meanings of the English word. In contracts, *consideration* should, therefore, be translated as *contraprestação contratual* and not as *consideração*. In the best reputed bilingual law dictionaries published in Portugal,[16] however, one of the meanings of *consideration* is still listed as *consideração* in the Chaves de Mello dictionary, 2nd, 3rd and 4th editions (respectively 1985, 2001 and 2008), and in the 1st and 4th editions of the Noronha dictionary (1993 and 2000), although Noronha's 2000 edition lists *consideration* as a false cognate.

[16] See Mello (1985, 2001, 2008); Noronha (1993, 2000). It should be noted that Mello (2008:13) and Noronha (2000:xxi) state that their dictionaries consider both the Portuguese and the Brazilian legal systems and varieties.

IATE, the EU's online multilingual term base, lists 25 entries for *consideration* in the Law domain. Five occurrences are, however, related to the common meaning of the word (e.g. *to have under consideration, under consideration*) and translate into *consideração*. None of the translation suggestions for the remaining 20 entries use *consideração*. Both these dictionary entries and my experience as a translator indicate that there may be little tolerance to interference in this case.

Second example: "joint venture"

Another illustration of ELF's influence and tolerance to interference from English in legal Portuguese is the case of *joint venture*. Portuguese law does not possess an equivalent to the English legal concept of *joint venture,* but joint venture agreements often have to be translated into Portuguese, because they govern international business relations.

For years, the difficulty in translation posed by the concept *joint venture* was left unresolved, and thus the English term started to be used in Portuguese contracts. The Portuguese use of *contratos de joint venture* for the English *joint venture agreements* has become common and the high frequency of this expression may also result from using Portuguese contract templates made available online.[17] In 1981, however, things seemed to change when Decreto-Lei no. 231/81 (DL), of 28th July, was enacted. It stated in its preamble:[18] "*Está internacionalmente em voga a expressão joint venture* [...] *e, se a expressão é pelo menos no nosso sistema, desprovida de conteúdo jurídico rigoroso, a realidade existe e deve ser reconhecida*"[19] (original emphasis).

Further on, this DL also states that the concept of "so-called *unincorporated joint ventures*" is under Portuguese law covered by the term *consórcio* (consortium). The preamble offers two reasons why, in the legislator's opinion, it is important to provide a Portuguese translation for the two English expressions. The first is that such realities exist and should be

[17] See e.g. the website NFS-Escritório de Advogados for an in-depth discussion of the translations laid down by Decreto-Lei no. 231/81 of *joint venture* and *unincorporated joint venture.*

[18] The full text of Decreto-Lei no. 231/81 of 28th July can be accessed from the website of Direcção-Geral da Política de Justiça – DGPJ –MJ, i.e. the Portuguese Directorate-General for Justice Policy.

[19] "The expression *joint venture* is often used internationally [...] and, if such expression is, at least under our legal system, void of rigorous legal content, such reality exists and should be acknowledged."

acknowledged, and the second is that litigation on this matter is frequent in Portuguese courts. Articles 21 to 31 of this DL lay down the rules for *contratos de associação em participação* (contracts of joint association), the Portuguese concept which is equivalent to the English *joint venture agreements*. Articles 1 to 31 provide the term *consórcio* (consortium) as an equivalent to *unincorporated joint venture*. Consequently, this DL lays down two Portuguese translations for joint venture: contrato de *associação em participação* (*joint venture* agreement) and *consórcio* (*unincorporated joint venture*) thereby rendering the use of the English expression unnecessary (and, if not explicitly at least implicitly banning it).

Reality has, however, proved to be somewhat different as illustrated by three different terminological sources. The above-mentioned 2000 *Noronha's Law Dictionary* lists five meanings for *joint venture*, two of which *associação* and *consórcio* are defined pursuant to DL no. 231 as *joint venture* and *unincorporated joint venture,* respectively. Mello (2008) also lists the meaning given by said DL for *joint venture*. According to the EU's multilingual term base IATE, there may nevertheless be other translations for *joint venture*. In fact, *joint venture* is listed by IATE in 23 entries in five different domains (Economics, Finance, EU Law, Law and Fisheries) while *unincorporated joint venture* is listed once (unspecified domain).

Considering the relevant domains, IATE's entries seem to indicate that translators should either keep the English term in *joint venture agreement* thus expressly ignoring *acordo de associação em participação* which is the official term laid down by DL no. 231/81; or translate the term as *empresa comum* (joint company) in three domains (Finance, EU Law and Fisheries).

No criteria are offered for these different confusing entries and this may be one of the reasons for tolerance of the English term *joint venture*, a case of direct interference, to use Even-Zohar's terminology (2005), of ELF in Portuguese. Specialists recognise and use the term in English in both translated and non-translated contracts originally written in Portuguese. This is a case where tolerance to interference and the prestige conferred to English are so high that the English terms apparently "dethrone" the officially recommended translation suggestion.

Concluding remarks

The prestige and influence of ELF as the first and dominant foreign language in the school national curriculum, and as the main SL in translation in vast domains such as cinema, television and book publications are examples of mass exposure to this vehicular language used by both native and non-native speakers for international communication in the general context in Portugal. As expected within this general context, the legal examples analysed and discussed in this paper in terms of their stylistic and lexical interference of English – *consideration* (*consideração*) and *joint venture* – show a high tolerance to interference by fostering a generalised use of a false friend and loan-word, respectively. This interference seems to be fostered by dictionaries, online databases and online contract templates currently used by translators and lawyers. The context and textual examples discussed in this paper suggest the relevance of further research on the interference of ELF in Portuguese legal language.

References

Advocatus, http://www.advocatus.pt [3 July 2012].

Alcaraz, Enrique/Hughes, Brian (2002) *Legal Translation Explained.* Manchester: St Jerome.

A.M. Pereira, Saragga Leal, Oliveira Martins, Júdice e Associados, Sociedade de Advogados R.L, http://www.plmj.com/ [3 July 2012].

Antonini, Rachele (2007) "SAT, BLT, Spirit Biscuits, and the Third Amendment. What Italians Make of Cultural References in Dubbed Texts". In Gambier, Yves/Shlesinger, Miriam/Stolze, Radigundis (eds.) *Doubts and Directions in Translation Studies: Selected Contributions from the EST Congress, Lisbon 2004.* Amsterdam-Philadelphia: John Benjamins, 153-167.

Barotchi, Maher (1994) "Lingua Franca". In Asher, Ronald E./Simpson, Seumas (eds.) *The Encyclopedia of Language and Linguistics.* Vol. 4. Oxford: Pergamon Press, 2211.

Barreto, António (2002) *Mudança Social em Portugal. 1960/2000.* Lisboa: Universidade Nova de Lisboa, http://www.fcsh.unl.pt/docentes [3 July 2012].

Bennett, Karen (2007) "Epistemicide! *The Tale of a Predatory Discourse*". *The Translator* 13:2, 151-169.

Berns, Margie (2009) "English as a Lingua Franca and English in Europe". *World Englishes* 28:2, 192-199.

Bhatia, Vijay K. (1997) "Translating Legal Genres". In Trosborg, Anna (ed.) *Text Typology and Translation.* Amsterdam-Philadelphia: John Benjamins, 203-211.

Bolton, Kingsley (2006) "World Englishes Today". In Kachru, Braj B./Kachru, Yamuna/Nelson, Cecil (eds.) *The Handbook of World Englishes.* Oxford: Blackwell Publishing, 240-269.

Bravenet Free Counter (1997-2012), counter13.bravenet.com/index.php [1 April 2011].

Cao, Deborah (²2009) *Translating Law.* Clevedon-Buffalo-Toronto: Multilingual Matters.

Crystal, David (1995) *The Cambridge Encyclopedia of the English Language.* Cambridge: Cambridge University Press.

Crystal, David (2001) "Global Understanding for Global English". *Moscow State University Bulletin* 19:4, 13-28.

Cuatrecasas, Gonçalves Pereira e Associados R.L. Sociedade de Advogados (2011), http://www.gpcb.pt/ [3 July 2012].

Decreto-Lei no. 231/81 (1981) Direcção-Geral da Política de Justiça – DGPJ–MJ, http://www.dgpj.mj.pt [3 July 2012].

de Swaan, Abram (2004) "Endangered Languages, Sociolinguistics, and Linguistic Sentimentalism". *European Review* 12:4, 567-580.

Diário Económico (2011) issue 5156, 14 April 2011.

Diário Jurídico (n.d.), http://diariojuridico.blogs.sapo.pt [3 July 2011].

Directorate General for Translation (DGT) (2011) *Studies on Translation and Multilingualism. Lingua Franca: Chimera or Reality?.* European Commission, http://ec.europa.eu/dgs/translation/publications/studies/index_en.htm [3 July 2012].

Even-Zohar, Itamar (2005) "Law of Cultural Interference". In Even-Zohar, Itamar (ed.) *Papers in Culture Research.* Tel Aviv: The Porter Chair of Semiotics, Tel Aviv University, 50-67.

Firth, Alan (1996) "The Discursive Accomplishment of Normality: On 'Lingua Franca' English and Conversation Analysis". *Journal of Pragmatics* 26, 237-259.

Graddol, David (²2000) *The Future of English. A Guide to Forecasting the Popularity of the English Language in the 21st Century.* The English Company, http://www.britishcouncil.org/learning-elt-future.pdf [3 July 2012].

Harvey, Malcolm (2002) "What's so Special about Legal Translation?". *Meta* 47:2, 177-185.

Henrique Abecasis, Andresen Guimarães, Pedro Guerra e Álvaro Roquette Morais Sociedade de Advogados R.L (2007), http://www.haaag.pt/ [3 July 2012].

House, Juliane (2003) "English as a Lingua Franca: A Threat to Multilingualism?". *Journal of Sociolinguistics* 7:4, 556-578.

House, Juliane (2010) "English as a Global Lingua Franca: A Threat to Multilingualism?". In Shiyab, Said M./Rose, Marilyn Gaddis/House, Juliane/Duval, John (eds.) *Globalization and Aspects of Translation.* Newcastle upon Tyne: Cambridge Scholars Publishing, 11-35.

IATE – Interactive Terminology For Europe (2007), http://iate.europa.eu/ [3 July 2012].

ICA – Instituto do Cinema e do Audiovisual (2009) *Anuário Estatístico/2009 Facts & Figures,* http://www.ica-ip.pt/ [3 July 2012].

Jardim, Sampaio, Magalhães e Silva e Associados, Sociedade de Advogados R.L. (n.d.), http://www.jsms.pt/ [3 July 2012].

Jenkins, Jennifer (2009) "English as a Lingua Franca: Interpretations and Attitudes". *World Englishes* 28:2, 200-207.

Kachru, Braj B. (1992) "Teaching World Englishes". In Kachru, Braj (ed.) *The Other Tongue: English across Cultures.* Champaign: University of Illinois Press, 355-366.

Mello, Maria Chaves de ([2]1985) *Portuguese-English English-Portuguese Law Dictionary.* Rio de Janeiro: Barristers.

Mello, Maria Chaves de ([3]2001) *Law Dictionary Portuguese-English English-Portuguese.* Lisboa: Dinalivro.

Mello, Maria Chaves de ([4]2008) *Law Dictionary Portuguese-English English-Portuguese.* Lisboa: Dinalivro.

Ministério da Educação (ME) (n.d.) "As Línguas Estrangeiras no Currículo", http://sitio.dgidc.min-edu.pt/linguas_estrangeiras/Paginas/LEstrang_curriculo.aspx [3 July 2012].

Mufwene, Salikoko S. (n.d.) "Language Endangerment: What Have Pride and Prestige Got to Do With It?", http://humanities.uchicago.edu/faculty/mufwene/langenda.pdf [3 July 2012].

Mufwene, Salikoko S. (2004) "Language Birth and Death". *Annual Review of Anthropology* 33, 201-222.

Nord, Christiane (1991) *Text Analysis in Translation. Theory, Methodology and Didactic Applications of a Model for Translation-Oriented Text Analysis.* Amsterdam: Rodopi.

Noronha, Durval G. (1993) *Noronha's Legal Dictionary.* São Paulo: Editora Observador Legal.

Noronha, Durval G. ([4]2000) *Noronha's Legal Dictionary.* São Paulo: Observador Legal Editora Lda.

NSF-Escritório de Advogados (2010), http://www.nfs-advogados.com [3 July 2012].

Oxford Advanced Learner's Dictionary (2011), http://www.oxfordadvancedlearnersdictionary.com/dictionary/ [3 July 2012].

Phillipson, Robert (2008) "*Lingua Franca* or *Lingua Frankensteinia*? English in European Integration and Globalisation". *World Englishes* 27:2, 250-267.

Rodrigues, Maria da Conceição Carapinha (2005) *Contributos para a análise da linguagem jurídica e da interacção verbal na sala de audiências.* University of Coimbra: PhD Dissertation.

Rosa, Alexandra Assis (forthcoming) "To Translate or not to Translate. Profiling Audiovisual Translation in Portugal: Some Figures".

Rosa, Alexandra Assis (in press) "A Long and Winding Road: Mapping Translated Literature in 20th-Century Portugal". In Pym, Anthony/Alexandra Assis, Rosa (eds.) *New Directions in Translation Studies, Special issue of Anglo-Saxónica* 3:3.

Šarčević, Susan (1994) "Translation and the Law: An Interdisciplinary Approach". In Snell-Hornby, Mary/Pöchhacker, Franz/Kaindl, Klaus (eds.) *Translation Studies. An Interdiscipline.* Amsterdam-Philadelphia: John Benjamins, 301-307.

Šarčević, Susan ([2]2000) *New Approach to Legal Translation.* The Hague: Kluwer Law International.

Seidlhofer, Barbara (2009) "Common Ground and Different Realities: World Englishes and English as a Lingua Franca". *World Englishes* 28:2, 236-245.

Seidlhofer, Barbara/Berns, Margie (2009) "Perspectives on English as a Lingua Franca: Introduction". *World Englishes* 28:2, 190-191.

Smaghi, Lorenzo Bini (2011) "Ireland's Taxpayers Must Share the Pain". *Financial Times* 14 April 2011, http://www.ft.com/intl/cms/s/0/15d8fbae-653e-11e0-b150-00144feab49a.html#axzz1lGivBAM0 [3 July 2012].

Swales, John (1997) "English as Tyrannosaurus Rex". *World Englishes* 16:3, 373-382.

Tardy, Charles (2004) "The Role of English in Scientific Communication: *Lingua Franca* or *Tyrannosaurus Rex*?". *Journal of English for Academic Purposes* 3, 247-269.

Uría-Menendez-Proença de Carvalho & Associados (n.d.), http://www.uria.com/pt/index.html [3 July 2012].

Vermeer, Hans (1992) "Is Translation a Linguistic or a Cultural Process?". In Coulthard, Malcolm (ed.) *Studies in Translation. Ilha do Desterro. A Journal of Language and Literature* 28. Florianópolis: Universidade Federal de Santa Catarina, 37-49.

White, James Boyd (1982) "Law as Language: Reading Law and Reading Literature". *Texas Law Review* 60, 415-445.

ISABEL FERRO MEALHA

University of Lisbon, Portugal

English as the Language of Science and Academic Discourse in (Non-)Translated Medical Portuguese: The Initial Stages of a Research Project

In a world where English has become the *lingua franca* of scientific communication, with Expanding Circle researchers opting for English owing to the greater impact and prestige associated with an international readership, one expects interference from Anglophone norms to occur in the target language, thereby leading to hybridisation of local discourse practices. Such is the general assumption underlying the author's research project on (non-)translated medical discourse. This paper begins by outlining the initial stages of the ongoing research, namely with regard to the project's background, main goals and central questions. It then focuses on the correlation between English Academic Discourse and English as the international language of science, a crucial issue in terms of worldwide dissemination of knowledge in a formal context. Lastly, the paper dwells on the impact of English as a *lingua franca* in Portugal and on medical Portuguese.

Keywords: medical translation, academic discourse, English as the international language of science (EILS), medical Portuguese, interference

Introduction

The contact of English with other languages has inevitably brought important changes both to the former and the latter. As Kachru and Smith (2009:2-3) point out:

> [T]here are two aspects to the impact of English in the world. First, English has been accultured and nativised in different linguistic, cultural, and regional contexts; second, world languages have undergone perceptible changes as a result of contact and convergence with English.

The first aspect is concerned with the emergence of world Englishes (e.g. Indian, Nigerian, or Singaporean English), each a legitimate variety of English with its own norms of use. The second aspect is related to the Englishisation of the world's languages and, as such, is the one that is more pertinent to my research project on (non-)translated medical discourse.

Indeed, as Neubert (1990:97) stresses "the enormous translational activity concerned with the propagation and dissemination of the procedures and results of the scientific and technical revolution has left indelible marks on many languages. And there is no doubt that the SL has been mostly English".

When transfer of information from one language to another takes place, some kind of cultural interference is bound to occur. Even-Zohar's (2005:50) definition of contacts and interferences sheds some light on this process:

> Contacts can be defined as a relation(ship) between cultures, whereby a certain culture A (a source culture) may become a source of direct or indirect transfer for another culture B (a target culture). Once this possibility is realized, interference can be said to have occurred. Interference is thus a procedure emerging in the environment of contacts, one where transfer has taken place.

The emergence and occurrence of interference can arise when a culture becomes a source by prestige (ibid.:53). This appears to be the case with medical Portuguese where a dominant, prestigious English-language culture has become the source of information transfer for a more peripheral target culture. In a world where English has become the *lingua franca* of scientific communication, with Expanding Circle[1] researchers opting for English owing to the greater impact and prestige associated with an international readership, one can assume that direct and indirect interference from Anglophone linguistic and rhetorical norms will occur in the target language (TL). The status of English as the preferred language of international medical communication (Maher 1986; Pilegaard 1997; Navarro 2001) conditions and changes textual conventions of both translated and non-translated TL texts. Such is the general assumption underlying this paper and my research project whose main aim is to determine whether the increasing dominance of English as a *lingua franca* can be said to influence medical discourse both originally written in Portuguese[2] and translated into Portuguese. The project's major goal is to find evidence for or against this assumption.

---

1 This term was coined by Kachru (1985:12-13) and refers to those countries where English is taught as a foreign language.

2 For the sake of brevity, the term "Portuguese" will be used throughout this paper in order to refer to the variety of European Portuguese.

The choice of this particular topic was motivated by two main considerations: on the one hand, the fact that non-translated medical Portuguese seems to employ a considerable number of English-language loanwords and phonological, morphological, syntactical and lexical calques, which makes one conjecture whether convergence with linguistic and culture-specific Anglophone norms might not go beyond the more obvious presence of lexical imports; on the other hand, the fact that hardly any systematic empirical research in this field of inquiry has been carried out to date in Portugal. To the best of my knowledge, the few existing corpus-based studies in the language pair English-(European) Portuguese are not specifically related to medical communication *per se*, except for Contente's (2008) doctoral dissertation on medical terminology. Hence, there seems to be sufficient justification for the research I would like to undertake. Indeed, as recognised by Baumgarten, House and Probst (2004:105), "research into how English as *lingua franca* influences other languages is a socially important field in both qualitative and quantitative translation and corpus studies". It is hoped that this research project, whose primary goal is to examine how far Portuguese medical texts are influenced by means of interference from English norms, may ultimately constitute one more piece, albeit a modest one, of the wider puzzle made up of existing and ongoing studies on how source-language-induced interference affects local discourse practices (the source language (SL) being English in this case) and whose main purpose is to achieve a better understanding of translational convergence and divergence phenomena between two languages.

Special reference should be made here to a major project that has already undertaken substantial research on the influence of English in its role as a global *lingua franca* on target text norms – the project Covert Translation (e.g. House 2003a, 2003b; Baumgarten/House/Probst 2004; Becher/House/Kranich 2009). According to House (2003a:169), the global hypothesis underlying this project is that, given the increasing dominance of English, "translations from English into German (French, Spanish) no longer employ a culture filter to account for local communicative conventions. Rather, translations from English will reflect Anglophone norms". Some recent results from the project (Becher/House/Kranich 2009:125) have shown that translation-induced convergence with Anglophone norms does not occur unconditionally: the analysis of popular science texts has provided evidence suggesting that while in some cases there might be a clear trend toward a decreasing application of a cultural filter (as is the case with

English and German concessive conjunctions) in others, local conventions prevail (as is the case with English and German lexicogrammatical means for expressing modality).

In view of the notion of "cultural filtering", i.e. "adapting the original text in accordance with conventionalized expectation norms of the target audience" (ibid.:125-126), I am particularly interested in discovering whether translated and non-translated texts in medical Portuguese employ a cultural filter to account for local communicative norms or whether they tend to give way to SL conventions. If the latter proves to be true, it may then be tentatively hypothesised that there is a drift toward English preferred usage patterns in medical Portuguese possibly brought about by the interplay of two main factors: (a) the prevalence and prestige of the SL, especially in its function as the *lingua franca* of science and, more specifically, as a vehicle for the advancement of medical knowledge across national/cultural boundaries; and (b) the fact that medical doctors and researchers represent one of the most globalised communities of practice in academia (Giannoni 2008:97) and, as such, are likely to adopt writing conventions and specialised terminology typical of their discipline rather than of their national languages/cultures. Indeed, and despite the fact that several contrastive studies on academic discourse have found that there is significant intercultural variation in the rhetorical preferences of national cultures (e.g. Johns 1992; Vassileva 1998; Salager-Meyer/Alcaraz Ariza/Zambrano 2003; Dahl 2004), writing conventions adopted in formal medical communication appear to be supranational. This claim is supported by evidence from Dahl (2004), who investigated metatext in English, French and Norwegian research articles belonging to three disciplines, economics, linguistics and medicine, and concluded that within medicine, and in all three languages, metatext was a marker of disciplinary culture.

The corpus on which the research will be based consists of medical research articles, considered to be "one of the more relevant and challenging medical text genres from a translation point of view" (Pilegaard 1997:163). Indeed, the medical research article is a highly structured text in which the different rhetorical sections (Abstract, Introduction, Methods, Results and Discussion) have distinct communicative functions and, as such, certain linguistic features tend to be distributed differently across the various sections (e.g. the use of hedges is especially marked in the introduction and discussion sections), which may pose further problems to the translator of medical texts. Hedging, as a resource for expressing tentativeness and open-mindedness about one's claims, plays a critical role in medicine where "writing is necessarily a balance of fact and evaluation, as the writer tries to present information as fully, accurately, and objectively as possible" (Hyland 2006:695).

The research articles will be analysed on the basis of a comparative method whereby translations will be compared with non-translated texts of the same kind in TL with the purpose of ascertaining what types of interference can be found in Portuguese written medical discourse. Franco Aixelá (2009:79) identifies four main reasons for interference in translation, adding that the last three are very common in scientific and technical translation: "the double tension intrinsically associated with translation, the creation and preservation of a specific terminology or jargon, the nonexistence of a given term or structure in TL, and the *prestige of the source culture*" (emphasis added). It is hoped that the analysis of the corpus will reveal whether these three variables apply, to some degree, to interference from English in Portuguese medical discourse and, if so, whether any of them proves to be more prevalent than the others. But, for the purpose of this paper, I would like to expand on the idea of the "prestige of the source culture", a context variable and socio-cultural factor that seems to play a critical role in the emergence of interference when there is transfer of information from a dominant culture to a more peripheral one, as is the case here. Thus, the paper focuses on some interrelated aspects pertinent to those two cultures and the point at issue here: the section "Science and *lingua franca*" addresses the correlation between English Academic Discourse (EAD) and the prevalence of English as the international language of science (EILS), as this is a crucial issue in terms of worldwide diffusion of knowledge which carries certain implications for national languages; and the section "The impact of English as a *lingua franca* in Portugal" dwells on the impact of English as a *lingua franca* in Portugal and on medical Portuguese.

Science and *lingua franca*

English academic discourse

The seventeenth-century western world witnessed a major revolution in the way reality was perceived and knowledge configured, which was accompanied by the birth of a new kind of prose style, scientific discourse. In a period that came to be known as the Scientific Revolution and which laid the foundations of modern science, the emergence of new ideas in astronomy, biology, chemistry, human anatomy, physics, and other sciences led to a rejection of doctrines that had prevailed since Antiquity. The new scientific paradigm challenged the Aristotelian system of deduction, which had been the basis of university education until then, and advocated the use of induction (combining the rational and the empirical) as the proper way to investigate nature (Bennett 2007:175). This change of attitude towards knowledge required a new type of discourse which could act as a vehicle for objective truth. Over the course of the eighteenth and nineteenth centuries, major events such as the Industrial Revolution and significant discoveries and theories (e.g. Faraday's on electricity, or Darwin's on evolution) contributed to the growing status of the natural sciences. In Britain, by the end of the nineteenth century, "there was a recognizable variety of scientific English [...], shaped by observations of grammarians, the expectations of the burgeoning scientific societies, and the style guides of the new academic journals" (Crystal 1997:87). The "authoritative plain style" (Venuti 1995:5) of the discourse of science had acquired prestige and began to spread to other areas of knowledge.

Today, this "style" is commonly recognised as English Academic Discourse and has become the dominant vehicle for the configuration and diffusion of knowledge in most of the English-speaking world, being adopted by scientific communities across the hard and soft knowledge fields. Publishing in academic journals demands that researchers display "a familiarity with the rhetorical conventions and social understandings of the community" which they belong to (Hyland 2001:209).

One of the prime vehicles for scholarly communication is the research article (RA) which has become increasingly standardised and rule-bound, especially in the hard knowledge disciplines including the health sciences where the IMRAD (Introduction-Methods-Results-and-Discussion) rhetorical structure is globally implemented. Yet, underneath the outward rigid format of the RA there is room for a wealth of disciplinary variation as revealed by an increasing number of studies on academic writing in English (e.g. Hyland 2001; Harwood 2005). Hyland (2001:217-218), for instance, investigated the use of self-mention in RAs from a broad range of disciplines. His findings showed that the use of "we" is favoured by single authors of hard knowledge papers as opposed to the use of "I" by single authors in the humanities and social sciences texts. Self-mention or authorial presence in RAs, which remains highly controversial (ibid.:208), is but one example of how an understanding of the writing practices underlying EAD is of paramount importance to academic success.

In sum, the process of gaining access to a particular research community seems to be dependent on awareness of and competence in the discourse styles and rhetorical structure typical of EAD and of the relevant discourse community (Dahl 2004:1808). The recognition of this fact has led to increasing standardisation and internationalisation in science writing (Kaplan 2001:14). Consequently, the role of English in international research mediation has acquired a growing importance and English has become the predominant language of science and technology. Some of the effects of this widespread use of English across language communities and countries will be discussed next.

English as the international language of science

It is commonly acknowledged that nowadays English plays a major role worldwide as an instrument of intercultural communication which takes place in and across all three Kachruvian circles: the Inner Circle, where English is a native language; the Outer Circle, where English is spoken as a second language, and the Expanding Circle, where English is still spreading and is taught as a foreign language, and where it is used as a vehicle for international communication in several domains (Kachru 1992).

In this sense, it can be said that English has achieved the status of a *lingua franca* in today's globalised world. The term *lingua franca* has been defined in different ways throughout history.[3] Yet, for the purpose of this paper and bearing in mind the prevalence and dominance of English in scientific oral and written communication, *lingua franca* will be perceived chiefly as a contact language, i.e. a vehicular language "which is used habitually by people whose mother tongues are different in order to facilitate communication between them" (Barotchi 1994:2211). The notion of English being used as a language for communication is introduced by House (2003b:562) who makes a distinction between "languages for identification – mother tongues, regional, local, intimate varieties of language" – and "languages for communication, such as English today", stressing that English as a *lingua franca* can

[3] For an overview of the different meanings of *lingua franca* see, for instance, the study published by the Directorate-General for Translation (DGT) of the European Commission (2011:7-51).

be regarded as "a useful instrument for making oneself understood in international encounters" (ibid.).

The use of English as the international language of science facilitates cross-cultural communication, enabling easy access to scientific information, but it also creates some situations in which Expanding Circle speakers may find themselves at a disadvantage, especially when it comes to the dissemination of knowledge in a formal context (Kaplan 2001). In fact, English is the language in which over 80% of the scientific information is published and the *lingua franca* most used at the vast majority of international scientific meetings and research exchange programmes. But "of the roughly 15 million people worldwide directly involved in scientific work, at least two-thirds are non-native speakers" (Montgomery 2009:6-7) and this has inevitable repercussions for national languages which might to a greater or lesser extent be influenced and affected by Anglophone norms. Moreover, the increased standardisation of scientific discourse according to the precepts of EAD may contribute to the gradual loss of specialised registers and genres in Expanding Circle national languages. Gatekeeping, through editorial boards and referees, is yet another factor that may affect periphery scholars' chances of divulging their work worldwide. Researchers face a great deal of pressure to publish in leading, usually peer-reviewed, international journals, most of which are now English language, for otherwise, they risk invisibility for themselves and their work (ibid.:11). Publication and citation practices are most often dictated by Inner Circle countries. Consequently, as noted by Kaplan (2001:18), "scientists who cannot write English to meet the standards of journal editors are deprived of the opportunity to have their views and contributions disseminated through the global information networks". This language bias in publication may have serious effects for science: not taking into account the work of scientists who have difficulty in publishing in English may lead to an incomplete and distorted view of scientific progress in any given field (Kaplan 2001; Navarro 2001; Tardy 2004).

There may be drawbacks to the use of EILS by Expanding Circle scholars, but the advantages of adopting a common language for disciplinary communication are widely acknowledged by scientists and professionals of different nationality groups (Tardy 2004:258). Medical communication is a case in point as it can be said that there has always been a *lingua franca* of medicine. The oldest written sources of Western medicine can be traced back to the Hippocratic writings of the fifth and fourth centuries BC (Wulff 2004:187). The Greek era of the language of medicine lasted well into the

Roman Empire since the Romans did not have a similar medical tradition. However, at the beginning of the first century AD, Celsus wrote *De Medicina*, a medical encyclopaedia based on Greek sources but written in Latin. During the Middle Ages, a third language gained importance as many classical Greek medical texts were translated into Arabic (Fischbach 1993:97). But in the Renaissance when knowledge of Greek began to decrease, both Arabic and Greek texts were translated into Latin, and the era of medical Latin started and lasted up to the early nineteenth century, according to Wulff (2004:187-188) who further explains that then came the era of the national medical languages, with a few of these, namely French, German and English, taking on the role of *lingua franca* of medicine at different moments in time. In the second half of the twentieth century, English gradually gained ground over the other languages and became the predominant vehicle for international communication and information access (Tardy 2004:248). It is hardly surprising, then, that medical Portuguese exhibits interference from English, given that Portugal is an Expanding Circle country where English is learnt as a foreign language and is increasingly used as a language for communication. The next section will briefly examine how English as a *lingua franca* impacts on the Portuguese language and culture in general terms and on medical Portuguese in particular.

The impact of English as a *lingua franca* in Portugal

The English language in Portugal

The English language currently enjoys a privileged position in most domains of Portuguese life and culture. However, this has not always been so. Up to the early 1970s, French was the first foreign language taught at school in Portugal: fresh out of primary school, ten-year-old pupils would start by learning French and two years later, they would take up English as a second foreign language. The influence of French culture was very much felt in all spheres of Portuguese life. But that state of affairs started to change after 1974 when Portugal became a democracy. French was replaced by English as the first foreign language and, as a result, amongst the younger generations, there are some who can hardly speak any French nowadays, because they chose to learn another second foreign language (e.g. Spanish). French culture lost importance as the Portuguese increasingly began to shift their attention towards Anglo-American cultural values. The music and film industries (most foreign films and TV shows are subtitled, not dubbed[4]) and later the Internet have played a major role in exposing people to English. As far as TV programmes are concerned, for instance, available data show that English is the SL which Portuguese broadcasting channels mostly translate from – with a high percentage of translation (70%) as opposed to that of the other languages also translated into Portuguese, e.g. Spanish, Italian, and German (Rosa forthcoming). In 1986, Portugal became a member state of the European Union (EU) and as such endorsed and enforced the EU policies, including those concerning languages. In a university context, the implementation of the EU Erasmus Programme has led to further contact with English as this is the language students (and teachers) resort to when they cannot speak each other's mother tongues.

The impact of the English language on Portuguese is also felt through the innumerable Anglicisms that proliferate in everyday usage. Words like *airbag*, *cheeseburger*, *cowboy*, *drive-in*, *e-mail*, *flirt*, *ketchup*, *laser*, *leasing*, and *roaming* are now part of Portuguese speakers' vocabulary. These linguistic imports, along with many others, were listed in the Lisbon Academy of Sciences' first complete dictionary which was published in 2001 (Casteleiro 2001).

To a certain extent, Portuguese academic discourse also appears to have been influenced by English paradigms as there is an increasing pressure to adopt writing conventions typical of EAD across the different disciplines. The writing styles of Portuguese-speaking scholars were investigated by Bennett (2008), who argues that there is no single dominant academic discourse in Portugal at present, but rather three different discourses labelled "modern", "traditional" and "postmodern".[5] Since the Scientific Revolution never really took place in Portugal, the scholastic/rhetorical tradition dominant throughout Europe in the Early Modern period was perpetuated over the centuries, retaining a central position up to the present time (Bennett 2008:208-209). This seems to account for the fact that two out of the three types of discourse identified rely on a very different epistemological framework to that underlying EAD.

[4] The only exceptions are animated cartoons for children under 6-7, and some children's shows which are dubbed into Portuguese.

[5] It should be noted that the three different kinds of Portuguese discourse are not static entities, and hybrid forms often occur. Features from the "traditional" style might unintentionally intrude upon a discourse that is attempting to be "modern".

The "traditional" style has its roots in the older humanities tradition and until very recently was the dominant discourse being produced across a wide range of humanities disciplines (ibid.:191). The governing principles of this kind of discourse are markedly different from EAD precepts: the style is more elaborate, erudite, rhetorical, poetic, subjective and less transparent. The "postmodern" style bears no resemblance at all to EAD. It shares many of the features of the "traditional" style, but "it is grounded upon a sign-based epistemology" and is very much fashioned like some of the texts of the French poststructuralists. Some extreme instances of this style can be found in art and architecture as well as in literary studies and music (ibid.:199-200). Finally, the "modern" style is the one that most closely resembles the EAD model, valuing clarity, precision, economy, and rational argument over aesthetic or interpersonal factors. This is obviously the type of discourse adopted by the hard sciences (engineering, economics and medicine) where factuality and authority need to be asserted. It only began being used more consistently in the final decades of the twentieth century. Within the specific context of medical communication and given the highly standardised format of the genre of medical RAs, the "modern" style appears to be used unconditionally. However, only an in-depth analysis, which is beyond the scope of this paper, will reveal whether Portuguese medical RAs are more closely related to the social and epistemological practices of the discipline or whether the Portuguese writers' rhetorical strategies are still partly conditioned by the local writing culture.

The English language in medical Portuguese

The English language occupies a central position in the life of medical students, doctors and biomedical researchers in Portugal. Most text books adopted at university are written in English. There are translations into Spanish or Brazilian Portuguese of several of them, but especially the latter are not to be recommended given that medical terminology in European Portuguese is different to that of Brazilian Portuguese. The pervasive influence of English on Portuguese medical discourse is felt not only through the use of lexical Anglicisms, many of which are already listed in the Portuguese dictionary of the Lisbon Academy of Sciences (e.g. *bypass, check-up, follow-up, pacemaker, rash, scanner, shunt*), but also through the use of syntactical Anglicisms (e.g. use of the passive) that may not be so immediately perceptible to the speakers but that could be taken as a clear sign that interference from English seems to go beyond the occurrence of loanwords.

Some of the most obvious examples of SL-induced interference, though, are related to lexical items. Hybrid expressions are often used in non-translated texts, e.g. *medidas de* outcome ("outcome measures"), bypass *aortocoronário* ("aortocoronary bypass"), shunt *bidireccional de* Glenn ("bidirectional Glenn shunt"). The use of calques is quite frequent too: for instance, "randomised (clinical trial)" becomes *(ensaio clínico) randomizado*, though *aleatório* would be more appropriate (and is, in fact, more often used); *evidências* ("evidence") and *achados* ("findings") are two examples of calques that have become common usage amongst physicians and medical researchers. A quick random look at translated RAs from the Portuguese edition of the *British Medical Journal* (2009 issues) has revealed that interference appears to be more visible in translations, with words and expressions, and sometimes even full sentences, being translated literally. By way of example, the following three instances of literal translation can be given: (a) both the adjective "severe" (e.g. "severe pain") and the noun "severity" (e.g. "severity of concomitant obstructive coronary disease") are sometimes translated as *(dor) severa*[6] and *severidade*, respectively – these translations are inadequate because, in Portuguese, the most common meaning of *severo* is "strict" (as in "a strict parent") whereas *severidade* usually means "excessive sternness", thus the two words do not match the meanings conveyed by the English terms ("intense" for a particular kind of pain and the "seriousness" of a given medical condition); (b) the collocation "distant metastases" is translated as *metástases distantes* in which the construction "noun + adjective" is maintained but the word order is reversed, as is more common in Portuguese – the correct expression would be *metástases à distância* (noun + adnominal adjunct); (c) the literal translation of "positively" as *positivamente* in "It is also positively related to oestrogen levels […]" renders the Portuguese sentence odd as the use of that adverb does not make any sense within the given context.

The transfer of discursive features and patterns of English academic discourse to medical Portuguese may be accounted for by the scientists' extensive reading of English-language medical literature and by the pressure to publish in English as a means of gaining recognition and prestige. Indeed, the scientific medical community has realised it can become more visible if

[6] Portuguese nouns have got two genders, the masculine (*-o*) and the feminine (*-a*) genders; adjectives agree in gender with the nouns they collocate with, e.g. *dor* is a feminine noun, therefore when the adjective *severo* is used as a qualifier to describe a particular kind of pain ("severe pain") it becomes *(dor) severa*.

it imitates the norms characteristic of the dominant foreign culture. Accordingly, most Portuguese medical journals now publish abstracts in English and have adopted the International Committee of Medical Journal Editors (ICMJE) requirements for manuscripts submitted to biomedical journals. The IMRAD structure typical of RAs is calqued from English and used consistently in Portuguese medical journals.

In sum, it can be said that Portuguese medical students, physicians and researchers all engage in some kind of formal or informal translation when it comes to knowledge transfer. Neubert (1990:97, original emphasis) refers to a "*translational discourse* integrated into the 'normal' (non-translated) discursive practice of native TL users". To put it simply, the knowledge input may be provided in English but the output is given in Portuguese. In the course of this process interference is bound to occur, brought about by "the importation, whether intentional or not, of literal or modified foreign words and phrases (lexical interference), forms (syntactic interference), specific cultural items (cultural interference, proper nouns included), or genre conventions (structural or pragmatic interference)" (Franco Aixelá 2009:75). In this sense, translation seems to play an important role in the process of the Englishisation of medical Portuguese.

Conclusion

This paper is based on the assumption that the widespread use of EILS results in the adoption of English preferred patterns by Expanding Circle speakers given the impact and prestige of English as SL. This trend seems to apply to the genre of medical research articles where disciplinary communicative preferences appear to play a greater role than national language and culture, as medical doctors and researchers represent one the most globalised communities of practice. The ongoing research project will attempt to establish whether Portuguese medical discourse (in translated and non-translated RAs) has given way to Anglophone linguistic and rhetorical norms or whether it still employs a "cultural filter" to account for Portuguese communicative conventions. At this stage, no findings can yet be produced, but it is hoped that the future analysis of the data will provide some answers as to whether convergence with English usage patterns occurs unconditionally or, as in Becher, House, and Kranich (2009), it only takes place in some cases while in others local communicative preferences prevail.

References

Baumgarten, Nicole/House, Juliane/Probst, Julia (2004) "English as *Lingua Franca* in Covert Translation Processes". *The Translator* 10:1, 83-108.

Barotchi, Maher (1994) "Lingua Franca". In Asher, Ronald E./Simpson, Seumas (eds.) *Encyclopedia of Language and Linguistics*. Oxford-New York-Seoul-Tokyo: Pergamon Press, 2211.

Becher, Viktor/House, Juliane/Kranich, Svenja (2009) "Convergence and Divergence in Communicative Norms through Language Translation". In Braunmüller, Kurt/House, Juliane (eds.) *Convergence and Divergence in Language Contact Situations*. Amsterdam-Philadelphia: John Benjamins, 125-152.

Bennett, Karen (2007) "Galileo's Revenge: Ways of Construing Knowledge and Translation Strategies in the Era of Globalization". *Social Semiotics* 17:2, 171-193.

Bennett, Karen (2008) *English Academic Discourse: Its Hegemonic Status and Implications for Translation*. University of Lisbon: PhD Dissertation.

Casteleiro, João Malaca (ed.) (2001) *Dicionário da Língua Portuguesa Contemporânea. Academia das Ciências de Lisboa*. Lisbon: Verbo.

Contente, Madalena (2008) *Terminocriatividade, Sinonímia e Equivalência Interlinguística em Medicina*. Lisboa: Edições Colibri/Universidade Nova de Lisboa.

Crystal, David ([2]1997) *The Cambridge Encyclopedia of the English Language*. Cambridge: Cambridge University Press.

Dahl, Trine (2004) "Textual Metadiscourse in Research Articles: A Marker of National Culture or of Academic Discipline?" *Journal of Pragmatics* 38, 1807-1825.

Directorate-General for Translation (DGT) (2011) *Lingua Franca: Chimera or Reality? Studies on Translation and Multilingualism*, http://ec.europa.eu/dgs/translation/publications/studies/index_en.htm [3 July 2012].

Even-Zohar, Itamar (2005) "Law of Cultural Interference". In Even-Zohar, Itamar (ed.) *Papers in Culture Research*. Tel Aviv: The Porter Chair of Semiotics, Tel Aviv University, 50-67.

Fischbach, Henry (1993) "Translation, the Great Pollinator of Science: A Brief Flashback on Medical Translation". In Wright, Sue Ellen/Wright, Leland D. (eds.) *Scientific and Technical Translation*. Amsterdam-Philadelphia: John Benjamins, 89-100.

Franco Aixelá, Javier (2009) "An Overview of Interference in Scientific and Technical Translation". *The Journal of Specialised Translation* 11, 75-88.

Giannoni, Davide Simone (2008) "Medical Writing at the Periphery: The Case of Italian Journal Editorials". *Journal of English for Academic Purposes* 7, 97-107.

Harwood, Nigel (2005) "'*We Do not Seem to Have a Theory... The Theory I Present Here Attempts to Fill this Gap*': Inclusive and Exclusive Pronouns in Academic Writing". *Applied Linguistics* 26:3, 343-375.

House, Juliane (2003a) "English as a Lingua Franca and its Influence on Discourse Norms in Other Languages". In Anderman, Gunilla/Rogers, Margaret (eds.) *Translation Today. Trends and Perspectives.* Cleverton-Buffalo-Toronto-Sydney: Multilingual Matters, 168-179.

House, Juliane (2003b) "English as a Lingua Franca: A Threat to Multilingualism?" *Journal of Sociolinguistics* 7:4, 556-578.

Hyland, Ken (2001) "Humble Servants of the Discipline? Self-mention in Research Articles". *English for Specific Purposes* 20, 207-226.

Hyland, Ken (^{2}2006) "Medical Discourse: Hedges". In Brown, Keith (ed.) *Encyclopedia of Language and Linguistics.* Oxford: Elsevier, 694-697.

Johns, Tim (1992) "*It Is Presented Initially*: Linear Dislocation and Interlanguage Strategies in Brazilian Academic Abstracts in English and Portuguese". *Ilha do Desterro: A Journal of English Language, Literatures in English and Cultural Studie*s 27, 9-32.

Kachru, Braj B. (1985) "Standards, Codification and Sociolinguistic Realism: The English Language in the Outer Circle". In Quirk, Randolph/Widdowson, Henry G. (eds.) *English in the World: Teaching and Learning the Language and Literatures.* Cambridge: Cambridge University Press, 11-30.

Kachru, Braj B. (1992) "Teaching World Englishes". In Kachru, Braj B. (ed.) *The Other Tongue: English Across Cultures.* Chicago: Board of Trustees of the University of Illinois, 355-366.

Kachru, Yamuna/Smith, Larry E. (2009) "The Karmic Cycle of World Englishes: Some Futuristic Constructs". *World Englishes* 28:1, 1-14.

Kaplan, Robert B. (2001) "English – the Accidental Language of Science?" In Ammon, Ulrich (ed.) *The Dominance of English as a Language of Science: Effects on Other Languages and Languages Communities.* Berlin-New York: Mouton de Gruyter, 3-26.

Maher, John (1986) "The Development of English as an International Language of Medicine". *Applied Linguistics* 7, 206-218.

Montgomery, Scott L. (2009) "English and Science: Realities and Issues for Translation in the Age of an Expanding *Lingua Franca*". *The Journal of Specialised Translation* 11, 6-16.

Navarro, Fernando A. (2001) "El inglés, idioma internacional de la medicina: causas y consequencias de un fenómeno actual". *Panace@* 2:3, 35-51.

Neubert, Albrecht (1990) "The Impact of Translation on Target Language Discourse: Text vs. System". *Meta* 35:1, 96-101.

Pilegaard, Morten (1997) "Translation of Medical Research Articles". In Trosborg, Anna (ed.) *Text Typology and Translation.* Amsterdam-Philadelphia: John Benjamins, 159-184.

Rosa, Alexandra Assis (forthcoming) "To Translate or Not to Translate. Profiling Audiovisual Translation in Portugal: Some Figures".

Salager-Meyer, Françoise/Alcaraz Ariza, María Angeles/Zambrano, Nahirana (2003) "The Scimitar, the Dagger and the Glove: Intercultural Differences in the Rhetoric of Criticism in Spanish, French and English Medical Discourse (1930-1995)". *English for Specific Purposes* 22, 223-249.

Tardy, Charles (2004) "The Role of English in Scientific Communication: Lingua Franca or *Tyrannosaurus rex*?". *Journal of English for Academic Purposes* 3, 247-269.

Vassileva, Irena (1998) "*Who Am I/Who Are We in Academic Writing*?: A Contrastive Analysis of Authorial Presence in English, German, French, Russian and Bulgarian". *International Journal of Applied Linguistics* 8:2, 163-190.

Venuti, Lawrence (1995) *The Translator's Invisibility. A History of Translation*. London-New York: Routledge.

Wulff, Henrik R. (2004) "The Language of Medicine". *Journal of the Royal Society of Medicine* 97, 187-188.

MATILDE NISBETH JENSEN

Aarhus University, Denmark; Macquarie University, Australia

Patient Information Leaflet Translators in the EU: Mapping the Hypothetical Competences of Professional Translators and Pharmacists-Cum-Translators

The last decade has seen an increased focus on health communication directed at lay receivers. The many challenges associated with effective expert-lay health communication are further compounded in an EU context as written mandatory patient communication is translated into all EU languages. Despite this increased focus on easy-to-understand health communication, many studies have shown that Patient Information Leaflets (PILs), the texts which in an EU context have to accompany all medication informing us about dosage, side effects etc., are often complex, and one study has indicated that PILs translated into Danish were even more complex than their English source texts. It has been assumed that this increase in complexity during the translation process is caused by the fact that the PILs translators were mainly pharmacists. Thus, this paper reports a preliminary study showing that pharmaceutical companies use either medical professionals or translators to an almost equal extent. The hypothetical translation competences of these two groups are then mapped against the PACTE competence model, and discussed from a theoretical perspective to explore whether the difficulties in the translated PILs could be linked to the translators in view of a further empirical investigation.

Keywords: medical translation, Patient Information Leaflets, expert-lay communication, translation competence, lay-friendliness

Introduction

Recent years have seen an increased focus on the importance of health communication, especially health communication for the general public. Patients today demand transparency and enough information in order to make informed choices about a proposed treatment option, or about taking a specific medication etc. The demand for patient information does not only come from patients, but also reflects a societal push to involve patients in their own health. Patient information also aims at optimising the use of a medicine (Raynor 2007:60), and at ensuring safe, effective and appropriate use once the decision has been made to take it (Raynor/Dickinson 2009:700). As a result of this recent demand for patient involvement, a great amount of legislation has been passed during the past 15 years, and pharmaceutical companies are now required to provide patients not only with explicit information, but with information that is lay-friendly,[1] i.e. information which is easy to read and understand for all receivers. The demand from authorities as well as from patients for pharmaceutical companies to provide easily understandable material has resulted in the production of an enormous amount of written patient information.

This need to produce lay-friendly health communication has led to new genres being created. One such genre is the Patient Information Leaflet (PIL),[2] which became mandatory in 1992 under EU law (Council Directive 92/27/EEC). A PIL must accompany all medication informing patients about dosage, side effects etc. The PIL is the most important source of information about a medication for the patient (Bjerrum/Foged 2003:58), and patients want the information provided in the PILs (Kenny et al. 1998:476). Lay-friendliness in PILs is extremely important, because it is essential for the correct use of medication, and in the event that the communication is not understood by the receiver, it could have significant consequences as it could for example lead to overdosing or failure to report serious side effects. Therefore, the EU has made it an explicit requirement that PILs are lay-friendly as stipulated in article 63(2) of EU Directive 2001/83/EC: the PIL "must be written and designed to be clear, understandable and enable the users to act appropriately". It is the responsibility of the pharmaceutical companies to ensure lay-friendliness, and it is a requirement for the granting of marketing authorisation. Despite the EU legislation, research conducted into the lay-friendliness of PILs has shown that patients struggle to understand the PILs, and that a large number of PILs are still not optimally lay-friendly and readable (e.g. Askehave/Zethsen 2000a, 2000b, 2002, 2003; Dickinson/Raynor/Duman 2001; MHRA 2005; Pander Maat/Lentz 2010).

---

[1] I would like to thank Professor Theo Raynor for introducing me to the term "lay-friendliness" in a personal communication, February 2011.

[2] PILs are also sometimes referred to as Patient Package Inserts or Package Leaflets. I have opted for Patient Information Leaflet as this term refers to the function of the leaflet, and not merely its location.

PILs have to be translated into all EU languages, and research in the Danish context has found that even when English source texts were quite lay-friendly, the Danish target texts were significantly more complex (Askehave/Zethsen 2003:40). It has previously been assumed that Danish PILs are generally translated by pharmacists and that this is one of the reasons for the increase in complexity (Askehave/Zethsen 2002:24). In order to shed light on this assumption, this article discusses the results of a survey of a large population of pharmaceutical companies seeking to investigate what kind of translator (medical professional or trained translator) they use. On the basis of this information, an analysis of the hypothetical profiles of the two translator categories is carried out using the PACTE model of translator competence (PACTE 2003, 2005, 2009). The main aim of this article is to analyse the hypothetical competences of typical professional translators and typical pharmacists, based on PACTE's competence model concerning their ability to translate for a lay audience and to discuss whether the decrease in lay-friendliness could be linked to the translators' sub-competences.

In order to examine the translation phase of PILs and hence the competences needed, the genre as well as the interlingual and intralingual translation complexity involved in its production process is further described. After this introduction to the PIL genre, an empirical study of who the translators are is introduced, and the results analysed in relation to medical translation competences needed for medical translation for lay receivers based on the PACTE translation competence model. Finally, the article ends with a discussion of whether the assumed competences of the translator types could be linked to the decrease in lay-friendliness in the translated PIL, and why it would be interesting to research the translation products from pharmaceutical companies using professional translators and pharmacists, respectively.

Patient Information Leaflets as a mandatory genre

The importance and complexity of lay-friendliness in PILs become apparent when investigating the production process and the legal requirements. Because the PIL is a mandatory genre, which means that it is a legally regulated genre (Askehave/Zethsen 2008:167), it is governed by several regulations and standards which influence the structure and content of the PIL, and therefore, also the translation of it. The most important legislative measures in connection with the production of PILs can be seen in Figure 1. One of these measures is the Readability Guideline which was issued by the EU in 1998. The guideline includes information to PIL producers on the use of headings, syntax, layout etc. Along with the guideline, PIL templates were produced in all Member State languages to ensure consistency across different medicines and across different languages (European Commission 2009:11). The template provides guidance for PIL producers, i.e. the pharmaceutical companies, but the template specifies headings, and the wording of specific sections, and alternative headings and wording can only be used in exceptional cases, and must be justified by the producers. It can therefore be assumed that pharmaceutical companies would stay very close to the template to ensure quick marketing authorisation. However, even though both the form and the content of the PILs are heavily regulated, it is still possible to make the PIL more lay-friendly while staying within the guidelines (Pander Maat/Lentz 2010:19). The most recent regulatory initiative came in 2005 when user-testing became a legal requirement. User-testing of one PIL must be conducted by the pharmaceutical companies prior to marketing authorisation. However, only one language version needs to be tested (European Commission 2006). Thus, the English version is most often the version which is tested as this version is the first to be produced and submitted, and furthermore, the results of the user-testing must be submitted in English to the European Medicines Agency (EMEA) (ibid.:21).

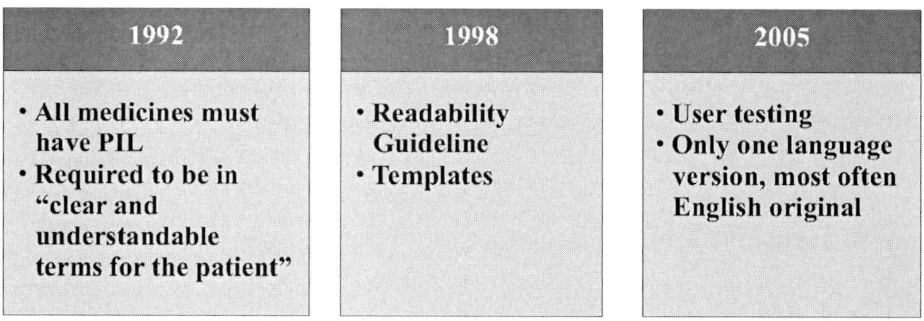

Figure 1: Legislative measures related to the production of PILs

Patient Information Leaflets and translation

The complexity of the PIL production is not only linked to the legal requirements, it is also emphasised by the knowledge asymmetry between the sender, a medical expert, and the receiver, a lay person. The receiver side of the communication process is very complex for PILs because the potential receiver group consists of a large heterogeneous group, who, in the reception situation, might feel anxious, stressed or insecure (Albin 1998:118). Even though the text producers might be aware that their potential receiver is a lay person, the receiver of many types of medications can potentially be the entire population, which means that the text producer can never really have a specific receiver in mind, and visualisation of the receiver can be extremely problematic to the text producer (Askehave/Zethsen 2003:26). In addition, research from other disciplines such as communication and psychology shows that experts are often unaware of what poses problems for lay people, and therefore, might overestimate the knowledge of their receivers (e.g. Hinds 1999; Nickerson 1999; Lentz/de Jong 2009), which might prove very detrimental to lay-friendliness.

As illustrated in Figure 2, the elaboration of a non-English language (e.g. Danish) PIL is the result of both an interlingual and intralingual translation. This is due to that fact that, following EU legislation, all PILs have to be based on, and closely linked to the report on the clinical studies, the Summary of Product Characteristics (SPC). This is the expert-to-expert text which in expert terminology describes contents, side effects etc. for a professional readership such as doctors. Furthermore, the SPC provides the authorisation body, EMEA, with information about the medicine in order for them to assess whether the medicine should be authorised. The intralingual translation of the SPC into a PIL comprises a change in receiver group from expert to lay person reflecting a knowledge asymmetry between the sender (producer of the SPC) and the receiver (reader of the PIL). This intralingual translation and the subsequent knowledge asymmetry could also contribute to the problems of lay-friendliness in the final non-English language PILs.

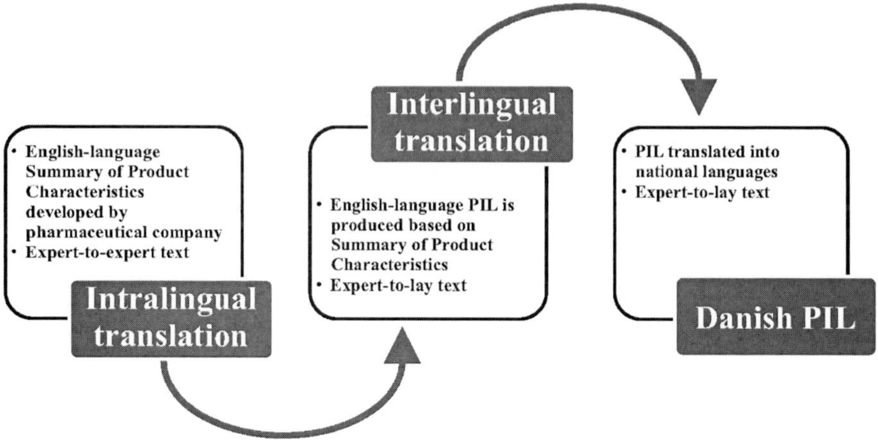

Figure 2: Production process of Danish PILs after a pharmaceutical company has developed a new medicinal product

The already complex problems of the communication process and the knowledge asymmetry between the sender and receiver are compounded further by the introduction of the translator who sits between the expert text producer and the lay text receiver. In the EU, all non-English language PILs authorised through the centralised procedure[3] are translations[4] as it is stipulated in EU Directive 2001/83/EC (Article 63(2)) that the PIL must be available in all the languages of the Member States in which the medicinal product is marketed. The translation issue and the complexity involved in it is overlooked by the EU; an example is that even though PILs are required to be available in all EU languages, the PIL only needs to be user-tested in one language version, and this is often the English, non-translated, version (Raynor 2008). The reason for this can be closely linked to EMEA's lay view of translation as there seems to be an assumption that a good, simple and lay-friendly English PIL automatically results in a good, simple and lay-friendly Danish PIL (Askehave/Zethsen 2002:26). This assumption can also be found in the requirement that solutions to the problems identified during

[3] Through the centralised procedure, the pharmaceutical apply for marketing authorisation to sell in all EU countries.

[4] English PILs are most often the source text for the 22 other European languages, because the English PIL must be submitted to EMEA earlier in the marketing authorisation process than other language PILs (European Commission 2005:26).

testing of the English version must be applied to the 23 other EU languages[5] by the pharmaceutical companies. This shows a lack of understanding and consideration of the variability of the 24 languages, and the different linguistics constraints and differences there might be between English and 23 other languages.

Due to the complexities discussed above in relation to the legal requirements, such as the template, the knowledge asymmetry between producer and receiver, and the fact that all non-English language PILs are translations, producing an optimally lay-friendly PIL can be difficult. Following EU legislation, all the Danish PILs which are translated versions of lay-friendly English PILs should be equally lay-friendly; however, Askehave and Zethsen (2003:40) found that "[o]n the basis of our contrastive analyses we were able to conclude that without exception the Danish PPIs[6] were more formal and dominated by expert syntax and terms than the English originals". An example taken from their study is the translation of: "xx[7] may cause drowsiness. If you feel tired, do not drive a motor vehicle or operate machinery" which was translated into Danish as "kan medføre døsighed, hvorfor forsigtighed tilrådes ved bilkørsel og maskinbetjening" (can result in drowsiness why carefulness is recommended in connection with car driving and machine operation; my translation). Instead of keeping the syntactical structure of the English source text, the translator has merged two sentences into one, and has also introduced nominalisations and a passive construction which is likely to make the sentence more difficult to understand.

Many of the above-mentioned studies into lay-friendliness in PILs have primarily looked at textual elements leading to non-lay-friendliness, whereas there seems to be a lack of empirical research investigating the contextual reasons why PILs are still not lay-friendly. Askehave and Zethsen (2002) assume that one reason for the decrease in lay-friendliness when a PIL is translated could be linked to many PILs being translated by pharmacists, but did not examine this systematically in their research. In order to shed light on whether the increase in complexity and decrease in lay-friendliness

---

[5] The EU has 23 official languages, however, one of them is Irish which is not translated into, and PILs are also translated into Icelandic and Norwegian.

[6] PPI (patient package insert) is identical with PIL.

[7] Name of drug deleted to ensure anonymity.

may be linked to the nature of the translators, I have investigated who do in fact translate the PILs.

Who are the translators of PILs into Danish and what translation competences do they possess?

In Translation Studies literature, it has been discussed who should translate medical texts, i.e. whether it should be medical professionals or professional translators. It is even said to be the oldest discussion in the medical translation field (Fischbach, qtd. in Márquez Arroyo 2007:74), and disagreement persists. Despite the importance of the question, there seems to be a lack of research investigating the medical translation product of professional translators and medical professionals to see if any differences are found.

Data collection

In an attempt to provide an answer concerning who is responsible for the interlingual translation phase of the PIL production, a study into the extratextual environment of the Danish PILs was conducted in 2010. 51 European pharmaceutical companies were contacted representing almost the entire population of pharmaceutical companies required to provide PILs in the EU. As it turned out that some of the contacted companies did not have any PILs in the EU, a study of all the PILs published on the EMEA website (about 580 PILs in July 2010) was conducted to count how many PILs each company had. Subsequently, all pharmaceutical companies with at least three PILs in the EU were contacted by email.[8] In this email, the pharmaceutical companies were asked what kind of translator they use for the translation of their PILs into Danish. The possible answer categories were "internal translation", which included "a person with a medical background", "a state-authorised translator", "a person with another language background", "a person with a different professional background – if so, which background?" and "external translation" which included the categories "state-authorised translator company in Denmark", "a translation company outside Denmark", "a freelance translator" and "a person with a different background – if so, which background?".

[8] There were five companies with three or more PILs which could not be contacted, either because it was not possible to find their contact details or because they had merged with other, already contacted companies.

40 companies responded (response rate: 78.43%). Three replies were discarded due to the fact that these three pharmaceutical companies did not have any translated PILs authorised in the entire EU,[9] leaving 37 usable replies. The results show that a slightly higher percentage of the contacted pharmaceutical companies use pharmacists for the translation of PILs into Danish, i.e. 15 of them or 41% (see Figure 3), whereas 13 (35%) pharmaceutical companies use professional translators. Of the pharmaceutical companies using translators, two of them use in-house translators only, and three companies use either an in-house translator or a freelance translator. The remaining eight companies using translators use only freelance translators. A small percentage of the contacted companies, 8% or three companies, have a co-production of the PIL in which both a professional translator and a pharmacist participate, which is what has been suggested by the literature (Askehave/Zethsen 2000a:36). The last 16%, or six companies, sometimes use one type of translator and sometimes the other. However, the majority of these six pharmaceutical companies said that they primarily use pharmacists. Another interesting finding was that several companies said that they used to use pharmacists, but now use translators. One company explains this by saying that a translator seems to make a better translation; however, the main arguments presented were that it is financially advantageous, or that the pharmacists do not have time for translation.

Even though the results show that pharmaceutical companies use either pharmacists or translators to an almost equal extent, it is important to note that when linking the authorised and published PILs with these contacted pharmaceutical companies, it is seen that the companies using pharmacists as translators have a greater number of PILs, which means that the majority of Danish EU PILs are translated by pharmacists.

[9] Not all companies get marketing authorisation through the so-called centralised procedure (i.e. authorisation to sell in all EU countries), but only sell their products in their national market or a few other markets.

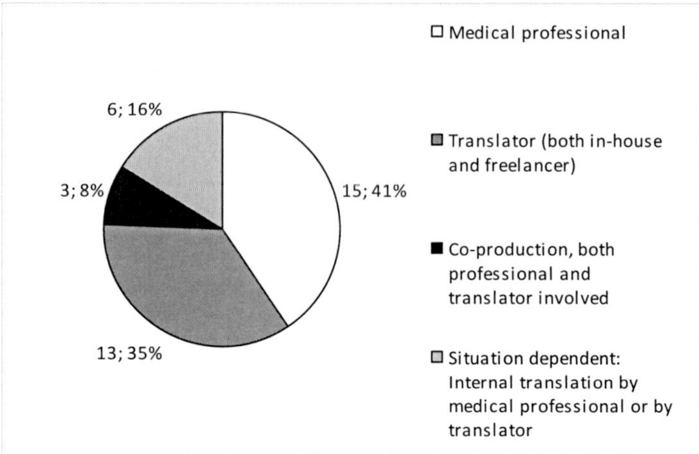

Figure 3: The translators of Danish PILs used in pharmaceutical companies

Profiles of Danish PIL translators

After this presentation of data on who is translating the PILs into Danish, in the following, focus will be placed on determining whether one group of translators translating PILs, i.e. professional translators and pharmacists, in theory, would be more suited to providing lay-friendly translations for a specific target audience than the other based on an application of the PACTE model. It should be made clear that the purpose of discussing the assumed competences of the two translator types based on the PACTE model is not to test the different sub-competences empirically, but to emphasise that there might be differences in relation to lay-friendliness in their translation products.

Before their assumed competences are discussed, the two translator groups and their background should be introduced further. As far as the pharmacists as a group are concerned, they typically do not have any translation courses or training during their education as pharmacists,[10] and furthermore, because each pharmaceutical company does not have many PILs in the EU, the typical Danish pharmacist is not likely to have much translation experience as s/he would not translate very often. Moreover,

[10] Information obtained from the websites on curriculum from the two universities training pharmacists in Denmark, i.e. Copenhagen University and University of Southern Denmark.

from the curriculum of pharmacists, it can be seen that no communication or linguistics courses are provided. As far as the translators are concerned, Denmark has been training and accrediting translators at MA level for the last 40 years and Danish translators are said to be "among the most well-educated in the world" (Dam/Zethsen 2009). Therefore, in order to work as a professional translator, an MA in Translation and Interpreting is a prerequisite to get a full-time translation job. This is of course only an overview of the profiles of the translators as *types,* but a necessary and useful prerequisite for the following analysis of PIL translators' sub-competences.

PACTE's competence model

Translation competence is a very complex concept within Translation Studies. It is a concept which has been widely discussed theoretically (e.g. by Wilss 1994; Chesterman 1997; Pym 2003) and researched empirically (PACTE 2003, 2005, 2009), and even though there is agreement that it involves more than L1 and L2 knowledge and skills, there is still a lack of consensus about the other abilities and skills required from a professional translator, and about how to define the concept of translation competence, and what such a concept includes and excludes.

In this study, the PACTE model of translator competence will be used as the framework for a comparative evaluation of the assumed competence of the translator types. PACTE's model has been chosen because of its holistic nature, empirical basis and its practical applicability. The model also aspires to describe the characteristics defining the professional translator (PACTE 2003:44) rather than defining competence for the purpose of translator education. Furthermore, PACTE's functional approach to translation "as a communicative activity directed towards achieving aims that involves taking decisions and solving problems, and requires expert knowledge" (ibid.) is relevant to how translation is viewed in this study. The functional approach is very relevant for the translation of PILs for lay receivers because of its emphasis on the role of the receiver and on the translation brief. Moreover, the fact that PACTE sees translation as a decision-making and problem solving process is relevant, the reason being that my study focuses on the decisions made by the translators when faced with translation problems, especially problems which influence lay-friendliness. The PACTE model is especially suitable for this study into lay-friendliness in translated PILs, as PACTE believes that competence is not only reflected in the process, but also in the product (PACTE 2009:209).

According to PACTE, translation competence is the underlying system of knowledge needed to translate. It consists of declarative and procedural knowledge, but procedural knowledge is predominant (ibid.:208). It includes the ability to complete the transfer process by understanding the source text and re-expressing it in the target language, taking into account the purpose of the translation and the characteristics of the target text receivers. As seen in Figure 4, the model consists of five main sub-competences: bilingual sub-competence, extra-linguistic sub-competence, knowledge about translation sub-competence, instrumental sub-competence and strategic sub-competence. PACTE also includes psycho-physiological components; however, these are not relevant here as it is not possible to discuss these when only knowing the translator *type*, not the individual translators. In the following, the five sub-competences will be briefly introduced with a main focus on the factors relevant for lay-friendly translation of PILs.

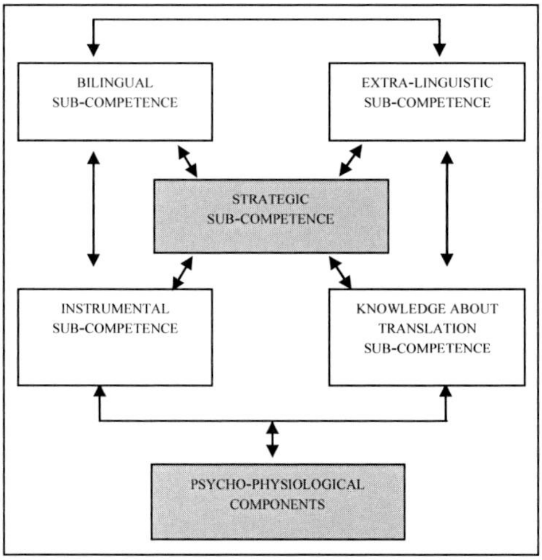

Figure 4: PACTE translation competence model (PACTE 2003:58)

The first sub-competence, bilingual sub-competence, logically deals with procedural knowledge needed to communicate in two languages; however, it is much broader than merely bilingual competence, because it also involves interference control (i.e. avoiding interferences between the two languages used), knowledge of pragmatic conventions that are acceptable in a given context, knowledge of socio-linguistic conventions, knowledge of language registers (variations according to field, tenor, mode), knowledge of texture, i.e. cohesion and coherence mechanisms, knowledge of genres and their conventions (structure, language features etc.) as well as knowledge of vocabulary, morphology and syntax. The extra-linguistic sub-competence is mainly declarative knowledge, both implicit and explicit knowledge about the world in general and specific areas of knowledge. The most relevant part of this sub-competence for the present study is specific subject knowledge, i.e. medical and pharmaceutical knowledge to ensure accuracy in the translation. The knowledge about translation sub-competence mainly includes declarative knowledge about translation and aspects of the translation profession, e.g. how to work with different types of translation units, strategies, techniques and types of problems. This sub-competence also involves knowledge about professional translation practice such as how to work with different types of briefs, clients and audiences. The instrumental sub-competence involves procedural knowledge related to the use of documentation sources, technologies and dictionaries, grammars and parallel texts. The fifth sub-competence, strategic sub-competence, includes the ability to evaluate the translation process and results as well as being able to identify translation problems and apply suitable procedures.

The following contains a data analysis in which the assumed competences of a typical pharmacist and professional translator, respectively, will be mapped against these five sub-competences. The mapping is based on knowledge about the profiles of trained translators and medical professionals functioning as translators.

Mapping the five sub-competences against the two translator profiles

Table 1 below shows an overview of the sub-competences that we could assume to be possessed by the two translator types based on the analysis described below. The "typical" Danish professional translator could be assumed to possess all the sub-competences because of their translation training and experience; however, they may only possess the medical extra-linguistic sub-competence to a lesser extent. The bilingual sub-competence could be assumed to be possessed by both translator types to some extent since they are both performing translation from English into Danish; however, they are not likely to possess it to an equal extent. To become English-Danish translators, the translators have had their bilingual competences tested and a certain level is a prerequisite to pass university exams. The pharmacists have not had their English language skills tested as an obligatory part of their job.

Sub-competence	**Medical professional**	**Professional translator**
The bilingual sub-competence	(X)	X
Extra-linguistic sub-competence	X	(X)
Knowledge about translation sub-competence		X
Instrumental sub-competence		X
Strategic sub-competence		X

Table 1: Overview of the sub-competences assumed to be possessed by medical professionals and professional translators[11]

The medical professionals are subject matter specialists because they are trained pharmacists, and therefore, specialised in pharmacology and the language used within this field; they would therefore possess the extra-linguistic competence to a very large extent. This sub-competence is extremely important for the translation of PILs because of the importance of terminology and accuracy. As far as the professional translators are concerned, unsurprisingly, they are not likely to have the same level of subject knowledge as the medical professionals. However, most Danish translators specialise after their MA in Translation, and would therefore have subject matter knowledge to some extent, though, much more limited than the pharmacists. Even when professional translators would possess some medical knowledge, some argue that they are not able to perform medical translation, because they are not subject matter specialists.

As the knowledge about translation sub-competence mainly includes knowledge about how to work with different types of translation units, strategies, techniques and types of problems as well as with different types of audiences, the pharmacists have no training or experience that would support this sub-competence. Professional translators, on the other hand, are

[11] "X" signifies a sub-competence, which the translator type is likely to possess, and "(X)" signifies a sub-competence, which the translator type is likely to possess to some extent.

trained in declarative knowledge about translation and in functional translation, and hence in translating for different audiences.

As far as the instrumental sub-competence is concerned, it has not been possible to know how much medical professionals use translation tools and instruments; however, as each pharmaceutical company has a limited number of PILs authorised through the centralised procedures and hence sold all over the EU, it is unlikely that the medical professionals have extensive experience translating as this would only happen quite rarely for each company. Translators, on the other hand, would be familiar with different translation instruments such as dictionaries and translation software through their training and professional experience.

One of the main elements included in the strategic sub-competence is the ability to evaluate the translation process and results as well as being able to identify translation problems and apply suitable procedures; therefore, it could be argued that the pharmacists would find this more difficult than trained translators as they are not trained in communication and translation strategies. As mentioned above, some think that translators cannot translate medical texts, because they are not subject matter experts; however, it could be argued that if the translator is not unsure of something, s/he has been trained to contact the client and ask for clarification.

Discussion

In the following discussion, based on the analysis, the five sub-competences will be individually discussed based on previous research with a view to discussing whether there might be any differences in the lay-friendliness of PILs from pharmaceutical companies that use professional translators and pharmacists, respectively.

Bilingual sub-competence

Previous research has shown that some medical professionals have weak interference control skills and that this may be one of the reasons for the unsuccessful target texts as they have a tendency to translate in an uncritical word-for-word manner (Askehave/Zethsen 2002:23). This can result in inelegant and sometimes incomprehensible texts (Gile 1986:28). Translators, on the other hand, are likely to have stronger interference control due to knowledge and experience about translating different genres for different receiver groups. In addition, they would have experience translating with variation in language register, such as tenor, which is important in PIL translation because there is an asymmetry between the expert sender and the lay receiver. They are also trained to know which pragmatic conventions are acceptable in a given context.

Extra-linguistic sub-competence

Translation businesses find that sometimes the challenge with medical texts is that translators without a medical background lack medical translation expertise (Andriesen 2001:5). One problem in relation to this is that a translator without extensive medical knowledge might have difficulties both in comprehending the source text and in re-expressing the meaning in the target text (Gile 1986:27). It could be expected that the medical professionals would be very knowledgeable of medical content and able to transfer the intended medical content.

Knowledge about translation sub-competence

Previous research suggests that some medical professionals lack knowledge about translation theory and methods, and therefore, they might have problems targeting a text at a specific receiver group (Askehave/Zethsen 2002:24). Besides, medical professionals have been shown to lack knowledge about what translation choice is acceptable in a given context, and how to translate for the correct receiver: "medical experts cannot free themselves from their own background knowledge and linguistic habits (and possibly expert status) and fail to reach a realistic perception of their audience" (Askehave/Zethsen 2003:39).

Furthermore, being able to translate for different audiences according to different briefs should lead to functional translations in which the translator focuses on the target text receiver. However, some medical professionals seem to have a more literal, equivalence-based approach to translation. Some medical professionals see literal translation as the ideal way of translating, i.e. keeping to the original and producing an accurate and precise target text in which no parts of the source text are lost (González Davies 1998:100). This could lead to the problems seen in Askehave and Zethsen's (2002:27) study in which the medical experts often uncritically, but "faithfully", transferred flaws found in the source text in the target text. Moreover, some medical professionals view specialised terminology as the most important factor in medical translation. This is seen for example in a study carried out by González Davies (1998) in which she had medical specialists assess students' medical translations. The specialists saw specialised terminology as of paramount importance, whereas syntax and grammar were the least relevant points, and cohesion and coherence were seen as of minor importance (ibid.:99-100). This primary focus on terminology could have consequences for lay-friendliness which is also linked to for example cohesion and syntax. Other researchers found that medical professionals have weak writing and translation skills, and they often have problems with simple items (O'Neill 1998:74). Furthermore, medical professionals' lack of translation competence can lead to target texts which are incomprehensible and contaminated by the source text language (Gile 1986:28).

The professional translators have both training and experience working with different briefs and targeting their translation to different audiences, whereas we must presume that medical professionals have very limited experience, and that instead of working with lay people, they generally work with other experts.

Instrumental sub-competence

As mentioned, it is not possible to know the extent to which pharmacists are used to using translation instruments, but professional translators would be familiar with different translation instruments because they would be required to use these in their daily translation work, which is why some scholars think that professional translators will produce better translations as they "[master] the techniques of translation, research and documentation" (Lee-Jahnke 2005:81).

Strategic sub-competence

Previous research shows that subject matter experts when producing texts have problems predicting reader problems (Lentz/de Jong 2009:119) and would therefore have problems evaluating their own process. Moreover, medical professionals tend to stick close to their expert language to ensure medical accuracy (Gal/Prigat 2005:489) and "lack the ability to down-grade their special language to accommodate the non-specialist target group" (Askehave/Zethsen 2000b:68), because they do not know what makes texts difficult to understand for lay people. Some medical professionals also struggle to apply suitable translation procedures, as they would not know "how to raise or lower the level of formality in a text" (Askehave/Zethsen 2003:39).

In conclusion, typical medical professionals are assumed to possess strong, extensive subject matter knowledge, which means that they will ensure accuracy in the translated PIL. Furthermore, they would possess the bilingual sub-competence to some extent, but they are not translation experts as they are likely to lack the translation specific sub-competences, which could lead to translation problems at several levels. Therefore, it might be argued that PILs translated by pharmacists-cum-translators might create lay-friendliness problems in their translations, as these translators are likely to mainly focus on transferring the propositional and medical content of the source text accurately. Moreover, they may not be able to assess the level of knowledge possessed by lay persons or to predict potential reader problems. Even if they are able to do so, they might lack the translational and linguistic knowledge, declarative and procedural, which is required to produce a translation which is easy to read, understand and act upon as is required by law. At the same time, we could argue that trained translators, because they might lack subject matter knowledge, might not always be able to transfer the medical content correctly and accurately. This is of course of utmost importance as giving patients a lay-friendly, but medically incorrect or inaccurate, text could have catastrophic consequences.

Based on this theoretical discussion of medical translation competence in relation to the translation of PILs, we could argue that there might be linguistic differences in the Danish PILs from pharmaceutical companies that use medical professionals and pharmaceutical companies that use professional translators, respectively, in relation to lay-friendliness.

Conclusion

The aim of this study was to determine whether there is likely to be an impact on the lay-friendliness of PILs translated by translators with potentially very different profiles. Based on the analysis and discussion, it can be concluded that differences in lay-friendliness in the translation products are likely to be found, and this is therefore an area that deserves further investigation.

The assumed translation competences of the two types of translators need to be further investigated empirically as the categorisation of the two translator groups and hence their competences are built on assumptions derived from previous research. Also, the two groups are not necessarily exclusive, and there could be some overlapping areas of sub-competence.

Identifying the ideal translator type for medical translation, i.e. whether it should be a medical professional or a translator, is said to be the oldest discussion within the medical translation field. Despite this, very limited empirical research has been carried out. A follow-up empirical study into the translation products from pharmaceutical companies that use professional translators and pharmacists-cum-translators, respectively, could provide useful empirical insights. Such an empirical study would also contribute to shedding further light on the translation products of pharmacists-cum-translators, i.e. non-professional translators who are professionals in another field and translate without having any translation training – an area within Translation Studies which has not been given a lot of attention.

References

Albin, Verónica (1998) "Translating and Formatting Medical Texts for Patients with Low Literacy Skills". In Fischbach, Henry (ed.) *Translation and Medicine.* Amsterdam-Philadelphia: John Benjamins, 117-129.

Andriesen, Simon (2001) "Medical Translations – a Job for Professionals". *The Industrial Pharmacist* 20, 5-6.

Askehave, Inger/Zethsen, Karen (2000a) *The Patient Package Insert of the Future. Report for the Danish Ministry of Health.* Aarhus: The Aarhus School of Business.

Askehave, Inger/Zethsen, Karen (2000b) "Medical Texts Made Simple – Dream or Reality?". *Hermes, Journal of Linguistics* 25, 63-74.

Askehave, Inger/Zethsen, Karen (2002) "Translating for Laymen". *Perspectives: Studies in Translatology* 10:1, 15-29.

Askehave, Inger/Zethsen, Karen (2003) "Communication Barriers in Public Discourse. The Patient Package Insert". *Document Design* 4:1, 23-41.

Askehave, Inger/Zethsen, Karen (2008) "Mandatory Genres: The Case of the European Public Assessment Report (EPAR) Summaries". *Text & Talk* 28:2, 167-191.

Bjerrum, Lars/Foged, Annette (2003) "Patient Information Leaflets – Helpful Guidance or a Source of Confusion?". *Pharmacoepidemiology and Drug Safety* 12, 55-59.

Chesterman, Andrew (1997) *Memes of Translation.* Amsterdam-Philadelphia: John Benjamins.

Council Directive 92/27/EEC of 31 March 1992 on the Labelling of Medicinal Products for Human Use and on Package Leaflets, http://eur-lex.europa.eu/smartapi/cgi/sga_doc?smartapi!celexplus!prod!DocNumber&lg=en&type_doc=Directive&an_doc=1992&nu_doc=27 [3 July 2012].

Dam, Helle V./ Zethsen, Karen Korning (2009) "Translators and (Lack of) Power: A Study of Danish Company Translators' Occupational Status". *Language at Work* 6, http://www.languageatwork.eu/readarticle.php?article_id=27 [3 July 2012].

Dickinson, David/Raynor, David K./Duman, Mark (2001) "Patient Information Leaflets for Medicines: Using Consumer Testing to Determine the Most Effective Design". *Patient Education and Counseling* 43, 147-159.

EU Directive 2001/83/EC of the European Parliament and of the Council of 6 November 2001, http://www.ema.europa.eu/docs/en_GB/document_library/Regulatory_and_procedural_guideline/2009/10/WC500004481.pdf [3 July 2012].

European Commission (2005) *2A Procedures for Marketing Authorization*, Chapter 1. Marketing Authorisation, November 2005, http://ec.europa.eu/health/files/eudralex/vol-2/a/vol2a_chap1_2005-11_en.pdf [3 July 2012].

European Commission (2006) "Guidance Concerning Consultations With Target Patient Groups for the Package Leaflet", http://ec.europa.eu/health/files/eudralex/vol-2/c/user_consultation_200605_en.pdf [3 July 2012].

European Commission (2009) "Guideline on the Readability of the Labelling and Package Leaflet of Medicinal Products for Human Use 1998". Revised 2009, http://ec.europa.eu/health/files/eudralex/vol-2/c/2009_01_12_readability_guideline_final_en.pdf [3 July 2012].

Gal, Iddo/Prigat, Ayelet (2005) "Why Organizations Continue to Create Patient Information Leaflets With Readability and Usability Problems: an Exploratory Study". *Health Education Research* 20:4, 485-493.

Gile, Daniel (1986) "La traduction médicale doit-elle être réservée aux seuls traducteurs-médecins? Quelques réflexions". *Meta* 31:1, 26-30.

González Davies, María (1998) "Student Assessment by Medical Specialists: An Experiment in Relating the Undergraduate to the Professional World in the Teaching of Medical Translation in Spain". In Fischbach, Henry (ed.) *Translation and Medicine.* Amsterdam-Philadelphia: John Benjamins, 93-104.

Hinds, Pamela J. (1999) "The Curse of Expertise: The Effects of Expertise and Debiasing Methods on Predictions of Novice Performance". *Journal of Experimental Psychology* 5:2, 205-221.

Kenny, Tim/Wilson, Rob G./ Purves, Ian N./Clark, Jill/Newton, Lynn/Newton, Doug P./Moseley, David V. (1998) "A PIL for Every Ill? Patient Information Leaflets (PILs): a Review of Past, Present and Future Use". *Family Practice* 15:5, 471-479.

Lee-Jahnke, Hannelore (2005) "Teaching Medical Translation: an Easy Job?" *Panace@* VI:20, 81-84.

Lentz, Leo/de Jong, Menno (2009) "How Do Experts Assess Usability Problems? An Empirical Analysis of Cognitive Shortcuts". *Technical Communication* 56:2, 111-121.

Márquez Arroyo, Cristina (2007) "Interview with Henry Fischbach". *Panace@,* VIII:25, 69-76.

MHRA – Medicines and Healthcare Products Regulatory Agency (2005) *Always Read the Leaflet: Getting the Best Information With Every Medicine.* London: The Stationary Office.

Nickerson, Raymond S. (1999) "How We Know – and Sometimes Misjudge – What Others Know: Imputing One's Own Knowledge to Others". *Psychological Bulletin* 125:6, 737-759.

O'Neill, Marla (1998) "Who Makes a Better Medical Translator: The Medically Knowledgeable Linguist or the Linguistically Knowledgeable Medical Professional? A Physician's Perspective". In Fischbach, Henry (ed.) *Translation and Medicine.* Amsterdam-Philadelphia: John Benjamins, 81-92.

PACTE (2003) "Building a Translation Competence Model". In Alves, Fabio (ed.) *Triangulating Translation. Perspectives in Process Oriented Research*, Amsterdam-Philadelphia: John Benjamins, 43-66.

PACTE (2005) "Investigating Translation Competence: Conceptual and Methodological Issues". *Meta* 50:2, 609-619.

PACTE (2009) "Results of the Validation of the PACTE Translation Competence Model: Acceptability and Decision Making". *Across Languages and Cultures* 10:2, 207-230.

Pander Maat, Henk/Lentz, Leo (2010) "Improving the Usability of Patient Information Leaflets". *Patient Education and Counseling* 80:1, 113-119.

Pym, Anthony (2003) "Redefining Translation Competence in an Electronic Age. In Defence of a Minimalist Approach". *Meta* 48:4, 481-497.

Raynor, David K. (2007) "The Importance of Medicines Information for Patients". *Prescriber* 18:2, 60-62.

Raynor, David K. (2008) "Testing, Testing. The Benefits of User-testing Package Leaflets". *Regulatory Focus*, 16-19.

Raynor, David K./Dickinson, David (2009) "Key Principles to Guide Development of Consumer Medicine Information – Content Analysis of Information Design Texts". *The Annals of Pharmacotherapy* 43, 700-706.

Wilss, Wolfram (1994) "A Framework for Decision-Making in Translation". *Target* 6:2, 131-150.

RAQUEL MARTÍNEZ MOTOS

University of Alicante, Spain

Models of Quality Assessment for Patient Package Inserts in English and Spanish: A Review from the Translation Perspective

The aim of this paper is to review the different models of quality assessment used in past decades to study patient package inserts in English and Spanish as well as to discuss their merits and apparent failure to fully achieve their communicative purpose. In recent years, there has been a noticeable upsurge throughout the world in the amount of research devoted to the study of patient package inserts, long acknowledged as a prototypical example of health care material with readability and user-friendliness problems. This paper points to the fact that, in spite of all the efforts made, there are still documents that do not meet readers' expectations, and raises the issue of whether the analysis of these texts should be tackled from a different perspective using an alternative quality assessment method in which translation is a key factor.

Keywords: medical translation, patient package insert, readability, user-friendliness, genre analysis

Introduction

Over the last ten years, a noticeable amount of research has been devoted to the study of readability and usability problems of health information materials (Askehave/Zethsen 2000, 2002, 2003, 2008, 2010; Svarstad et al. 2003; Clerehan/Buchbinder/Moodie 2005; Clerehan/Hirsh/Buchbinder 2009; Connor et al. 2010). Such materials include documents like health promotion leaflets, on-line health and drug information, package patient inserts, etc. Two of the reasons why research communities throughout the world have shown interest in this topic are firstly, that "patients are gaining control over their health as a result of a patient empowerment process within the health care system facilitated by means of a wide range of empowerment tools" (Askehave/Zethsen 2010:105). That is, patients no longer have a passive role in their health management but a very active one. As a result, healthcare changes have been introduced to achieve a more patient-centred care approach, including the adoption of what Hall (2006:271) defines as "policies which mandate that adequate information be made available about treatments, medication and surgical procedures so that people can participate in an informed way in the management of their own health". Secondly, "in spite of all the intentions, complex and ambiguous texts still abound in expert writing for the general public" (Askehave/Zethsen 2002:15), that is, many texts are still not easily read by the layman. This voluminous literature published in recent decades shows that there continues to be a debate about the readability and user-friendliness of health education materials. This could be considered somewhat perplexing, given the availability of a wide variety of guidelines to improve their design and test their readability and communicative effect (Tutty/O'Connor 1999; EU Directive 2004; FDA, US Food and Drug Administration 2006).

Given the linguistic and political specificities of my country of origin, Spain, as well as the space limits to which this work is subject, I will necessarily focus on a specific case of health information material, i.e. patient package inserts. It should be added that, as with other types of health information materials, patient package inserts are produced to help patients make informed decisions about their health but, "the degree to which a patient comprehends written messages related to prescription medications may be an important factor influencing patients' adherence to directives about medication use" (Connor et al. 2008:117). In other words, there is a strong correlation between patients' understanding of the information and adhering to treatment given the fact that "the safe and correct use of all medicines depends on users reading the labelling and packaging carefully and accurately and being able to understand and act on the information presented" (European Commission 2006:2). What is more, according to Connor et al. (2010:89), "treatment non-adherence is considered a major public health problem" as it results in very high financial costs and poorer health outcomes. This alone would seem sufficient reason to continue to work towards a clearer understanding of the factors that help to make documents comprehensible to their intended audience and so avoid treatment non-adherence.

Therefore, at this point, the question to ask is why do we still find documents of this type that fail to fulfil their apparent communicative purpose? As mentioned above, this should not be the case given the increasing awareness of the need to improve readability and user-friendliness of health information materials in general and package inserts in particular, as shown by the numerous studies published throughout the world. Some such studies use readability formulas that estimate the level of comprehensibility and readability of the documents (Ley/Florio 1996; Buchbinder et al. 2001; Hedman 2008); some use a more linguistic approach focusing on qualitative textual analysis (Askehave/Zethsen 2000, 2003; Mercado 2004; Clerehan/Buchbinder/Moodie 2005; Connor et al. 2008; García Izquierdo 2008); while yet others have opted for consumer-testing methods (Svarstad et al. 2003; Wolf et al. 2007; Askehave/Zethsen 2008; Hirsh et al. 2009; Connor et al. 2010). Undoubtedly, these methods of analysis have provided very valuable information about health information materials. However, it could be argued that more needs to be done, given the abundance of documents that are difficult to understand by patients, which in the specific case of package patient inserts could have fatal results.

This has led us to the conclusion that the topic may need to be approached from a different perspective. So, the aim of this article is to revisit the different approaches taken so far to the study of patient package inserts in English and Spanish, to discuss their merits and possible failures and, ultimately, to propose a potential alternative for future study. I will first provide a brief introduction to the specific genre under investigation, patient package inserts, followed by a description of the context in which this form of written patient information has developed in the US-American and European legal framework in general and in Spain in particular. In the second part, I will review the different models of quality assessment that have been applied by other authors throughout the world. In the third part, I will propose a new analytic framework for quality assessment of patient inserts in which translation plays a major role.

Patient package inserts as a genre

Interest in genres has rapidly grown over the past decades partly due to the theoretical insights they offer into the study of language and communication, especially for researchers working in areas such as language for specific purposes, discourse analysis, language teaching, literary studies or translation. Patient package inserts are conceived as a genre and defined as "highly conventionalized and extremely structured multifunctional texts" (Cacchiani 2006:28), thus the relevance of a brief review of the evolution of this concept. Over the years, genres have been defined from different perspectives but with one idea in common i.e. the assumption that a communicative situation, a communicative purpose and a discourse community are the key features of genres. Swales (1990:58) puts special emphasis on these aspects in his definition and claims that:

> A genre represents a class of communicative events, the members of which share some set of communicative purposes. These purposes are recognised by the expert members of the parent discourse community, and thereby constitute the rationale for the genre. This rationale shapes the schematic structure of the discourse and influences and constrains choice of content and style. […] [E]xemplars of a genre also exhibit various patterns of similarity in terms of structure, style, content and intended audience.

Yates and Orlikowski (1992:305) focus on their emergence and evolution and add a sociological and historical perspective by stating "that genres emerge within a particular sociohistorical context and are reinforced over time as a situation recurs". Bazerman (1998:24) conceives a genre as a process defining it as:

> A kind of activity to be carried out in a recognisable textual space. That activity embodies relations with the readers and kinds of messages to be developed in order to carry out generically appropriate intentions and interactions – to complete the rhetorical and social possibilities of the genre. Thus genre presents an opportunity space for realising certain kinds of activities, meanings, and relations. Genre exists only in the recognition of typicality by writers and readers – it is the recognisable shape by which participation is enacted and understood.

Unlike Bazerman, Trosborg (1997:ix) conceives genres as products of dynamic societies, which change simultaneously:

> Genres are sites of contention between stability and change. As products of dynamic societies, they are influenced by social structures, by changing social systems and not least by the rapid growing technological development in modern society. As dynamic constructs, genres change with changes in society, and new genres emerge as a product of new technology. This creates a continual need for research in the changing nature of old genres and the emergence of new ones.

I agree with García and Borja (2008:3-4) who, after revisiting the different approaches made by other genre theorists, conclude that:

> As members of a cultural community we are capable of recognizing that a certain text belongs to a genre (from a particular socio-professional domain) thanks to the features of prototypicality and recurrence which are displayed in different micro- and macrostructural levels.

However, I also agree with Askehave and Zethsen (2008:168) who point out that "it is not always the case that genres emerge and evolve naturally over a period of time in response to community members' social action". Following the definition of Swales' (2004:4) newly-introduced term *generification*, they make reference to the fact that communities are "increasingly introduced to and governed by regulated, official, and quasi-official arrays of genres". This would be the case of patient package inserts, additionally classified by Askehave and Zethsen (2003:28) as a *mandatory genre* and a prototypical example of public communication. By mandatory genre, these authors mean legally regulated texts, that is, they are not only "introduced by external mandate" but producers are also obliged to "adhere to particular guidelines to the rules and communication patterns stipulated in a legal document". A prototypical example of public communication would satisfy the following criteria: (a) it is aimed at a large audience, often potentially the entire population of a country; (b) the audience is extremely heterogeneous; (c) the sender-receiver relationship is asymmetrical, that is, the sender is usually an expert and the receiver is a layperson; (d) the sender is unknown to the reader; (e) interaction between sender and receiver is practically nonexistent; (f) the channel through which the communication is transmitted is often the genre itself; (g) genres often, but not always, come into being as a result of legislation; (h) the purpose of public communication is functional, that is, the receiver is not only informed about something but is often supposed to use the document to perform some kind of action (ibid.:24-25). More specifically, the purpose of patient package insertsis to inform consumers about the safe use of a medicinal product and how to gain the most benefit from it, as well as to protect them against medication errors.

After this brief approach to the concept of genre, I will now take a closer look at the legal framework that regulates the genre patient package insert in the United States and the European Union, with special emphasis on Spain. My choice of countries is based mainly on the fact that my working languages are English and Spanish and, although Spain has a pharmaceutical industry, it is a country that receives medicines produced abroad, mainly in the US and Western European countries.

US-American legal framework

In the US, the Food and Drug Administration (FDA) is responsible for the protection and promotion of health. Over the years, the FDA has undertaken a number of efforts to improve the system to help ensure that users are provided with useful written information. Since 1968, FDA regulations have required that patient package inserts be distributed as part of the drug package only for prescription medicines with estrogens and oral contraceptives. In 1982, after the withdrawal of a comprehensive patient package insert programme proposed in 1979, private voluntary programmes were developed as an alternative. However, none of these could be considered a comprehensive programme designed to improve patient knowledge, although, according to Svarstad et al. (2003:383) "the percentage of patients receiving written drug information in community pharmacies in the United States increased nearly fourfold from 15% in 1982 to 59% in 1994". Wolf et al. (2007:293) point out that very often "the prescription container label, in particular, is often the sole, tangible source of specific dosage/usage instructions given to and repeatedly used by the patient". In other words, very often patients do not receive any kind of written drug information except for the brief dosage instructions included in the container label.

In 1995, the FDA proposed a regulation entitled *Prescription Drug Product Labelling: Medication Guide Requirements*, which required that a thorough plan be developed and set the goal that by 2006, 95% of health consumers should receive some form of useful written patient information when buying drugs. On the one hand, the law required manufacturers to prepare and distribute Medication Guides (MedGuides) for products that, according to the FDA, pose a serious and significant public health concern. These guides, which generally focus on a specific risk and how to avoid it, are subject to FDA revision and approval and pharmacists are required to provide them when dispensing drugs. On the other hand, it was also compulsory by law for another type of written information called *Consumer Medication Information (CMI)* to be developed and distributed by individuals and organisations other than manufacturers, e.g. pharmacies or health care associations. This type of written information is neither reviewed nor approved by the FDA, and it is voluntarily provided by pharmacies with new prescription medicines.

In 2001, the results of a national study conducted by the National Association of Boards of Pharmacy (NABP) showed that, although 89% of the patients received some form of written medication information, the average *usefulness* of the information was only 50%.[1] In response to these results, the FDA (2006) published a document named *Guidance on Useful Written Consumer Medication Information* intended to provide developers of CMI with a series of nonbinding recommendations to ensure that their CMI was useful for consumers. However, this attempt also failed as shown by a study according to which the goal set by the FDA was not met, since by 2006, although 94% of consumers received CMI with new prescriptions only about 75% of the CMI met the minimum criteria for usefulness.

In light of these results, the FDA (2010) recently determined that "the current system is not adequate to ensure that patients receive the essential medication information that is needed to use the drug safely". Consequently, they held a 2-day public hearing on September 27-28, 2010 to obtain input on a potential new framework for the adoption of a single, standardised document called *Patient Medication Information (PMI)* (that would correspond to what we know as PPI) to avoid the current situation where patients receive information developed by different sources, i.e. consumer medication information, medication guide and patient package insert. This situation clearly differs from the much more evolved one in the member states of the European Union for the reasons stated below.

European legal framework

In the European Union, member states are subject to both European and their own domestic legislation regarding the production, distribution and use of medicinal products. European authorities have mainly legislated in the form of Directives, which are only binding as far as the intended result is concerned, thus leaving their implementation in domestic law to the corresponding national authorities.

The main difference between the United States and the European Union lies in the fact that in the latter, a single, standardised document is provided with prescription and non-prescription drugs. Another difference is that in Europe only drug manufacturers are responsible for the production and distribution of package inserts. Council Directive 92/27/EEC was the first European norm to establish the obligation of member states to include a package leaflet (known as Patient Information Leaflet, PIL) with all medici-

---

1 Useful medication information was defined as that which enables the consumer to use the medicine properly and appropriately, receive the maximum benefit, and avoid harm (FDA 2006:4).

nal products, unless all the information required is directly conveyed on the outer packaging or on the immediate packaging.[2] It was later repealed by EU Directive 2001/83/EC, which established in article 8 that an application to obtain authorisation to place the medicinal product on the market should be made either to the competent authority of the Member State concerned (national, decentralised and mutual recognition procedures) or the European Medicines Agency (centralised procedure) and this application must be accompanied by the above-mentioned package leaflet (among other documents). In other words, PILs must be approved by the competent authority together with the medicinal product to which they refer.

Regarding the information included in the PIL, article 59 of the same directive established that it shall be in accordance with the summary of the product characteristics. In order to ensure that the statutory information is set out in a particular order and written in terms which the patient could understand, Member States and the European Medicines Agency agreed on harmonised Quality Review of Documents (QRD) templates. However, after the introduction of EU Directive 2004/27/CE amending EU Directive 2001/83/EC, compliance with the QRD templates does not exempt from the obligation to undertake consultations with target patient groups to ensure that the final document is legible, clear and easy to use. That is, prior to marketing approval, a performance-based testing of one of the language versions of the PIL must be carried out in order to ensure its readability and usefulness. Furthermore, producers are required to follow particular guidelines, otherwise, pursuant to article 61, "the competent authority shall refuse the marketing authorization if the labelling or the package leaflets do not comply with the provisions".

So, going back to Askehave and Zethsen's (2003:28) idea that package inserts are a mandatory genre and an example of public communication, I agree when they state that:

> The result is that public communicators produce a document that adheres to the rules and communication patterns stipulated in a legal directive, and the main concern (and covert purpose) of the communicators becomes that of observing the legal requirements. This in turn makes it very problematic for

[2] In the European context, the term patient information leaflet, PIL, refers to the information included in the medication package, whose content is mandated by regulatory guidelines. It is the same as what I call patient package leaflet. In the Australian and US-American context, authors use the term PIL to refer to the leaflets provided by doctors as an adjunct to verbal exchange at the time the medication is prescribed.

> the mandatory genre to appear as a useful or purposeful genre in its proper environment. The tone and style of the document preserve a social identification with the community of experts, which means that the document fails to achieve its proper goal in the public context.

To sum up, as a mandatory genre, PPIs are subject to a series of legal constraints. This makes it more problematic for producers to achieve their main communicative goal. Furthermore, very often package inserts do not only have to adhere to the communication patterns stipulated in a legal document but also have to undergo a translation process, thus adding an extra difficulty.

Package inserts from the translation perspective

According to EU Directive 2004/27/EC article 63 (2), patient package inserts marketed in Europe must be written in the official language of the market in which the drugs are sold:

> The package leaflet must be written and designed to be clear and understandable, enabling the users to act appropriately, when necessary with the help of health professionals. The package leaflet must be clearly legible in the official language or languages of the Member State in which the medicinal product is placed on the market.

That is, it is a legal requirement that the language be clear and understandable. The above paragraph refers to the final document, but in the process of application for marketing authorisation a testing of multiple language versions of the package leaflet must be carried out and, according to the European Commission (2006:4):

> Results of such consultation should be presented in English for the centralised, decentralised and mutual recognition procedure, or in the national language for national procedures to permit the assessment of the test to be undertaken by competent authority responsible for granting the marketing authorisation.
>
> In the centralised, decentralised and mutual recognition procedure, only the English language version of the package leaflet will be agreed during the scientific assessment. […]
>
> Following the grant of the marketing authorisation, the responsibility for the production of faithful translations will rest with the marketing authorisation holder in consultation with the Member States/European Medicines Agency.

According to this, the language of the package leaflet presented in the process of application for marketing authorisation depends on the procedure, i.e. English in the centralised, decentralised and mutual recognition procedure and the national language in the national procedure. Since Spain, like other European countries, is a non-English-speaking country that imports pharmaceutical products, many package inserts have to be translated from English into Spanish. Regarding products manufactured in other European countries, translation from English into Spanish would be necessary when the medicine was produced by a British pharmaceutical company and the marketing authorisation granted by the competent national authority, the Medicines and Healthcare products regulatory Agency (MHRA), or when it was produced in another European country and approved by the EMEA through the centralised, decentralised and mutual recognition procedure. The package inserts of pharmaceutical products produced in other English-speaking, non-European countries such as the United States or Australia would also need to be translated.

Coming back to the above quote, the marketing authorisation holder, that is, the pharmaceutical company is responsible for the "faithful" production and thorough revision of the translation of the package leaflet. According to Askehave and Zethsen (2002:16) "the pharmaceutical industry is painfully aware that package inserts are notoriously difficult to understand" and "blame the authorities, legislation, standardisation, etc." for this. In a study carried out by the same authors (Askehave/Zethsen 2000), two main factors concerning translation were pointed out as causes for unsuccessful package inserts: inter-generic translation or translation between genres, which takes place when the information extracted from the summary of the product characteristics (considered as a genre itself) is transferred to the package insert when it is first drawn up; and inter-linguistic translation, referring to translation in the traditional sense of translation between languages.

Similarly to the Danish case studied by Askehave and Zethsen (2000), we could state that these types of translation are also involved in the creation of Spanish inserts in two different ways: (1) when the package insert is originally produced in English, the information included is transferred from the English-language product summary (inter-generic translation). Once the product has been granted marketing authorisation, the insert is translated into Spanish (inter-linguistic translation); (2) when the package insert is originally produced in Spanish, the information included is transferred from the Spanish-language product summary (inter-generic translation). To sum up, two kinds of patient inserts are available for the Spanish consumer: Spanish originals and translations.

Current models for assessing the quality of patient package inserts

As stated in the introduction, the number of studies on healthcare literature quality conducted in the last twenty years has dramatically escalated. Not all focus on the same aspects, nor were they carried out under the same conditions or with the same methodology. What is more, they do not focus on package inserts alone but cover a variety of patient information materials. However, the analysis of their merits and apparent failures may be of great interest for future studies.

Some studies use readability formulas as an assessment tool for healthcare materials for the general public (Ley/Florio 1996; Buchbinder et al. 2001; Hedman 2008). These formulas have been increasingly applied to written healthcare material to give a statistical estimate of the grade level of education an average reader needs in order to be able to read and comprehend them. This score is obtained by applying a mathematical equation mainly based upon sentence and word length. There is a variety of readability formulas but the most widely used in the healthcare sector are the Dale-Chall Formula, the Flesch Formulas, the Fog Index, the Readability Graph and the SMOG Grading Formula (Ley/Florio 1996). Despite their popularity and ease of use, their validity has been questioned by authors such as Clerehan and Buchbinder (2006:40) for whom

> they [readability formulas] take no account of nontextual dimensions such as context (prior knowledge, purpose for reading), cultural differences, and visual elements. They do not measure any of the top-down factors involved in reading comprehension such as recognizing the structure and organization of a text, or such bottom-up decoding factors as density of information (not word length) and appropriateness of language.

Other authors (Barber et al. 2009) have taken a more patient-centred approach by testing health literacy with a group of selected subjects. This method does not improve the quality of the document but helps to identify where the problematic aspects are and, in the case of package inserts and other types of drug information materials, the patients' motivations for adherence or non-adherence to treatment. Moreover, different methods have been applied for consumer testing of texts e.g. observational studies

(Svarstad/Mount 2001; Svarstad et al. 2003) or interviews (Dickinson/Raynor/Duman 2001; Connor et al. 2010). These provide very useful information about consumers' perception on the quality of the documents and allow identifying and improving those aspects that pose an additional difficulty for patients' correct understanding of the information. However, these methods disregard other extratextual elements that also have an impact on the final document, both at production and reception level.

Clerehan, Buchbinder and Moodie (2005), Clerehan, Hirsh and Buchbinder (2009) and Clerehan and Buchbinder (2006) proposed a new analytic approach for drug information materials provided by doctors based on systemic functional linguistics. According to this linguistic framework, the interaction between text and context enables the reader to construct meaning, so any analytical tool to assess a text should take into account the situational variables of the context and how these impact on the text. This model is also based on the assumption that genres are expected to show a conventional text structure according to their specific purpose and that the comprehensibility of the information conveyed depends to a great extent on whether they show the generic patterns expected by the reader. Clerehan and Buchbinder (ibid.:42) agree with that as they consider that the analysis of the degree to which medication information leaflets provided by doctors (regarded as a subset of the genre of health care materials) follow their conventional patterns is of great importance when trying to find out whether they meet their readers' expectations, in other words, whether they are effective functional texts. According to Clerehan, Hirsh and Buchbinder (2009:118),

> [u]sing an SFL-based approach, the following aspects of the leaflets were identified and analysed: generic structure, rhetorical elements, metadiscourse, headings, technicality of lexis, lexical density, writer-reader relationship and factual content.

But, as Clerehan and Buchbinder point out (2006:60-61) "a linguistic theory is not enough. Alternative media and document design issues and, crucially, a strategy for patient evaluation also need to be addressed". Moreover, in a later study, Hirsh et al. (2009) validated this Evaluative Linguistic Framework (ELF) by obtaining feedback on a set of leaflets, some of which had been developed taking into account the ELF, by means of interviews, focus group discussions and self-administered questionnaires.

An additional issue worth mentioning is that in some cases, the studies were not conducted by linguists or by translators, but by health care professionals and researchers or members of national and international committees of political relevance (Svarstad et al. 2003; Blancafort/de Cambra/Navarro 2005; Barber et al. 2009), whose main interest lies in discovering the reasons for patients' non-adherence to treatment and improving written communication for patients, i.e. their aim is reader-focused. This is not the case of other authors with a more linguistic/translation background (Askehave/Zethsen 2000, 2002, 2010; Ruiz/Fortanet/Palmer 2008; Hirsh et al. 2009; Connor et al. 2010) who also based their studies on the assumption that package inserts, like other health information materials, are a conventionalised genre, but from a different perspective. Their research has mainly focused on a comparative analysis of package inserts in different languages (Danish, English, Spanish and Italian) in search of textual and cultural differences and with the improvement of the translation process of these texts as their main objective. However, most of them tend to focus on the analysis of the linguistic elements of texts and disregard the possible causes for comprehension failure among patients at the production level.

Only Askehave and Zethsen (ibid.:15) point at translation as the possible cause of patients' misinterpretations or lack of understanding of package inserts:

> While most studies assert that the scarcity of user-friendly inserts is due to experts' difficulties in adjusting their language for the benefit of non-experts (i.e. they are incapable of writing plain English), the studies overlook another important reason why inserts are hard to understand, namely that in non-English-speaking countries which import medical and pharmaceutical products from the Anglophone world, many inserts are translated from one language (English) into another one.

After carrying out an analysis of the most common mistakes in the translation of English inserts into Danish, Askehave and Zethsen (2002:27) conclude that "most *de facto* translators of package inserts are specialists who on the one hand have the advantage of possessing expert knowledge of the field in question, but who on the other hand lack linguistic and translational competence", that is, they are not experts in translation. So, according to this statement, the problem mainly lies in the asymmetrical relationship that exists between sender and receiver in expert-to-layman communication, and the lack of linguistic and translational competence among expert producers.

Although the authors also add that "apart from translation-related problems there are problems with layout, legislative requirements, standardisation and the relationship between the medical industry and the approving

EU authorities" (ibid.), they go no further to establish a link between these factors, which could also be of great interest with a view to improving the assessment models used so far.

To summarise, if one thing has been made clear by the studies carried out so far it is that, despite the legislation covering package inserts at the European level, these still fail to meet users' needs. So, taking a step further the main question would be, which package inserts are less readable and user-friendly, the original ones or those that have been translated? In other words, is the translation process a key factor in the production of good quality inserts? To what extent does translation affect the readability and user-friendliness of a document? In the case of translations, does the main problem lie in the original draft of the document that is later translated or in the translation itself? Up until now, these questions have only been partially addressed by some authors but a more comprehensive approach that includes both originals and translations would be necessary to give a more specific answer to these questions.

Proposal of a comprehensive model for the future assessment of patient package inserts

As mentioned above, Spain, like many other countries, is a non-English-speaking country that, despite having its own pharmaceutical industry, also imports medical and pharmaceutical products. As a result, two types of package inserts coexist: those originally written and approved in Spanish and those that are translations, of which I will focus on translations from English. As stated in the above paragraph, evaluation of the role played by the translation process in the production of package inserts with readability and user-friendliness problems could be part of an alternative model for future assessment of patient package inserts in Spain, whose results could perhaps be extrapolated to other countries in a similar situation.

For this purpose, a corpus comprising three sub-corpora of package inserts should be compiled: those originally written in Spanish, those originally written in English and those that are translations of the latter into Spanish. Two types of analysis would be carried out, one at a textual level and another at an extratextual level. Regarding the textual level, the corpus analysis would be aimed at establishing the genre conventions of original documents, that is, those inserts originally written in English or Spanish. When I say genre conventions, I am not only referring to the conventions imposed by regulations, guidelines and so on, to which this type of mandatory text is subject, but also to the linguistic and format patterns normally used by authors and translators despite these regulations. Once the conventions were established, they would be compared with the patterns generally found in Spanish translations in order to determine whether they are closer to Spanish or English conventions. In this way, I would attempt to determine whether translations follow target language conventions or stick to those of the original. The second step would consist in the analysis of the texts in Spanish and would involve user-testing of a group of inserts, both originals and translations, by means of a questionnaire. The results of this method of quality assessment would then be applied to determine whether originals or translations are more readable and, ultimately, in relation with the results obtained in the analysis of conventions, whether there is any correlation between the conventions and these results.

As far as the extratextual level is concerned, this would consist of a case study aimed at describing the real professional setting in which the translations are carried out. As previously specified, package inserts in Spain are a mandatory genre subject to legislative requirements and standardisation, but little has been said about the constraints to which translators are subject regarding their daily work. Although Askehave and Zethsen (2002) already pointed out that very often translations are carried out by experts in the field of pharmacy who lack the necessary linguistic and translational competence, I think that other factors such as time pressure, contractual situation, etc. could also have a great impact on the final product.

Conclusion

As stated in the introduction, the aim of this paper is to review the different models of quality assessment used in the past decade to study patient package inserts in English and Spanish as well as to discuss their merits and apparent failure to fully achieve their communicative purpose. After doing so, this paper has concluded that, in spite of all the efforts made, there are still documents that do not meet readers' expectations, and raises the issue of whether the analysis of these texts should be tackled from a different perspective using an alternative quality assessment method in which translation is a key factor. The specificity of this new framework would lie in the pre-eminent role granted to translation and the combination of some of the approaches previously taken by other authors. Although this new analytic framework would be designed to provide a specific tool to assess and produce package inserts that meet Spanish readers' needs, it could also be partially applied in the case of other countries in the same situation and with other linguistic combinations.

References

Askehave, Inger/Zethsen, Karen K. (2000) "Inter-generic and Inter-linguistic Translation of Patient Package Inserts". In Mayer, Felix (ed.) *Language for Special Purposes: Perspectives for the New Millennium.* Tübingen: Gunter Narr, 882-887.

Askehave, Inger/Zethsen, Karen K. (2002) "Translating for Laymen". *Perspectives: Studies in Translatology* 10:1, 15-29.

Askehave, Inger/Zethsen, Karen K. (2003) "Communication Barriers in Public Discourse: The Patient Package Insert". *Document Design* 4:1, 22-41.

Askehave, Inger/Zethsen, Karen K. (2008) "Mandatory Genres: The Case of European Public Assessment Report (EPAR) Summaries". *Text & Talk* 28:2, 167-191.

Askehave, Inger/Zethsen, Karen K. (2010) "Check it Out" - The construction of Patient Empowerment in Health Promotion Leaflets". In Ruiz Garrido, Miguel F./Palmer Silveira, Juan C./Fortanet Gómez, Inmaculada (eds.) *English for Academic and Professional Purposes.* Utrecht: Rodopi, 105-119.

Barber, Melissa N./Staples, Margaret/Osborne, Richard H./Clerehan, Rosemary/Elder, Catherine/Buchbinder, Rachelle (2009) "Up to a Quarter of the Population May Have Suboptimal Health Literacy Depending Upon The Measurement Tool: Results From a Population-Based Survey". *Health Promotion International* 24:3, 252-261.

Bazerman, Charles (1998) "Emerging Perspectives on The Many Dimensions of Scientific Discourse". In Martin, James R./Veel, Robert (eds.) *Reading Science. Critical and Functional Perspectives on Discourses of Science.* London-New York: Routledge, 15-28.

Blancafort, Sergi/de Cambra, Salomé/Navarro, María D. (eds.) (2005) *Funciones y utilidad del prospecto del medicamento.* Barcelona: Fundació Biblioteca Josep Laporte/Universitat Autònoma de Barcelona.

Buchbinder, Rachelle/Hall, Stephen/Grant, Gail/Mylvaganam, A./ Patrick, Mark R. (2001) "Readability and Content of Supplementary Written Drug Information for Patients Used by Australian Rheumatologists". *Medical Journal of Australia* 174, 575-578.

Cacchiani, Silvia (2006) "Dis/Similarities between Patient Information Leaflets in Britain and Italy: Implications for the Translator". *New Voices in Translation Studies* 2, 28-43.

Clerehan, Rosemary/Buchbinder, Rachelle/Moodie, Jane (2005) "A Linguistic Framework for Assessing the Quality of Written Patient Information: Its Use in Assessing Methotrexate Information for Rheumatoid Arthritis". *Health Education Research* 20:3, 334-344.

Clerehan, Rosemary/Buchbinder, Rachelle (2006) "Toward a More Valid Account of Functional Text Quality: The Case of the Patient Information Leaflet". *Text & Talk* 26:1, 39-68.

Clerehan, Rosemary/Hirsh, Di/Buchbinder, Rachelle (2009) "Medication Information Leaflets for Patients: The Further Validation of an Analytic Linguistic Framework". *Communication & Medicine* 6:2, 117-127.

Connor, Ulla M./Ruiz-Garrido, Miguel F./Rozycki, William/Goering, Elizabeth/ Kinney, Eleanor D/Koehler, Julia M. (2008) "Patient-Directed Medicine Labelling: Text Differences Between the United States and Spain". In *Communication & Medicine* 5:2, 117-132.

Connor, Ulla M./Goering, Elizabeth M./Matthias, Marianne S./Mac Neill, Robert (2010) "Information Use and Treatment Adherence Among Patients With Diabetes". In Ruiz Garrido, Miguel F./Palmer Silveira, Juan C./Fortanet Gómez, Inmaculada (eds.) *English for Academic and Professional Purposes.* Utrecht: Rodopi, 89-104.

Dickinson, David/Raynor, David K./Duman, Mark (2001) "PILs for Medicines: Using Consumer Testing to Determine the Most Effective Design". *Patient Education and Counseling* 43:2, 147-159.

EU Directive 2001/83/EC of the European Parliament and of the Council of 6 November 2001 on the Community Code Relating to Medicinal Products for Human Use.

EU Directive 2004/27/EC of the European Parliament and of the Council of 31 March 2004 amending Directive 2001/83/EC on the Community Code Relating to Medicinal Products for Human Use.

European Commission (2006) *Guidance Concerning Consultations With Target Patient Groups for the Package Leaflet.* Article 59 (3) and 61 (1) of Directive 2001/83/EC as amended by Directive 2004/27/EC.

FDA, US Food and Drug Administration (1995) "Prescription Drug Product Labelling; Medication Guide Requirements", http://www.federalregister.gov/ articles/1995/08/24/95-21020/prescription-drug-product-labeling-medication-guide-requirements [3 July 2012].

FDA, US Food and Drug Administration (2006) *Guidance on Useful Written Consumer Medication Information,* http://www.fda.gov/downloads/Drugs/Guidance ComplianceRegulatoryInformation/Guidances/UCM080602.pdf [3 July 2012].

FDA, US Food and Drug Administration (2010) "Development and Distribution of Patient Medication Information for Prescription Drugs: Public Hearing", http://www.fda.gov/Drugs/NewsEvents/ucm219716.htm [3 July 2012].

García, Isabel/Borja, Anabel (2008) "A Multidisciplinary Approach To Specialized Writing And Translation Using A Genre Based Multilingual Corpus Of Specialized Texts". In *LSP & Professional Communication* 8:1, 39-63.

García Izquierdo, Juan M. (2008) "Estudio descriptivo del prospecto de medicamentos desde una perspectiva traductológica". In Campos, Miguel A./Gómez, Adelina (eds.) *The Language of Health Care: Proceedings of the first International Conference on Language and Health Care, Alicante, 24-26 October 2007*. Alicante: IULMA. CD-Rom.

Hall, David R. (2006) "Medical Leaflets, Empowerment and Disempowerment". In Gotti, Maurizio/Salager-Meyer, Françoise (eds.) *Advances in Medical Discourse Analysis: Oral and Written Contexts*. Frankfurt am Main-Berlin-Bern-Bruxelles-New York-Oxford-Wien: Peter Lang. 271-288.

Hedman, Amy S. (2008) "Using the SMOG Formula to Revise a Health-Related Document". *American Journal of Health Education* 39:1, 61-64.

Hirsh, Di/Clerehan, Rosemary/Barber, Margaret/Osborne, Richard H./ Buchbinder, Rachelle (2009) "Patient Assessment of Medication Information Leaflets: A Reader-Focused Strategy to Validate an Analytic Linguistic Framework". Patient Education and Counselling 77, 248-254.

Ley, Philip/Florio, Tony (1996) "The Use of Readability Formulas in Health Care". *Psychology, Health & Medicine* 1:1, 7-28.

Mercado, Sebastián (2004) "El análisis de géneros aplicado a la traducción: Los prospectos de medicamentos de Estados Unidos y España". *Linguax: Revista de lenguas aplicadas* 2:2, 3-21.

Ruiz, Miguel F./Fortanet, Inmaculada/Palmer, Juan C. (2008) "El prospecto de medicamentos en España y EEUU: utilización de viñetas y abreviaturas". In Campos, Miguel A./Gómez, Adelina (eds.) *The Language of Health Care: Proceedings of the First International Conference on Language and Health Care, Alicante, 24-26 October 2007*. Alicante: IULMA. CD-Rom.

Svarstad, Bonnie L./Mount, Jeanine K. (2001) "Evaluation of Written Prescription Information Provided in Community Pharmacies. Final Report to the US Department of Health and Human Services and the Food and Drug Administration", http://www.fda.gov/AboutFDA/CentersOffices/OfficeofMedicalProductsandTobacco/CDER/ucm169753.htm [3 July 2012].

Svarstad, Bonnie L./Bultman, Dara C./Mount, Jeanine K./Tabak, Ellen R. (2003) "Evaluation of Written Prescription Information Provided in Community Pharmacies: A Study in Eight States". *Journal of the American Pharmacists Association* 43:3, 383-393.

Swales, John M. (1990) *Genre Analysis: English in Academic and Research Settings*. Cambridge: Cambridge University Press.

Swales, John M. (2004) *Research Genres. Exploration and Applications*. Cambridge: Cambridge University Press.

Trosborg, Anna (1997) "Text Typology: Register, Genre and Text Type". In Trosborg, Anna (ed.) *Text Typology and Translation*. Amsterdam-Philadelphia: John Benjamins, 3-23.

Tutty, Linda/O'Connor, Geraldine (1999) "Patient Information Leaflets: Some Pertinent Guidelines". *Radiography* 5, 11-14.

Yates, Joanne/Orlikowski, Wanda J. (1992) "Genres of Organizational Communication: A Structural Approach to Studying Communication And Media?" *Academy of Management Review* 17:2, 299-326.

Wolf, Michael S./Davis, Terry C./Shrank, William/Rapp, David N./Bass, Pat F./Connor, Ulla/Clayman, Marla/Parker, Ruth M. (2007) "To Err Is Human: Patient Misinterpretations of Prescription Drug Label Instructions". *Patient Education & Counseling* 67, 293-300.

List of contributors

Roxana-Mihaela Antochi is a research assistant with the *BITRA* (Bibliography of Interpreting and Translation) project at the Department of Translation and Interpreting, University of Alicante, Spain. Her current project is a PhD thesis on drama translation in Communist Romania. Her research interests include translation and censorship, translation and ideology, drama translation.

E-mail: roxana_antochi@yahoo.com

Giovanna Di Pietro is a PhD candidate in Translation Studies at the Department of Anglo-German and Eastern European Studies at the University of Bari "Aldo Moro", Italy. Her research focuses on dubbing, humour studies, film studies, intercultural communication, (non)verbal communication and multimodal analysis. She is currently working as a teacher and a translator.

E-mail: giovanna.dipietro85@gmail.com

Beatrice Fischer is a PhD student at the Department of Translation Studies at the University of Graz, Austria. She completed a Master's degree in Interpreting (2008) and in Gender Studies (2009), both at the University of Vienna. Currently, she is working on her dissertation project dealing with the development of gender-sensitive translation didactics. Her main research areas are: feminist translation studies, translation didactics and gender studies. She has published articles in various essay collections.

E-mail: beatrice.fischer@uni-graz.at

Isabel Ferro Mealha is a lecturer at the University of Lisbon. She teaches English for Medical Students, and Scientific and Technical Translation, especially medical translation. Her main research areas are technical and scientific translation, English as a Lingua Franca and English for Specific Purposes. She is currently working on medical discourse in (non-)translated Portuguese for her PhD.

E-mail: mealha.isabel@gmail.com

Ana Isabel Foulquié Rubio is an Associate Lecturer at the University of Murcia, where she teaches translation and interpreting. Furthermore, she works as a freelance translator and interpreter. She holds a Degree in Translation and Interpreting, a Postgraduate Degree in Aliens Law and a Postgraduate Degree in Intercultural Mediation. Currently, she is also working on her PhD thesis.

E-mail: ana.foulquie@um.es

Rosario Garnemark is a Doctoral Research Fellow at the Department of Literature, Area Studies and European Languages (ILOS), University of Oslo. Her research focuses on the rewritings of Ingmar Bergman's filmography for Spanish audiences during the Francoist regime, especially on the impact of censorship in translation.

E-mail: rosario.garnemark@ilos.uio.no

Franziska Heimburger is currently finishing her PhD in history at the EHESS Paris where she also holds teaching duties. Her main area of research is the Allied coalition during the First World War. She is also working on languages in conflict more generally and connections between history and translation/interpreting.

E-mail: research@franziska.fr

Raquel Martínez Motos is a lecturer and PhD student in the English Department at the University of Alicante. She is currently writing her PhD on translation in the field of Pharmacy. She co-authored a specialised bilingual dictionary of Pharmaceutical Sciences (with Enrique Alcaraz Varó and Alfonso Domínguez-Gil Hurlé, 2007). Her main research areas include terminology and terminography, specialized translation, discourse analysis and language for specific purposes.

E-mail: raquel.motos@ua.es

Dainora Maumevičienė is a PhD student in Translation Studies at Kaunas Faculty of Humanities at Vilnius University. She also works as a lecturer teaching translation and translation technologies in Kaunas University of Technology and works as a translator/interpreter in various national and international projects. Her research interests are translation and localisation, interpreting, distance learning and English for Specific Purposes.

E-mail: dainora.maumeviciene@ktu.lt

Eduarda Melo Cabrita is a lecturer at the University of Lisbon. She teaches English, Legal English and Scientific and Technical Translation (legal translation). Her main research areas are technical and scientific translation, English as a Lingua Franca and English for Specific Purposes. She is currently working on legal discourse in (non-)translated Portuguese for her PhD.

E-mail: melocabrita@gmail.com; mcabrita1@campus.ul.pt

Elisa Moroni has recently completed a PhD in Translation Studies at Bologna University. She wrote a thesis on the translation of Russian folk epics. She holds an MA in Russian and English from Bologna University and co-edited an anthology of translations of Russian epics with E. T. Saronne.

E-mail: elisa.moroni@gmail.com

Nicole Nolette is a doctoral student in French language and literature at McGill University, in Montreal, Canada. Her research interests include Translation Studies, performance studies, multilingual theatre and Canadian francophone literature. She currently holds a Social Sciences and Humanities Research Council of Canada doctoral scholarship.

E-mail: nicole.nolette@mail.mcgill.ca

Matilde Nisbeth Jensen is a doctoral student affiliated with the Research Group for Translation and Interpreting at Aarhus University in Denmark and the Centre for Translation and Interpreting Research at Macquarie University, Australia. Her main research interests include expert-lay communication, medical translation, plain language, patient communication.

E-mail: matnj@asb.dk

Irina Elena Tiron is a PhD student working jointly with University Alexandru Ioan Cuza of Iaşi, Romania and Katholieke Universiteit Leuven, Belgium. She is part of the Centre of Translation Studies (CETRA); her research focuses on the sociology of translation and the publishing policies practiced in the post-communist Romania.

E-mail: irina.tiron@student.kuleuven.be

Janko Trupej graduated in translation and interpreting (English and German) from the University of Maribor, Slovenia, and is currently a PhD student at the Department of Translation of the Faculty of Arts, University of Ljubljana, Slovenia. His main research interests are norms in translation and translating popular literature.

E-mail: janko.trupej@gmail.com

Subject Index

P

R

S

T

U

W

Name Index